CATALONIA

Landscapes of the Imagination

CATALONIA

A CULTURAL HISTORY

Michael Eaude

2008

OXFORD
UNIVERSITY PRESS

Oxford University Press, Inc., publishes works that further
Oxford University's objective of excellence
in research, scholarship, and education.

Oxford   New York
Auckland   Cape Town   Dar es Salaam   Hong Kong   Karachi
Kuala Lumpur   Madrid   Melbourne   Mexico City   Nairobi
New Delhi   Shanghai   Taipei   Toronto

With offices in
Argentina   Austria   Brazil   Chile   Czech Republic   France   Greece
Guatemala   Hungary   Italy   Japan   Poland   Portugal   Singapore
South Korea   Switzerland   Thailand   Turkey   Ukraine   Vietnam

Published by Oxford University Press, Inc.
198 Madison Avenue, New York, New York 10016

www.oup.com

Oxford is a registered trademark of Oxford University Press

Co-published in Great Britain by Signal Books

Library of Congress Cataloging-in-Publication Data
Eaude, Michael.
Catalonia : a cultural history / Michael Eaude.
    p. cm. —(Landscapes of the imagination)
Includes bibliographical references.
ISBN 978-0-19-532797-7
1. Catalonia (Spain)—Civilization I. Title.
DP302.C616E38 2007
946'.7—dc22   2007005776

9 8 7 6 5 4 3 2 1

Printed in the United States of America
on acid-free paper

Contents

CONTENTS

CONTENTS

Preface and Acknowledgements

I first became aware of Catalonia as a country that had a specific identity apart from Spain on 9 April 1973. The moment is fixed in my mind. I had gone to see Antoni Turull, Lecturer in the Spanish Department at Bristol University, with a view to attending his course on Cuban literature. This was our first meeting. Antoni, white hair straggling to his shoulders though he was only forty, greeted me with what I came to know as his characteristic warm extravagance: "Our great Picasso is dead." That day I was made aware of three things: that Catalonia was a nation; that Catalans could legitimately claim Picasso as a wonderful adopted son; and that Catalan was a rich language and taught in some British universities, such as Bristol. Antoni was one of those pioneer teachers. He continued trying to educate my ignorance on our occasional meetings until his early death in January 1990.

I am grateful, too, to my other early Catalan friends, Rosa Blanch and Toni Tulla, whose mother and then sister, Assumpció, ran the beautiful, old-fashioned chess bar, the Oro negro, in Barcelona's Carrer Aribau. Rosa and Toni kindly had me to stay in Barcelona on several occasions, including stressful weeks towards the very end of the dictatorship. Then activists in what was quite the best of the Catalan radical groups, the LCR, "la Lliga", they explained Catalan politics to me and introduced me to embotits and the beautiful music of Lluís Llach. The sound of 1975 and the death of Franco are captured for me in Llach's intimate and soaring voice singing that allusive political anthem, *Voyage to Ithaca: Més lluny, sempre molt més lluny. . . Further, always much further on. . .*

I would like to thank, too, the following who generously helped me on specific questions concerned with this book: Andy Durgan, Jude Egan, David C. Hall, Stephen Hayward, Vicky Hayward, Carol O'Brien, John Payne, Gabriel Sempill, Paddy Woodworth and Simon Wynne-Hughes. All errors are, of course, my fault and responsibility.

I am particularly grateful to Marisa Asensio, who encouraged me and is responsible for most of the photographs.

Introduction
Thoroughfare and Nation

Many foreigners visit Catalonia today for art. Its capital, Barcelona, has risen in the last twenty years to stand alongside Venice or Paris as one of Europe's great destinations for cultural breaks. Catalonia's architecture, combining medieval Romanesque and twentieth-century Art Nouveau, is an experience difficult to find elsewhere. And Salvador Dalí, despite his complexity and sexual explicitness, is an extremely accessible and popular painter.

Architecture and painting give Catalonia its prestige. Most visitors, though, come for cheap alcohol and sun holidays. Millions are drawn to the coastal beaches and towns. More Britons know the Costa Brava than Paris or Rome. A linked attraction today is the reputation of Catalonia as a place to live well, with great bars in the beautiful surrounds of Barcelona's Born, *mestissa* music, famous and original food. It is the modern version of the Latin poet Martial's dream of Tarragona: here we know how to live, not too hot, not too cold, with sea and mountains, working hard yet knowing how to relax. . .

Catalans often refer to their own country as a *terra de pas*, a place people pass through, a thoroughfare. It is a comforting view of the homeland. It implies that they are open, a mix, with people passing through down the centuries, each leaving their traces behind. This feeling of being a *terra de pas* is represented most dramatically by Josep Maria Sert's startling paintings in the cathedral of Vic, Catalonia's religious capital, of pagan Hannibal's elephants, which passed through 2,200 years ago. It is also reflected in the melting-pot of Catalan food, fusing Italian, French and Spanish styles into an original cuisine.

Catalans counterpose the *terra de pas* to more fundamentalist views of identity, such as that in the Basque Country, often evoked as moulded by remote valleys uncontaminated by outsiders; or of the fierce Castilian tableland in the centre of Spain, freezing in winter and scorched in summer.

There is little genetic nationalist pride in Catalonia; all those who live and work in Catalonia, and ran the slogan of Jordi Pujol, Catalonia's first elected post-Franco president, are Catalans. The Catalan language is the distinguishing feature of Catalan nationalism, and anyone who comes and lives here can and should learn the language. Thus the definition of Catalonia as a *terra de pas* is transferred easily into a complacent modern view of an easy and hospitable people welcoming newcomers into a tolerant, liberal country. The *terra de pas* also implies that the country is a *terra d'acolliment*, a land of welcome.

The story, of course, is never as simple as people's views of their best selves. Africans and Asians today, picking fruit in Lleida for two scorched months a year, do not feel welcomed, but exploited. Many of the migrants to Catalonia, driven off the land by famine in other parts of Spain during the twentieth century, did not feel that working for rock-bottom wages in a Catalan factory was much of a welcome. Nevertheless, signalling the strength of Catalan identity, and to the credit of both the migrants and indigenous Catalans, in the 1960s and 1970s they united in a huge movement of unions and residents' associations against the dictator Franco. The immigrants recognized the justice of the demand for Catalonia's national rights.

There is another side to the *terra de pas*, chillingly posed by Claudio Magris, writing about Romania: "The evil is that of having too much history, being a crossroads, or at least an optional stop on the route of universal history, along which the slaughterhouses work overtime even in the minor centres." This certainly applies to Catalonia, the minor centre squeezed between two major states, France and Spain. The violence of its history can be envisaged dramatically on the great hill on which the cathedral of Catalonia's main inland city, Lleida, is built. Around the cathedral still lies the crushed rubble where the old town was destroyed after Spanish conquest in 1714 and the citadel of the occupiers was raised. Then this latter was itself sacked by French invasion in 1810.

Present-day Catalonia's peaceful feel and the apparent calm and sense of its people belie this particularly violent and bloody history. Its repeated attempts and failure to become an independent nation state have led to wars and centuries of suppression, culminating in the ten-week siege of Barcelona in 1714 and subsequent suppression of all national rights, and in Franco's attempt to wipe out Catalan identity after 1939.

From the nineteenth century onwards Catalonia's industrial revolution made it the richest and most developed part of the Spanish state, leading also to the world's biggest anarchist movement and, in 1936, to what Andreu Nin called "a deeper revolution than Russia in 1917". Much of this book will examine the great artists whom modern Catalonia has produced, but none of them can be understood without reference to these linked struggles: the fight of an oppressed nation for its national rights and the fight of a militant working class for social justice.

The 1936 revolution attracted George Orwell to Barcelona. His classic, *Homage to Catalonia*, a hymn to socialist revolution, has done more than any other book to make English-speakers aware of Catalonia. No-one actually wants to experience a revolution on their holidays, but it is fascinating to reflect in Barcelona's comfort on the idealism and conflict of the 1930s.

The book is divided into three sections. It starts at the frontier town of Portbou, a *terra de pas* and a good place for a monument that reminds us of the slaughterhouses of history. The description of Portbou goes back (with Stephen Spender) to the Spanish Civil War, an event that still stirs many visitors to Catalonia, and (with Walter Benjamin) to the post-war period that still underlies Catalan politics today. The 1939 victor of that war, Francisco Franco, ruled Spain until 1975, long after his contemporaries and sponsors, Hitler and Mussolini, had died violently. I return to the Civil War in later chapters, but the first section goes on to look at Catalonia's history: its Greek and Roman prehistory, seen as marks in the sand at lonely Empúries and in its glory in imperial Tarragona; then the birth of Catalan as a written language and of Catalonia as an independent state in the Pyrenees about 1,000 years ago, at much the same time as other European states were emerging. The Romanesque churches of the mountain valleys, Catalonia's first indigenous architectural style, flourished at this time. It dwells then on Catalonia's imperial conquests in the Mediterranean in the fourteenth century, when the Catalan flag flew on Athens' Parthenon for seventy years. Accompanying this imperial expansion, a literature flowered: chronicles, poetry, philosophy and one of the first modern novels, Joanot Martorell's *Tirant lo Blanch*.

Catalonia's defeats at the hand of Spanish forces in the 1640s and especially in 1714 are still seared into the minds of modern Catalans. Their rights were suppressed, their language banned, their wealth reduced. The most interesting period follows: the Catalan renaissance in politics, art and language of the second part of the nineteenth century, coinciding with its industrial revolution. When Catalans talk of the *renaixença*, they are talking of this proud rebirth, not the postmedieval period we think of as the Italian Renaissance. The *renaixença* laid the basis for the painting and architecture that has made Catalonia's capital, Barcelona, one of the world's art-tourism capitals. This story is told by chapters on Catalonia's national poet, the priest Jacint Verdaguer, and on its most famous architect, Antoni Gaudí, both sponsored by wealthy industrialists.

The middle section of the book tackles directly the famous twentieth-century visual artists of Catalonia, all deeply attached to their local landscapes: Gaudí from the southern town of Reus, the painters Ramon Casas and Santiago Rusiñol at Sitges, Picasso (whose passage through Barcelona's slums was so fertile), Salvador Dalí from Figueres and Joan Miró, who settled near Reus at Montroig. The last chapter of the second section looks at music, an important component of Catalan culture, and focuses on Raimon, the most influential of the *cantautors* (singer-songwriters) who revolutionized Catalan culture and politics in the 1960s and 1970s.

The third and last part discusses Catalonia in the twentieth century: Barcelona's *barrio chino* (Chinatown), made famous by Jean Genet and other French lovers of low-life, the Ramblas and Gothic Quarter, one of Europe's finest ensembles of medieval buildings, along with the city's outlying suburbs where most people actually live. Chapters cover mass tourism, whose infrastructures have ravaged the beautiful Costa Brava; Catalonia's unique anarchist-led workers' movement and the Civil War that destroyed it; Catalan food, closely linked to its long coastline and mountains, and suddenly world-famous in the last decade; and FC Barcelona, 2006 European soccer champions and, historically, a repository of Catalan nationalist aspirations. The last section covers, too, the inland orchard on the plain around Lleida, and Catalonia's great river, the Ebro, site of the Civil War's longest and most terrible battle in 1938. The Ebro ends in the unique landscape of its large though shrinking delta, the flat antithesis to the Pyrenees.

It is a source of lament to Catalans that many foreign visitors who know that they are in Barcelona, Salou or Lloret think that they are just in Spain. They may not realize they are in Catalonia at all. This book aims to contribute in a small way to explaining an unusual, stateless country. A *terra de pas* for tourists does not have to be a place we know nothing about.

CATALONIA

FRANCE

Perpignan

Roussillon

Pyrenees

Vall de Boí

ANDORRA

▲ *Mt.Canigó*

Portbou

Cap de Creus

SPAIN

Segre

Ripoll

Cadaqués

Figueres

Besalú

Empúries

Berga

Llobregat

Ter

Girona

Costa Brava

Vic

Manresa

Besós

Tossa de Mar

Montserrat

Terrassa

Blanes Lloret de Mar

Lleida

BARCELONA

Poblet

Sitges

N

Reus

Montroig

Salou

Terra Alta

Tarragona

0   30

km

Corbera

Tortosa

Ebro

Ebro Delta

Mediterranean Sea

Sant Carles de la Ràpita

FRANCE

Catalonia

PORTUGAL

Madrid

SPAIN

AFRICA

Part One

Birth and Rebirth of a Nation

Chapter One

Portbou and Montserrat: Sea and Mountain

Portbou is the first town in Spain, if you are approaching from the South of France. From Cerbère on the French side, the train rumbles through a long tunnel into an enormous station with a roof of pale cast-iron beams arching over the platforms. This Euston-like structure looks so metropolitan that, if you woke suddenly and glanced out of the window, you might think you had already reached Barcelona.

Ghost Town

It has always been a strange place, this gateway to Spain accustomed to its name on the destination boards of railway stations in Paris, Milan and Geneva. Because of the wider gauge with which the Spanish railway system was built—to prevent invasion by train from France—Portbou was not just a stop on the line, but a destination where the train halted. Everyone had to change.

It is not just an evocative name for travellers from abroad, but within Catalonia too. Josep Pla (1897-1981), the most officially "boosted" writer of twentieth-century Catalonia (and despite his being so "official" one of the best), expressed a general feeling: "Port-Bou has been, in the lives of many of us, a magic word with many different meanings: the illusion of leaving or the sadness of leaving, delight in return or regret at returning."

Throughout the 1950s and 1960s the emigrants fleeing the hunger of Franco's Spain with their knotted bundles and string-tied cardboard suitcases for jobs in German factories had to file through the enormous customs hall and have their hard-acquired passport scrutinized. Juan Goytisolo remembered it then:

> The station was a shabby, inhospitable place, with a strictly military air: the traces of a recent past were still to be seen: barbed wire, sentry boxes, forts, protective sanitary cordon, fear of guerrillas filtering in, omnipresent police: grey caps, military stripes, three-cornered hats, sinister offices, corridors with benches for waiting on.

Portbou is the first, or last, town in Spain, but not in Catalonia, for French Catalonia—Roussillon—adjoins Spain to the north. The Pyrenees seem like the natural border between Spain and France, making Spain for most Europeans a homogeneous near-island south of the mountain range. History, though, has worked against geography, for both the Basque Country on the Atlantic coast and Catalonia on the Mediterranean are partly in Spain and partly in France. The French state has succeeded in imposing a uniform, centralized model, to the envy of Spanish nationalists. Spain, despite centuries of autocratic monarchy and even, on occasions, open warfare against Catalonia, is not at all homogeneous and has signally failed to suppress its several minority nationalities.

Portbou today is a ghost town. If you get off here, by the time the train has disappeared into another tunnel, you are likely to be the only person on the platform, alone beside the huge Customs offices, canteen and the 26-track-wide marshalling yards crammed onto a narrow plateau. A surrealist dream: just one passenger in an empty station. It is not surprising that French art critic and sex memoirist Catherine Millet found the platform a good place to be photographed naked, though not easy to see how she could satisfy her exhibitionism where so few spectators are to be found.

Portbou seems especially ghostly on a day that the *tramuntana*, the cross-mountain north wind that blows for a sixth of the year, keeps everyone indoors. The steep streets leading from the station down toward the sea are pot-holed; the steps where the terrain is too steep for streets, crumbling. The church, built of the same off-white stone blocks as the railway offices, is locked. The Hotel i Restaurant Portbou in the main square is now given over to seagulls and feral cats. Window-panes are broken, doors on the balconies have fallen in, shutters bang as reminders of a busier past. There has been no vandalism. It is just that when the European Union opened its internal frontiers in 1992, most of the custom agencies closed and 500 people went with them. On the front, an old man told me: "We lost a frontier and gained a town. This place was a mad-house before. Now it's peaceful." "It's peaceful alright," his friend laughed, "because it's going nowhere."

It is not only the opening of the frontier and closure of the customs agencies that have depressed Portbou. The steady shift over the last decades from rail to road has also contributed to its decline. La Jonquera, the frontier-town on the inland motorway pass over the Pyrenees, is busier than ever, with its lorry-parks full of juggernauts that haul fruit from Murcia and Valencia to Northern Europe, while their drivers doze in the cabs or the decidedly non-tourist hotels. At weekends up to 3,500 trucks fill La Jonquera's parking-lots, as French law stops them driving. In addition, the town's half mile-long high street is packed with wholesalers from France filling their vans with cheap wine and spirits. Common prices have still not reached the Common Market. As if to symbolize the mercantile nature of this new frontierless Common Market, in which goods and white tourists pass freely while black people are still routinely stopped and searched, La Jonquera's main multi-storey customs agency has been converted into what is reputedly the biggest brothel in Spain. The women who work there are the new slaves, mostly paperless Romanians working off the "debts" they acquired for their trip to Western Europe.

Portbou inhabits another world: a side-entrance into Spain, a town of no more than 1,500 people huddled between the mountains and a small bay. Inland, scruffy and low round-topped Mediterranean pines are the only trees that cling to the steep slopes of scrub and broken, black rock. Portbou is where the jagged end of the Pyrenees drops into the sea. Bare rock is part of the Spanish countryside, hardly seen in England, which is dressed demurely with trees and grass. It is part of the eternal attraction of Spain to foreign travellers. English novelist James G. Ballard, modern master of the power of landscape on the human mind, said: "Mountainous Catalonia is a dramatic landscape close to the central nervous system: what English meadows and rolling hills aren't." Around Portbou black cliffs rise straight up from tiny coves. Everywhere you look inland from the village, the splintered rock climbs into the low clouds. Here the Costa Brava really earns its name: the Rugged Coast.

It is well worth getting off the train, for Portbou boasts a formidable work of art that takes full advantage of this wild coast. Most of the town is shut up out of season, consisting of holiday flats for Barcelonans. The few shops round the waterfront are living off the last gasps of cross-border traffic, selling to the French cheap tobacco, perfumes and alcohol (mainly appallingly bad, cheap whisky in five-litre bottles).

Stephen Spender's Divided Heart

Portbou does not have the space of Lloret, Platja d'Aro, Blanes, Calella and other notorious names of the Costa Brava package holiday boom, and is undeveloped. Fishing-boats are still pulled up on the beach. It is not even especially picturesque. The narrowness of the bay, the grey shale and pebbles of its beach, and its remoteness have ensured its peace. If it wasn't for the wind and the lowering hills that mean the sun sets too early, it could have become a very pleasant secluded resort for the rich: not unlike Cadaqués just down the coast (see Chapter Nine).

The village covers the slope from the railway down to a little bay. An ox horn-shaped bay, thus the name perhaps, *bou* in Catalan meaning ox, though it is as likely to refer to the technique of fishing off a small boat with a long line, also called *bou*. If the name is known other than by train-passengers creeping under the edge of the Pyrenees, it is for Stephen Spender's poem "Port Bou". Spender spent his first day in Spain here, in February 1937. He had come to serve as an ambulance-man on the Republican side in the Civil War, but despite his new and public commitment to the Communist Party he was in private profoundly uncertain of what he was up to.

In his autobiographical *World within World* (1951) Spender recalls how he sat on the parapet above the pebble beach and answered—or failed to answer adequately, which is the theme of his poem—a lorry-load of militiamen, "smiling flag-like faces like one face" eager for war news. "Port Bou" describes how:

> ...the earth-and-rock arms of this small harbour
> Embrace but do not encircle the sea
> Which, through a gap, vibrates into the ocean,
> Where dolphins swim and liners throb.

That is just how Portbou's small, natural bay is. In the carefully structured poem Spender makes the circling bay that does not quite close correspond to his "circling arms" around a newspaper and to his failure to connect with the militiamen who ask him for news, but are unable to read the French paper held out to them or to understand Spender's words.

The image of Spender and the smiling militiamen, still waving as the lorry jerks away, is reminiscent of another famous Civil War encounter. On the very first page of *Homage to Catalonia* (1938), George Orwell is deeply moved by an Italian militiaman he meets by chance in the POUM's Lenin Barracks in Barcelona. The Italian gripped Orwell warmly by the hand, though neither spoke each other's language. Orwell wrote later, in 1943, of this as one of his two basic memories of the Civil War: "This man's face, which I saw only for a minute or two, remains with me as a sort of visual reminder of what the war was really about. He symbolizes for me the flower of the European working-class, harried by the police of all countries..."

These two Englishmen meeting militia on their first day in Catalonia are both honest in their different ways. Whereas Orwell's powerful, romantic and revolutionary vision is expressed with a decisive hand-shake, Spender's doubt is reflected by his inability to connect with the militia. Orwell's book has done more than anything or anyone else to make the name of Catalonia known to English speakers. Its description of the anarchist revolution that erupted in 1936 has associated Catalonia with red politics to this day, even though the sympathies of most visitors are more likely to lie with Spender's ambivalent liberalism. Indeed, Spender's Civil War poems are outstanding precisely because, avoiding Stalinist panegyrics about the working class, he expressed this ambivalence.

Spender's intensely personal poem continues with the militiamen driving out to the Portbou headlands, where the circling arms of the bay nearly meet. They start target practice.

> I assure myself the shooting is only for practice
> But I am the coward of cowards. The machine-gun stitches
> My intestines with a needle, back and forth;
> The solitary, spasmodic, white puffs from the carbines
> Draw fear in white threads back and forth through my body.

The machine-gun bullets close the circle. The connection made is not a frank hand-shake, but rather the fear of the lanky Englishman watching from the parapet above the beach. This poem about doubt and cowardice seems brave today; in the middle of a war where a pose of public heroism was demanded, Spender remains in his poetry true to his "divided heart", giving an anti-heroic response to the Civil War.

Trapped: Walter Benjamin's Last Night

The parapet and "the childish headlands of Port Bou" are still there. Indeed, Portbou must be the least changed of any town on the Costa Brava in the last sixty years. By sitting on the wall above the beach, visitors can have the rare pleasure of reading a fine poem in the precise geographical position described. But there is no mention of Spender today in Portbou. All the leaflets in the hotels, shops and Town Hall concern another literary figure, the German philosopher Walter Benjamin. Benjamin, along with the cheap whisky, has become the town's minor industry. Just as down the coast, at L'Escala, they sell Spain's best anchovies, here they sell Benjamin and Spain's best anti-fascist monument.

Like Spender, Benjamin spent just one day at Portbou; but unlike Spender, who lived a long and prosperous life, Benjamin had the ill fortune to die there, and his name was thus linked forever to an obscure border town. Fleeing the Gestapo in 1940, Benjamin crossed the

Pyrenees on foot from Vichy France. Three years later than Spender, he was greeted by no smiling militiamen full of the optimism of the still unlost war, but by those fearsome victors of the war and patrollers of rural Spain, the Civil Guard with their polished three-cornered hats. With his two chance travelling companions, Henny Gurland (later wife of Benjamin's colleague, Erich Fromm) and her teenage son, Benjamin took a room at the Fonda de Francia for the night of 25 September 1940.

The three applied for permission to cross Spain to Lisbon, from where Benjamin intended to embark for the United States to meet up with his colleagues of the Frankfurt Institute of Sociology, Theodor Adorno and Max Horkheimer, already safe in New York exile. Though Benjamin and his fellow refugees had a transit visa for Spain, they were trapped by having no exit visa from France. Unknown to them, just the day before—one more link in this unfolding chain of ill luck—Spain had agreed with Germany not to allow people into the country who had their papers not fully in order. The three were told they would be returned to France the following day. Three policemen guarded the group in the hotel that night. It was Benjamin's bad luck that the hotelier Juan Suñer was a fascist. The police and Gestapo—who at this time, after the fall of France, openly wandered through this border town in uniform, even though Spain was neutral—habitually drank there, a presence that could hardly have eased Benjamin's terror on the last night of his life.

On reaching the Fonda de Francia (now the Fonda Internacional) Benjamin, who suffered from a number of ailments, including angina, and had just made a strenuous seven- or nine-hour (accounts vary) journey on foot cross-country through the Pyrenean foothills, felt ill and had a doctor called. According to Henny Gurland, Benjamin told her he took morphine after this medical visit. There is no reason to doubt her, though otherwise the evidence of suicide is circumstantial. No autopsy was conducted and the death certificate recorded "cerebral haemorrhage". Bertolt Brecht summed up the desolation of his friend Benjamin's death in a concise couplet:

Then at last, brought up against an impassable frontier
You passed, they say, a passable one.

In a savage twist of fate, Henny Gurland and her son were granted permission to travel on to Lisbon the day after Benjamin died. Perhaps he would have had a visa, too, or perhaps it was the shock of Benjamin's death that moved the authorities to waive the new ruling. Certainly they had nothing against Benjamin: they had registered him by a bureaucratic error as Señor Benjamin Walter. Benjamin is a common Spanish first name; he had not been identified as a Jew or a famous German Marxist.

Walter Benjamin, Jewish atheist, was interred in a niche of the Catholic cemetery at Portbou. Because of the Second World War no family or friends came to collect his remains or renew the rental on the niche. As is customary in such cases, after five years the niche was cleaned and re-let, and his bones thrown into the ossuary. With its white-washed walls and cypresses, Portbou's classic Mediterranean hilltop cemetery, overlooking the sea and black cliffs and surrounded by twisted prickly pears, is the most beautiful part of this ugly town. In autumn soft red fruits can be pulled gently from among the piercing prickles of the cactus, sweet trophies to reward patient picking. The beauty of the cemetery hillside is not smooth or delicate. This is, remember, the Costa Brava, with days on end of fierce seas and winds that drive the inhabitants, as the saying goes, "either mad or taciturn".

With the approach of the 1992 centenary of Benjamin's birth—coinciding with the opening of Europe's internal borders under the Schengen agreement—a memorial was commissioned from the Israeli artist Dani Karavan "in memory of Walter Benjamin and the European exiles of 1933 to 1945". The scheme was co-funded by the German government and the government of Catalonia.

Though statues of General Franco still abound in Spain, there are few official anti-fascist monuments. Two of the very best are in Catalonia: one in Barcelona at the quarry site of executions behind the Montjuïc mountain and Karavan's at Portbou, finished in 1994. Karavan's piece of landscape art, called *Passages*, took full advantage of the cemetery's setting. Outside its main gate he had a rusted iron corridor drilled down at a 45-degree angle through the cliff. Stepping down the corridor through the rock, the only thing visible below at the end of the dark tunnel is the turbulent sea. In this low corridor you feel as trapped as Benjamin. Then the corridor's roof ends and a sudden marvellous view opens of the sea (that ocean outside the harbour encircled by the bull's horns) and the hills across the bay. Thick glass, invisible from higher up, stops you stepping off the cliff into the waves. On this glass is cut, in German, Catalan and Castilian, famous words of Benjamin's:

> It is a more arduous task to honour the memory of the anonymous than that of the famous. Historical construction is consecrated to the memory of those who have no name.

The monument is a direct and militant use of art that is uncommon today. Not ironic and not self-observing, it harks back to the internationalist spirit of the 1930s. It can be weighed against Spender's more ambivalent view of the world, and indeed against the complex philosophy of Benjamin himself.

Apart from the corridor, there are three other component parts of Karavan's memorial, which surrounds, without entering, the cemetery. The water swirling hypnotically in and out of the rocks, seen by the visitor stepping down the rusty corridor, forms a second part. By the front gate of the cemetery an olive tree has been planted. And on the hill overlooking the cemetery a large platform with an empty plinth has been placed. The platform, made of the same simple hard rusted metal as the corridor through the cliff, is brilliantly simple, its sharp rectangular lines set boldly in the dramatic setting. The plinth faces the mountain, just as the corridor faces the sea.

On the memorial slab to Walter Benjamin inside the cemetery is carved his most famous aphorism: "There is no document of civilization that is not at the same time a document of barbarism." The aphorism is famous partly because it is not immediately clear what it means, though it certainly sounds good. Nevertheless, the context of the quote does clarify its meaning. Benjamin is explaining that all those who paid money for what we think of as the great achievements of our civilizations were barbarians. For barbarians, read generals, statesmen and ruthless businessmen, who did not care a fig for culture, except for how it could immortalize their names. We will meet some of these in the form of the industrialists who had made their money out of slavery and financed the *modernista* architecture that is one of Catalonia's claims to fame (see Chapter Six).

Benjamin was a man obsessed by history. Indeed, it is often asserted that the lost contents of the suitcase he carried with him over the Pyrenees were his *Theses on the Philosophy of History*. For him, as for Adorno and other members of the Frankfurt School, history was dark. He probably needed no profound analysis to reach this conclusion; the circumstances of his life as a wanderer and then as an exile from Nazism were sufficient. Yet (unlike Adorno) he was not a pessimist. He encouraged his readers to fight constantly over the interpretation of history because if the ruling class's version prevailed, it would consolidate in the present, in each new generation, the unjust power of that class. Thus he coined a beautiful phrase, in the same paragraph as the quote above, that historians should seek to "brush history *against the grain*."

Historians should tell the story of those who have no name or an unofficial story, which is usually the history of how history is falsified. Despite Benjamin's growing fame, which has turned Portbou into a site of pilgrimage, the poignant destiny of his salt-bleached bones in the ossuary makes him an apt representative of nameless victims.

Official Catalonia is fond of over-promoting its great figures, its "universal Catalans", rather than let them stand by themselves. And they certainly could stand by themselves: Gaudí, Casals, Picasso, Miró, Dalí are towering figures of modern art. Over-promotion is a tic characteristic of a small nation having to fight for its identity. To some extent Benjamin has become a posthumous victim of this mythologizing, despite his tenuous relationship with the country. Few people could tell you anything he had to say, but he adds to the general aura of leftist victims of oppression that is part of modern Catalonia's view of itself.

The emotion associated with Benjamin for Catalans is that his death at Portbou took place when Catalonia was buried under the barbed wire that the earlier quote from Goytisolo refers to. Its freedoms had been crushed by the victory of fascism in the Civil War of 1939, the same wave of fascist victories in Europe that led to Benjamin's death. Catalan President Lluís Companys, the only democratically elected president of a European country to be executed in these dark years, was shot at Montjuïc only a few days after Benjamin's death.

Dark Lady of the Mountains: Montserrat
If Catalonia is coast, it is also mountain. If it is famous for its revolu-

The Abbey of Montserrat

tionary traditions, it also has a rich religious history. A month after Benjamin's death and a few days after Companys' murder, Heinrich Himmler visited the holy mountain of Montserrat.

Montserrat, "serrated mountain", is a huge outcrop of conglomerate stone some thirty miles inland from Barcelona, by the road to Manresa. (A huge outcrop or small range, for the mountain is several miles long.) From all sides it can be seen from a distance, often through cloud or haze that adds to its magical status. From the grape country round Sant Sadurní (home of Catalan *cava*), the farm-worker in the fields can look up and see what Jan Morris called a "pile of queerly serrated jags, bumps, and crevices".

Himmler was in Barcelona to discuss security arrangements with Spain's Foreign Minister Serrano Súñer. While the rest of the German delegation went off to take part in Hitler's famous meeting with Franco at Hendaye, Himmler stayed behind in Catalonia. Despite his fame as a highly efficient chief of Nazi Germany's police, Himmler was fascinated by the legend of the Holy Grail. As in the *Indiana Jones* films, some Nazis took seriously the possibility of the power they could wield on finding it. Wagner placed, in *Parsifal*, the secret hiding-place of the Holy Grail on the mountain of Montsalvat. It may have been Wagner himself, but it is more likely to have been the Catalan admirers of Wagner, who spread the idea that Montsalvat was Montserrat. Wagner became the object of a cult in Catalonia; his operas were for decades the most popular at Barcelona's Liceu. At Montserrat Himmler questioned the abbot about the abbey's history. Doubtless the abbot told his visitor the legends of the Black Virgin, but Himmler failed in his search for the Grail, just as at Hendaye Hitler failed to persuade Franco to let his troops march through Spain.

Whereas Portbou is empty, Montserrat is bustling. The abbey is one of the special sanctuaries beloved of the Church, full of smiling and busy priests, with long queues to kiss the statue of the Black Virgin, and massive car and coach parks, cafeterias, hotels, restaurants and religious trinket shops. The complex's only parallel in Catalonia is the pagan Dalí Museum and its surrounds at Figueres. Today the drive up is on a winding, fairly hair-raising road or the totally hair-raising funicular from the train station (from Barcelona, catch the train at Plaça d'Espanya). If you wish to keep closer to the earth, you could walk up barefoot like Queen Violante in the fifteenth century.

The red-brick abbey buildings are singularly ugly. The excuse is that it was sacked by the French in 1811. It is uglier from a distance, perched two-thirds of the way up the mountain. Once onto the great main square, the utilitarian brick is no longer visible and the rebuilt Benedictine church with its rounded arches echoes the huge bare boulders like nail-less fingers pointing at the sky.

Montserrat has been one of the Christian world's great places of pilgrimage. Legend has it that the statue of the Black Virgin revered at the shrine was carved by St. Luke, brought to Catalonia by St. Peter and then hidden during the Moorish occupation. In the ninth century the statue was discovered by shepherds. When priests tried to bear it off the mountain to Vic, it grew so heavy that it could not be moved, so indicating that a shrine should be built. Thus, the Church subtly created a popular religious legend with an anti-Church undercurrent. Modern tests have shown that the Black Virgin dates from the twelfth century. Its blackness comes not from being buried for several centuries or from any African origin, but because the smoke of the votive candles has darkened the wood.

Catalonia's national poet Jacint Verdaguer (see Chapter Five) wrote in his *Virolai*, which is sung each day by the famous Boys' Choir, the *Escolania*, at Montserrat and has become one of Catalonia's best-known songs:

> Rose of April, dark lady of the mountains
> ...
> with a golden saw the angels carved
> these hills to give you a palace.

(The *Escolania* still sing every day at 1pm and 8pm. It is worth timing a visit to hear them.)

On a freezing day, the heat of the thousands of candles in the dark lady's shrine is welcome. The long queue moves slowly up the stairs and round behind the altar where the pilgrim, or visitor, can kiss the Virgin's hand, which protrudes from the glass case protecting her. A severe monk makes sure you do not linger in lengthy adoration. The Mare de Deu (Mother of God, the words in Catalan for the Virgin) de Montserrat holds Jesus on her lap and the whole world in her right hand. Like so

13

many icons, the statue's eyes are wide and soft and her look open. Montserrat, or its abbreviation Montse, is by far the most popular girl's name in Catalonia.

The mountain was covered with hermitages in medieval times. Today one can walk to the Santa Cova, Holy Cave, where the image of the Virgin was supposedly found. On the way, fifteen sculptures mark the fifteen mysteries of the rosary, and several of these are by famous early twentieth-century Catalan sculptors such as the Llimona brothers, Gaudí and Puig i Cadafalch. Towards another hermitage, Sant Miquel, you pass a statue of St. Francis and one of the cellist Pau Casals. Here Catalan art has been closely and carefully associated with the mountain and the legend of the statue.

One of the surprising features of the abbey is its art museum, with Grecos, a Caravaggio and a Dalí, and even works by such notorious atheists as Ramon Casas, Nonell and Picasso. The apparatus of ultra-religious mysticism, the cult of the Virgin, is given a modern, practical tinge.

Himmler was not the only famous visitor. The Emperor Charles V visited nine times, some pilgrims have climbed the mountain on their knees, and league-winning Barcelona football teams offer their victories here. Don Juan of Austria, the victor of the decisive Battle of Lepanto over the Moors in 1571, dedicated his victory and spoils of his victory to the Virgin. Ignatius Loyola, the Basque converted like St. Paul on the road, laid his sword before the altar in 1522. The fanatical convert, like many converts "more papist than the pope", had passed months wrestling with his conscience in a cave near Manresa with a view of the whole Montserrat range. Now he renounced military arms to take up spiritual weapons and to found the Jesuit order that played a key part in Portugal and Spain's conquests in the Far East.

St. Ignatius' visit coincided with Montserrat's least Catalan period. After Ferdinand and Isabel had united Spain in 1492, they insisted on appointing a Castilian Spanish-speaking abbot in 1494, part of the centuries-long struggle that Isabel initiated to weaken Catalan power by trying to destroy its language. This is why civil servants, governors and military officials were all appointed from outside Catalonia at this time. At Montserrat Catalan penitents were urged to confess after 1494 "in a Christian language", i.e. in Castilian Spanish. It was the chilling forerunner of the famous insult to Catalan speakers from Franco's officials and police in the 1940s: *Habla en cristiano*... Speak in Christian.

In the Civil War the Black Virgin was hidden again and became a new source of feeling and legend when once more it was put on display. In the 1936 Revolution, many of Montserrat's Benedictine monks were killed and the monastery was turned into a convalescent home. The Catalan Church lives within the contradiction between its intrinsically conservative ideology and its status as a church of a nation without a state. As Catalonia's most eminent contemporary historian of the Church, Hilari Raguer, summarizes: "In Catalonia, the reds burnt the churches in 1936, but the whites burnt the Church in 1939."

The story of the Federation of Young Christians of Catalonia is illustrative of this contradiction. Many of this Catholic Youth Group fled revolutionary Catalonia at the start of the Civil War and enlisted in the Our Lady of Montserrat Regiment of Franco's army. Several died in the Battle of the Ebro in 1938; various individuals and the regiment collectively were decorated by Franco. After proudly re-entering Catalonia with Franco's victorious army in 1939, they renewed their Catholic propaganda activities. To their shock, these Franco loyalists were at once banned by the authorities because they wrote leaflets and spoke in Catalan. Cardinal Díaz de Gómara announced that they were a "separatist" organization and obliged them to join the Spanish Youth for Catholic Action, administered from Madrid and exclusively, of course, in Castilian Spanish. This is what Raguer means by the Church being "burnt by the whites". The totalitarian nature of Franco's regime is highlighted by the way it treated its own supporters.

After the Civil War, every activity at Montserrat, as everywhere else, had to be conducted in Castilian. There were abstruse disputes between Catalan Church and Spanish State on the pronunciation of liturgical Latin. Drawing on papal guidelines, the Abbot of Montserrat defended the Roman pronunciation, closer to the Catalan. Díaz de Gómara, who like Franco only obeyed the pope when it suited him, insisted on the Castilian pronunciation. The monks of Montserrat resorted to what Franco's Civil Governor called "slyness" when the *Escolania* sung chants in Catalan in the early 1940s because they had "no music scores in Castilian".

For several years, half the bishoprics in Catalonia were unfilled because of conflict between Franco and the pope over who could nominate bishops. Franco, who kissed the Black Virgin's hand on nearly all his visits to Catalonia, had convinced the Catalan Church of the justice of his crusade, but failed to convince it of the peace he imposed. By the late 1950s and 1960s, the national question led many priests and even sections of the hierarchy to oppose the regime actively. The Church understood that it had to distance itself from the regime or lose its base. In the 1960s it became a focus of the internal opposition to Franco. The Montserrat Abbey press, forbidden of course to publish in the 1940s, issued extensive literature in Catalan and protected dissidents. In 1970 the abbot allowed the monastery's use for the world-famous protest of intellectuals and artists (including the painters Joan Miró and Antoni Tàpies) against Franco's Burgos trials of ETA militants. This occupation led to the Catalan Assembly, which united Catalan left and right behind the slogans "Liberty, Amnesty, Statute of Autonomy" in a powerful movement that climaxed with the downfall of the dictatorship after Franco's death.

The contradiction between ideology and Catalanism has resurged recently with the Spanish-nationalist anti-Catalan campaign waged by the Spanish Church's radio station, the COPE, and the main conservative party, the confessional Partido Popular, against socialists and Catalan nationalists. Despite sharing nearly all the COPE's ultra-rightwing positions—on abortion, homosexual marriage, the family, palliative treatment for the terminally ill etc.—the Archbishop of Barcelona, in early 2006, admitted to feeling "embarrassment" at the belligerent Spanish centralism of the COPE's broadcasts.

Despite its coach- and car-parks and souvenir shops, Montserrat is not a recently invented cult, like Lourdes in southern France or the Virgin of Fatima in Portugal. Nor is it a dark and sinister place of worship, like some of the Castilian cathedrals that reek of the Inquisition's torture chambers. Its history is intimately tied to the history of Catalonia, as this brief outline has shown. In Catalan life respect for the Abbey of Montserrat and its monks runs far beyond Catholic militants. "Neither the symbolic nor the real role of this place in Catalan national life should ever be underestimated," noted Alastair Boyd.

Chapter Two
Mediterranean, the Centre of the Earth: Tarragona

The City that Speaks Latin

Just behind Tarragona on the Autopista-7, the motorway of the Mediterranean cutting right through Catalonia and down the east side of Spain from the Pyrenean pass of La Jonquera to Valencia and beyond, is a sign with a lay-by for the Pont del Diable, the Devil's Bridge. Many great works are known as the Devil's, perhaps because God's Church has been so diabolical in Spain. Curiously, drivers can stop in the motorway lay-by and walk into the woods to see, and cross, this impressive 700 foot-long, two-tier aqueduct across a valley. It is part of a twenty-mile channel and gives some idea of the scope of Roman civilization in what is today Catalonia.

A stop at the Pont del Diable is a visit to a point balanced between three worlds. The Roman aqueduct itself is made of great blocks of reddish sandstone shading off into grey. During the visit to this 2,000-year-old engineering masterpiece in the woods, the clunk of tyres over the joins in the motorway and the hum of fast traffic are a constant reminder of the industrial world: to the right, the slum tower-blocks on the outskirts of Tarragona are visible. Then there is a third world, even more ancient than the Devil's Bridge: of vegetation. This is typical Mediterranean *selva*—jungle—with pine forest dense with low scrub, sarsaparilla, yellow broom, rock rose. It burns easily, a periodic feature throughout the history of Mediterranean landscape. It is nature's way of clearing the scrub and initiating rebirth. Now, though, the constant summer fires in an epoch of less rain and more concrete—viz the advancing tower-blocks of Tarragona—have become an ecological disaster, baring the earth to be washed away by the torrential autumn rains.

At the time that Rome began to occupy the Iberian Peninsula, some 200 years BC, Julius Caesar had still not conquered Gaul. Thus it was by

The Devil's Bridge, Tarragona

sea that the Romans had to come rather than through the hostile lands of what is now southern France. The main port became Rome's capital in northern Iberia: imperial Tarraco, modern Tarragona. The Devil's Bridge brought water from the nearby mountains to Tarraco, a city by the time that Christ was born of some 200,000 people. Tarraco's ruins are the most impressive Roman ruins in Spain and, many say, of the whole Mediterranean shore.

Tarraco was the earliest city in the peninsula to be Romanized. Scipio moved his troops southwards from Empúries to winter here in 211 BC during the second war with Carthage for domination of the western Mediterranean. Scipio's army overran the Celtiberian village at Tarragona and built on the existing walls of the fortified city. In 197 BC, it became capital of Hispania Citerior, Nearer Spain, one of the two provinces into which Iberia was divided. Tarraco, *urbs opulentissima*— most opulent city—remained Roman for six centuries and became not just a capital, but a fashionable coastal resort for the Romans. This has always been a beautiful coast with an enviable climate; far enough south not to freeze in winter, but not so far that it bakes in summer. The wind that assails Portbou and the Costa Brava has blown out here.

The poet and often obscene punster Martial, who retired after 35 years in Rome to his native town of Bilbilis in inland Spain, wintered here, fed up with harsh winters and too much country life:

> But when white, grizzly December, feeble with winter sun,
> Moans with the hoarse north wind,
> Then you will seek again the sunny shores of Tarraco...

Martial shows that tourism to the Mediterranean coast started early. Tarraco was a Rome from Rome, a sophisticated imperial city whose citizens had "toga" rights, giving them equal status with the inhabitants of Rome itself. The Emperors Augustus, in 26 BC, and Hadrian spent winters in the resort. According to Quintilian, the *Tarraconenses* over-flattered Augustus by erecting a temple to him as a "god" while he was still alive. After he had left the city, though, the sycophants let a palm-tree sprout on his neglected altar. "How little you have sacrificed to me," Augustus commented dryly on his return. The Via Augusta, named after him, ran down through the city from Gaul, newly conquered by

Augustus' time, for the legions to march into Spain: still in Barcelona there is a major street called the Via Augusta. The coast and the hills were scattered with villas, much as they are now. In the Priorat range behind, wine was produced to supply the villas, also much as it is today. Martial liked to hunt stags and boars in those hills. The stags are gone, but wild boars, considered a delicacy throughout Catalonia, are still prolific.

Tarragona today is a provincial city of some 100,000 people, long overtaken by Barcelona. I was going to say "quiet" provincial city and it is, but to the south the chemical works spill contamination into the sky. Tarragona is one of those Mediterranean cities of golden light, but it is also a polluted dump. Down the coast is the nuclear reactor of Vandellós, a similar design to that at Chernobyl. One of its reactors was closed after a fire and serious leak in October, 1989. There is a saying in this southern province of Tarragona about the four provinces into which Catalonia is currently divided: "Girona for tourism, Barcelona for industry and commerce, Lleida for agriculture, and Tarragona for the shit."

Arriving by train—just an hour's ride from Barcelona—the visitor walks up a wide flight of steps to the parapet, or, as it is known, "balcony of the Mediterranean" that overhangs the sea. From the balcony, where the statue of the great medieval admiral (or pirate) Roger de Llúria stares along the main street, the Rambla Nova, Tarragona looks down on Homer's beautiful wine-dark sea, the centre of the earth, *Medi terrae*, for the Romans. It is immediately striking how Tarragona, unlike Barcelona seventy miles up the coast, faces the Mediterranean. Barcelona was long separated by walls from the sea, but Tarragona from its heights embraces it. Below the "balcony" curls the half-moon of the restored Roman amphitheatre. From the top of the theatre's tiers of seating, the view over the back is of the sea: this was a city built to welcome what came from the sea, from Rome.

For the writer-traveller Rose Macaulay, obsessed with the ancient world sixty years ago in a way that few in our generation are, Tarragona "is possibly the most grandly poised city in Europe. The shape formed by the steep walls that encircle it and the climbing mass of the ancient town crowned by the cathedral on its summit, is theatrically superb." If you come, like her, towards Tarragona along the coast road from the north—the Via Augusta—you pass three dramatic Roman monuments. The Arc de Berà, an arch restored with ugly blocks on top to keep out the rain, celebrated some long-forgotten military triumph. Till recently the main road ran through the middle of it; now it stands among four olive trees on an island in the middle of the two lanes. Rub your hand over the worn, pitted surface of the limestone blocks whose erosion has lasted two thousand years.

Closer to Tarragona is the quarry from which the stone for the arch and for much of the city was mined. Its main access, strangely and reminiscent of access to the Pont del Diable, is through the Mèdol motorway service station, where rubbish is scattered over the eating area and the juggernauts are parked in oily rows. Yet half a mile down a path lined with cypresses the quarry itself is a wild, raw place. Bushes run riot in the damp protection of its vertical walls, like some craggy Alpine valley in a romantic painting. Vegetation, scrub and slim pines reaching up for the light have taken over the quarry, from which 50,000 square metres of rock were cut: on the quarry walls, chisel marks are still visible.

In the middle of the quarry, L'Agulla del Mèdol, the Mèdol Needle, marks its depth. The finely balanced obelisk, consisting of one long slim rock left as a marker, shows the desire of the Romans to remind subsequent generations what they had achieved. Yet the effect is different; it reminds of suffering as much as glory. This great hole in the ground is evidence of the sweat and blood of the Empire's slaves, the conquered Iberians, to build the arch or the villas and theatre of Tarragona. The needle was an industrial site; here you step behind the pomp and glory of imperial Tarraco.

The third monument is the Torre dels Escipions, Tower of the Scipios, a funeral sarcophagus, though nothing to do with Scipio the founder of the city. A two-storey tower with two sculpted figures on the front, it stands on a hill above the main road and sea. Rose Macaulay caught its grandeur in the 1940s, in the decade before mass tourist development transformed this entire coast:

> The Torre de los Scipiones... stands brown and solid among cypresses, pines, ilex, juniper and aloes on the baked hill-side; from it one has a superb view of Tarragona and its coast, the blue and green and peacock sea stretching beyond the grey shimmer of the twisted olives round the deep bay, Tarragona at its far end, magnificently piled on its rocky hill sheer above the sea.

Tarragona was, on its hill, defensible from the sea, yet easily accessible. Rose Macaulay's is the romantic view of the Mediterranean, as the title of her book about the Spanish coast *Fabled Shore* indicates. This is the Mediterranean that has enticed northerners for several centuries, where you can sit in shirt sleeves sipping wine by the pine-ringed beach and feel you have escaped from the chill, repressed north to the sun. This dream has several forms: the sex and booze nightlife that Salou, on the coast just south of Tarragona, and Lloret de Mar have made famous, or Macaulay's more intellectual approach to the origins of Western civilization, to the same sea that Homer sang of. There is another form of the dream, which the wealthy have made real by building classy houses in protected surroundings. Sitges and Cadaqués are the best-known such enclaves on the Catalan coast. Another is the Roc de Sant Gaietà, a fantasy development mixing Moorish, Andalusian and Roman architecture. It is built among fountains and luxuriant vegetation on a natural salient of rock jutting into the sea. This invented dream of a Mediterranean village has a small Dalí Museum, with original pieces by him. Needless to say, this luxury enclave is not cheap, but access is free. The Roc de Sant Gaietà is worth a look on a visit to the Arc de Berà, just half a mile inland.

Tarragona is famous for its golden light, a soft light that the pale local sandstone, hard as all stone is yet soft-looking, diffuses. John Payne perceptively suggested another reason:

> ...the Rambla, the broad avenue with its central pedestrian walkway... slopes slightly upwards towards the sea. Perhaps it is this sloping towards the sea on a due north-south axis that helps to give the Rambla its special quality of light, a luminosity, an absence of shadows, and yet also oblique as if caressing everything it touches.

The beauty spots on the coast near Tarragona still do exist, though you need to wear blinkers so as not to see the building with which Catalonia, like the rest of Spain, has adorned its shores. Bare rock, scrub and insects are not well-loved; and many Catalans agree with builders that the earth should be covered with a good layer of concrete for living and driving on. More of that in Chapter Fourteen, but in imperial Tarraco on its hill you can still sense the ancient lure. And though romanticism was an invention of nineteenth-century rebels against industrialization, Tarraco's life as a resort 2,000 years ago shows that the fabled Mediterranean shore was not just a northerners' dream.

Making your way through the narrow, twisting streets up the hill from the Rambla Nova towards the cathedral, you can see the Roman presence in the numerous slabs of stone at the bottom of the walls of the houses. Many of them have Latin inscriptions, bearing out Richard Ford's words: "The Roman inscriptions embedded here and elsewhere are so numerous that the walls are said to speak Latin."

One needs be careful with Roman ruins, though. The buildings were often used as a quarry for later building, like the Forum in Rome itself. The Roman stones in the houses that Ford saw and you can still see are undoubtedly Roman, but after their extraction from the Mèdol quarry may not have started their useful life where you see them today. Much of the port was built with Roman masonry removed from the amphitheatre, which by the nineteenth century was a heap of rubble. Today the amphitheatre stands entire, beautifully outlined against the sea, so that a naïve visitor could think, as I at first did, it was unrestored, for nowhere is the repair work acknowledged.

Despite this caveat, history can nonetheless be read from the ruins. The layers of occupation can still be perceived, for the strange pillars on the sand of the amphitheatre are Christian church ruins from a later date. The city walls of Tarragona up on the hill are huge. "Cyclopean" is the word used in the tourist leaflets for these granite blocks reminiscent of the Inca walls of Cuzco and reputed to be pre-Roman. On the base they form lie the Roman sandstone slabs, the same soft-looking, light-filled stone seen in the Cistercian monastery of Poblet thirty miles inland.

On the west of the city, by the small Francolí river that runs down from its source by Poblet, is the Roman-Christian necropolis. Used between the third and sixth centuries, it was only rediscovered in 1923 when the tobacco factory was being built. Over 2,000 tombs have been identified, along with mosaics and funeral art, including a figure of a woman in a transparent dress. It is believed that the necropolis began to be used in the third century AD, along with a church that stood beside it in memory of Bishop Fructuos and his two deacons, executed in the amphitheatre. Thus the necropolis marks the conversion of the Roman

Empire to Christianity. As Tarragona entered its decadence, along with the fall of the Roman Empire, so the necropolis ceased to be used.

The Christian Visigoths who occupied Spain for three centuries before the Moors came in the eighth century left few traces of their occupation, but did not destroy Roman Tarraco. When relative peace reached the area after the Moorish-Christian wars, the building of the present cathedral began. In this sense, Tarragona is a Roman and medieval city, with an interregnum of several hundred unrecorded years in between.

The cathedral on top of the hill dominates the town, with steps leading up to it, as in other parts of Catalonia such as Girona. The citizens approach the House of God as if they were climbing a little closer to heaven. Sacheverell Sitwell described it in his self-consciously poetic prose:

> The cathedral of Tarragona is built, principally, from blocks of Roman stone. It rises, in Catalan fashion, down the narrowest of streets, at the head of a splendid flight of steps, so that the beautiful rose window, and then the statues and doorways, reveal themselves, golden stone by stone.

Started in 1171, in the century after the Moors were expelled, it was not completed until 1331. The long time it took to be completed explains its not uncommon mix of Romanesque and Gothic styles. The fear of the Moors returning also explains its resemblance to a fortress. There had always been temples on this hill—to the Iberian Gods and then to Jupiter. On the right of the door is a fourth-century sarcophagus with detailed sculptures of biblical stories. Christ is riding into Jerusalem on a donkey, which underlines both how the Biblical stories had arrived in Roman times and how the medieval builders valued too their Roman past.

Tarragona cathedral is something of an architectural mish-mash, the Gothic austerity of its lines clashing with its varied remodellings and adornments. It underlines the huge scale on which building was undertaken in this Spanish provincial town. "The Spaniards, beyond argument, have been the greatest builders after the Romans," wrote Sacheverell Sitwell. In Tarragona today you can see this Spanish tradition alongside, and on top of, its Roman beginning.

Façade of Tarragona Cathedral

Empúries: "whispering centuries of ghosts"

There is an even earlier presence on the Catalan shore, the settlement at Empúries founded by Phoenician traders, developed by Greeks and then taken over by Romans as their first beach-head in Iberia before Tarraco was developed. A hundred years ago, Empúries was completely forgotten, buried beneath the sands, but in the twentieth century it was excavated, and the lay-out and ruins of this ancient city revealed.

Right beside Empúries is the medieval hamlet of Sant Martí. This used to be an island, and it was here about 550 BC (the date is known from the pottery found) that the first Phoenician trading settlement was established. After Scipio's armies arrived in 211 BC it became Roman and there are descriptions of it in the work of Livy and Strabo. Both remark that Empúries was two towns separated by a wall: the "fierce and warlike" (Livy) Iberians on one side; the cultured, trading Romans on the other. Walls were common in the ancient world, when the vanguard of a conquering people arrived and established an enclave. Yet the whole point of the Phoenicians' and Greeks' outpost at Empúries was not to conquer (that came with the Romans), but to trade, to make money.

Indeed, the very word *emporion* means market place in Greek, related to our "emporium". The Greeks brought olive trees (and with them, oil), wine, ceramics and coins to Iberia. Salted fish, which could be kept for months and so transported into the hills, also came with the Greeks. Salted fish, especially the anchovies bottled in nearby L'Escala, is still common in Spanish diet today.

The stronger civilization, of course, traded on advantageous terms. The gate of Empúries was wide open during the day for buying and selling, but it was locked shut and the walls patrolled at night for protection against those the traders had fleeced by day. When Scipio arrived, it was to make money, too, but the Romans had another longer-term plan: to wrest control of parts of Iberia from the Carthaginians and conquer the rest of it.

The remains of these walls and civilizations can be trod at Empúries. Unlike Tarraco, occupied continuously over the last two and a half millennia, by the ninth century Empúries had been abandoned. It was to be covered by the sands for ten centuries. Its "whispering centuries of ghosts" haunt the ruins. Rose Macaulay, searching for the roots of Western civilization, found what she wanted:

> Ampurias to-day is a place inexpressibly moving in its beauty and desolation. Along the intricate criss-cross of the streets that run between the vanished houses, cypresses darkly and necropolistically stand, and fig trees sprawl stickily in the sun. The columns of arcaded porticoes and of temples rear broken stumps against sky and sea.

Despite her awkward language, Macaulay catches the point of visiting Empúries: to reflect on the past. Sitting up near the top of the ruins, looking out over the curve of the Bay of Roses in the Mediterranean light, it is a place of great natural beauty. Combine this with the melancholy that ruins inspire—the evidence of death and of time that cannot ever be recovered. Josep Pla wrote: "Probably the most Greek thing about Empúries is the invitation its setting offers of contemplating the outside world with a wide, long and clear look... Here you can feel physically, without sophistication, the ancient world."

The Roman presence was not restricted to Empúries or Tarragona.

There are remains all over Catalonia. There is a magnificent bridge (restored), also called the Devil's Bridge, in the Seat car-factory town of Martorell. There are thermal baths at Sant Boi, Caldes de Montbuï and Caldes de Malavella (*caldes* means "hot springs"). At Vic there is a Roman temple; and at Badalona, an industrial city joined to Barcelona on its north side, is a Roman museum in a villa with baths, mosaics and the headless and armless, yet still beautiful "Venus of Badalona" statue. The Roman presence was so long and extensive—some 600 years—that nearly every town boasts remains.

In the heart of Barcelona, just behind the Plaça Sant Jaume, are pillars of an old temple in the Carrer Paradís (Paradise Street—religious name or shades of Roman orgies?). This is one of the dark, often deserted streets that counter-point so startlingly Barcelona's bustle. The pillars mark the highest point of the old Roman city, known as Mont Taber, ironically one assumes as it reaches only 55 feet above sea level. Barcelona's Via Laietana, constructed about 100 years ago, recalls the Roman name of the city, and still today a favourite Catalan forename is Laia.

Of course, Catalonia did not exist in Roman times. The area was a province of Rome, as later after 1714 and then under Franco, Catalonia was to be a province of Madrid. But the pleasure that many Catalans take in a Roman history, in being part of Europe's greatest empire, is that Madrid did not exist then. Today's state capital was just a wind-swept steppe. Catalonia's Roman history underlines how it is so much closer to the Mediterranean, to the "centre of the earth", the heart of Western civilization—and how its people are mixed. Carthaginians, Romans, Celtiberians, Greeks... even 2,000 years ago these had all passed through. Such thoughts of greater depth and fuller history do not help you eat, but have been comforting to Catalan nationalists in long decades of being dominated by the Spanish state's power.

Wetlands: the Empordà

Unlike Portbou among its black cliffs or Tarragona on its fortified hill, Empúries lies on a flat coast, to the south of the long curve of the Bay of Roses. To the north of the ruins are the wetlands of the Empordà, where two rivers, the Ter and Muga, run into the sea. These wetlands, *aiguamolls* in Catalan, are characteristic of the near-tideless

Mediterranean. Here, instead of a delta protruding into the sea, a network of shifting pools and lakes has formed, ideal for wildlife. If you are an ornithologist, you can do worse than pitch your tent at the Nautic Almatà campsite on the wetlands. It is a good site for lovers of mosquitoes, too. Not only flamingos and herons adore shallow, near-stagnant water.

Look north from the ruins across the wetlands and you see the tower-blocks of Empuriabrava. When J. G. Ballard and his young family holidayed at this area north of the *aiguamolls* in 1962, it was just sand and rock: "untouched by the feet of holiday-makers, the white sand was like fluffed sugar. I stepped out of the water and sank into its soft quilt," he wrote in his autobiographical *The Kindness of Women* (1991). This was the moment just before the change. Even then, as a friend explained to Ballard:

> "This island will vanish, literally turn into cement. They'll up-end the beach into half a mile of hotels and apartment houses." He pointed to the pine posts like so many gibbets which the surveyors had staked into the dunes... "They plan to consolidate the waterways with promenades of boutiques and bars, then sell off the housing plots to all those Dusseldorf dentists. Three years from now the place will be a film set, with a series of mock-antique Catalonian villages along the speed-boat canals."

We are more than forty years further down that road now and Ballard's friend was right: Empuriabrava was constructed as a kind of Little Venice. Canals ran up from the sea and the wealthier of Spain's expanding middle class (and German dentists too, perhaps) could moor their boats by the back gate and park their cars at the front. Here incidentally lies the source of Ballard's ferocious Mediterranean novels, *Cocaine Nights* (1996) and *Super-Cannes* (2000). The towns in these novels are fortified estates of bored foreigners playing murderous games because there is nothing else to excite them. Outside the towns is the apocalyptic beach, "a forlorn shelf of ochre sand littered with driftwood and water-logged crates, like the debris of a ransacked mind." The shock is that Ballard is not delineating a sci-fi fantasy, but describing Spain's coast as much of it is today.

In the 1970s a more proletarian part of Empuriabrava was put up: eighteen-storey tower-blocks of tiny one-bedroom flats just to the north of the mouth of the Ter. These were the weekend bolt-holes of couples from working-class suburbs of Barcelona or Girona. Now they are full of immigrants from Eastern Europe. In 2004 they hit the news because several migrants died in a fire; there are no safety doors or fire-escapes and cooking was done on butane stoves.

Just as Empúries takes us back 2,500 years, Empuriabrava provides the perfect metaphor for changes over the last fifty years on this coast. First isolated fishing villages, a joy for the first tourists and a prison for the young fishermen; then classy marina developments for a new middle class; next, working-class holiday flats; and finally today's death-trap slums for the poorest of the poor. If you are reading this in a generation's time, the ill-constructed tower-blocks may well have come down, to be covered by the sands as Empúries once was.

In the wetlands between Empúries and Empuriabrava, the Generalitat has constructed a nature park with tracks and hides. From the tower-blocks of Empuriabrava, a bird-loving paperless Romanian immigrant who can afford binoculars and manages to get back from a twelve-hour day before dark, can see numerous flocks of ducks and flamingos landing on the lagoons, storks nesting on the top of electricity pylons and (my favourite) long-necked white egrets riding on the backs of cows.

The Romanesque church at Llanars (Pyrenees)

Chapter Three
Romanesque Catalonia: The Pyrenees

Hispanic Marches

From Barcelona, the current capital of Catalonia, a train runs up to Ripoll, the Pyrenean birth-place of Catalonia a thousand years ago. This scenic route continues on to the Catalan Pyrenean border town of Puigcerdà and down towards Foix and Toulouse in France. It is an attractive, slow back door into or out of Catalonia. The train climbs first to Vic, said to be the religious and linguistic heart of Catalonia (in contrast to godless, half-Spanish speaking Barcelona). Vic is situated on a plain full of pig farms and prone to fog. If the fog lifts, you see on the treeless plain the strange flat-topped mud hills, remains of primeval deltas.

From Vic the rail and road follow the River Ter rapidly upwards to Ripoll, passing several abandoned textile mills, which used the mountain waters to drive the machinery. They are the ghosts of Catalonia's industrial revolution (see Chapter Five). Ripoll is a scruffy market-town today, often shadowed by the steep mountains above its valley. Ripoll's iron, coal and water gave it a considerable pistol-making industry in the seventeenth and eighteenth centuries, reflected in its provincial museum. The town's claim to fame, however, is not guns, but peace: the monastery of Santa Maria, consecrated in 1032 under the renowned Abbot Oliva and burial-place of the early counts of Barcelona and Besalú, among them the semi-mythic "founder" of Catalonia, Guifré el Pelós or Wilfred the Hairy.

In the time of Abbot Oliva, friend of popes and the learned men of the day, Bishop of Vic and Abbot of Ripoll from 1008 to 1046, Ripoll was one of the great intellectual centres of Europe. It was under Oliva that the abbey promoted at a congress in 1027 the *Pau i Treva de Déu* (Peace and Treaty of God). This argued for conflicts to be settled by negotiation rather than violence. Among its most notable principles was the establishment of the inviolability of refuge in a church and the suspension of war on Sundays, new ideas that became accepted gradually throughout Europe. Before the *Pau i Treva de Déu*, the counts and landlords would pursue opponents into churches and often kill them there. To this day in mostly godless Europe killing someone in a church is still considered worse than killing him or her in the street. The Church was beginning to use its powerful threat of excommunication to defend its own lands and staff. The Catalan cellist, Pau Casals, referred to the treaty in his famous 1971 address to the General Assembly of the United Nations:

> Today Catalonia is a group of provinces in Spain. But before Catalonia was a nation. Perhaps it was the greatest nation in the world. I'll tell you why; Catalonia had the first Parliament, long before England. And it was in Catalonia where the "United Nations" started. All the authorities of Catalonia met in the eleventh century at Toluges [near Perpignan, in the Roussillon], a city that today belongs to France but used to belong to Catalonia, to talk of peace. They introduced the Treaty of God.

Casals exaggerated to correct the world's ignorance of Catalonia. The treaty is a key part of Catalan nationalists' view of themselves as a peace-loving people, given to negotiation.

When Abbot Oliva died, the abbey library possessed 246 volumes and scholars travelled from all over the continent to study at its school (remember that Latin then was Europe's common language of writing). Whereas the Church vigorously crusaded to expel the Arabs from Spain, it just as energetically appropriated their more advanced culture. For example, Arabic numerals, the ones we use today, spread through Europe via Ripoll. Much medical knowledge was conserved through translation from the Arabic in monasteries such as Ripoll. The whole area, what is now the north-eastern part of modern Catalonia, was known as the Hispanic Marches and acted as a buffer between Al-Andalus—Moorish Spain in modern Andalusia—and the Franks to the north. A porous buffer, for it was also a thoroughfare, a *terra de pas*, with the border moving several times and mutual influence passing between the two cultures.

There is not much of Ripoll's original abbey left, save the great front porch and the cloisters. It suffered from an earthquake in the fifteenth century and was destroyed on the dissolution of the monasteries in 1835. The late nineteenth-century restoration was poorly done. However, the porch with friezes on either side of the door, remarkably saved from anti-clerical rage and now protected by glass against pollution, is a peak of Romanesque sculpture. The door is framed by the characteristic half-a-dozen rounded pillars, each slotting within the next. On both sides of the door run six ribbons of decorated friezes. These tell the Biblical stories to those who did not read, as is common on the façades of great medieval churches.

In Catalan history Guifré or Wilfred the Hairy is like King Arthur in England, a founding father of the nation. Guifré was a real enough historical figure, but his deeds merge into legend. The Hispanic Marches were divided in the ninth century into numerous small counties, gov-erned by often warring counts. Count of Ripoll, Guifré was created Count of Barcelona by Charlemagne's grandson, Charles the Bald, in 874. In about 880 he founded the original Ripoll monastery and is buried there. By conquest, marriage and inheritance Guifré managed to combine several Pyrenean counties, and his will left the counties of Barcelona, Girona and Vic undivided, thus laying the basis for a united country. When he died in battle in 897 on a raid against the Moors, it is said that Charles the Bald dipped his fingers in Wilfred the Hairy's blood and traced four red lines (four rivers of blood, in Raimon's words, see p.161) on his golden shield. These lines became the four red stripes on the yellow flag of Catalonia, which today flies over every public building and adorns nationalist balconies on feast days.

The Moors made their last incursion into the Marches in 985, sacking Barcelona, and in 988 Count Borrell of Barcelona did not renew his oath of allegiance to the Frankish king. What was the point, if the Franks could not defend the area from the Moors? More to the point, the Franks were too weak to do anything about his rebellion. The inde-pendence of Catalonia can be dated from then.

Barrel Vaults and Towers
The last chapter dwelt on Roman Tarraco and Greek Empúries on the Mediterranean coast, objects of intense romanticism from Martial to

Rose Macaulay. Within Catalonia itself the steep valleys and mountains of the Pyrenees are objects of romanticism even more than the coast: the lure of snowy peaks above green valleys, of eagles swirling above and of cow-bells echoing across the high, flower-filled pastures. The mountains of Catalonia also harbour a great artistic tradition: Romanesque architecture, the austere style summarized in the slender, tall, rectangular church tower above a hamlet perched on a high slope.

This chapter goes inland, into the Pyrenees, where the modern nation of Catalonia first started to take shape a thousand years ago. The Christians built in the out-of-the-way Pyrenees, hard of access to the Moors who were a threat for at least a century after 985, but who never controlled the mountain valleys. These fastnesses are where the early Romanesque churches are to be found. In Romanesque architecture today's frontier between Spain and France is of no consequence. Wilfred the Hairy was also Count of Carcassonne; Abbot Oliva of Ripoll was also Abbot of Cuixà, now in France; similar abbeys and churches were built on both sides of the Pyrenees. In these mountains not just a particular version of Europe-wide Romanesque architecture developed, but a special art of wall frescoes and paintings on wood, as well as the stone sculptures seen in the porch of the abbey at Ripoll.

There are some 2,300 Romanesque churches and hermitages in Catalonia, as well as hundreds of other Romanesque buildings, such as castles, bridges and houses. This is a greater density than anywhere else in the world and makes Romanesque the characteristic style of Catalonia. It was a team led by Puig i Cadafalch, the Art Nouveau architect, which first studied and listed these buildings a hundred years ago. It is probably no accident that of the famous Art Nouveau architects Puig is the most obviously influenced by medieval styles (see Chapter Six). Most Pyrenean villages have a Romanesque church, its slim tower often highlighted against a valley or the sky. In *The South* (1990), the Irish writer Colm Tóibín's first novel, his spare, simple—Romanesque, one could say—prose describes the village of Pallosa first seen through the eyes of a foreigner:

> The village was sheltered below the summit in a small dip; it stretched out beyond a stone church and a narrow street of houses towards a valley. The houses had been built from the yellow-brown stone of the

mountains and the rock behind the village was bare so that it was difficult at first to make out some of the houses.

Inside, such stone churches are dark and unornamented, with just one window and high rounded roofs. They are damp and cold as if they were extensions of the ground. They have none of the baroque luxury and adorned side-chapels of later Catholic churches.

Romanesque architecture spread through Europe around the tenth century with the rise of the monks of Cluny, who became in the early Middle Ages the continent's driving artistic and intellectual force. Roughly similar to what is known as Norman in England, Romanesque's distinctive feature is the round barrel- or tunnel-vault, so-called because the roof is curved like a tunnel, whereas in the later Gothic style architects used counter-weighing buttresses to push the roof up to a point.

In some of these Pyrenean churches, frescoes were painted around the altars. In later centuries they were whitewashed over, not to be rediscovered until Puig i Cadafalch's investigations at the start of the twentieth century. Indeed, some were not found until 1970.

The "rediscovery" of these twelfth- and thirteenth-century wall paintings coincided with the rise of Art Nouveau in Catalonia. These are the two high-points in Catalan architecture and art: the Romanesque, as the new state was forming; and Art Nouveau or *modernisme* from about 1880 to 1920, the fruit of re-birth after centuries of decline. Puig i Cadafalch, as well as being a major *modernista* architect, was also a conservative Catalan nationalist politician. The 1907 publication of his team's report-catalogue was key to the remarkable work conducted in the 1920s to remove the wall-paintings from many Pyrenean churches and bring them down to a museum in Barcelona. The removal required skill and patience, for these fragments of frescoed walls had to be transferred bit by bit to plaster. They are housed now in the National Palace on Montjuïc and make up the greatest exhibition of such art in the world. Art critic Robert Hughes affirmed: "They are the finest group of 'primitive' (pre-Giotto) painted murals in Europe... [though] the word 'primitive' hardly applies to artists who had such a... learned grip of the principles of Byzantine style."

What strikes visitors to the National Palace museum is the bright freshness of the murals' colours. A fresco is painted into wet plaster, so these unnamed artists had to work fast to do the work that has then lasted eight centuries. Gold and red dominate, alongside the blue of lapis lazuli. The faces and gestures are much more expressive than those normally seen in such early painting; the forms, anti-naturalist and geometric. Some say Picasso saw his Cubist geometry in them: if so, this was at Gòsol in the Pyrenees where he spent several weeks in the summer of 1906. Robert Hughes thought that the "strong look" of the paintings, "the gaze of power and appropriation", was pure Picasso.

The faces of the frescoes look straight at the viewer, who is drawn into the painting by such directness. The long-faced Christ in Majesty, from Sant Climent at Taüll, stares severely, mouth closed, cheeks red and big eyes steady. He wears a finely drawn, blue rich cloak. There is also multi-coloured painting on wood from the church of Santa Eulàlia at Erill-la-Vall; and from Sant Joan in Boí, camels and an entire bestiary alongside religious pictures.

Just as intellectuals came from all Europe to study at Oliva's Ripoll, so the unnamed artists travelled from Lombardy or Burgundy to carve and paint in the remote mountain valleys. The painting is too sophisticated to be only local. Neither artists nor materials came cheap, which underlines the wealth of the local Church and land-owners.

A polemic still lingers as to whether these frescoes should have been removed from their original Pyrenean sites at all. The museum authorities explain that they would have been lost otherwise: there was not the money to restore, outfit and secure the churches in situ. There was also a fear of Americans roaming Spain and snapping up treasures cheaply. And agents for Paris or Turin dealers were steadily removing Spanish art works from remote churches for no payment at all, especially after Puig's catalogue alerted the trade to these Pyrenean masterpieces. The New York Metropolitan Museum's famous Cloisters on northern Manhattan with its authentic Romanesque cloisters and apse, brought in the 1920s partly from Sant Miquel de Cuixà on the flanks of Mount Canigó in French Catalonia, illustrates the danger.

Certainly Barcelona's National Palace, built for the Spanish monarchs as part of the 1929 Universal Exposition, is a good museum for the frescoes. The palace is an enormous pompous building of domes and high ceilings on the flanks of the Montjuïc mountain. Its rooms, never used by King Alfonso XIII and his English Queen Victoria Eugenia, as they were expelled in 1931, have found a nobler purpose: they are so high and wide that small Pyrenean church interiors with their murals were reproduced to the original scale inside them.

The lament of critics of the frescoes' transfer is that a museum deadens them, isolates the art from daily life. In the churches this was collective art, open to all. Art was used as mass education in spiritual questions. The 1989 Nobel Prize-winning novelist Camilo José Cela, visiting the Pyrenees in 1955 to write one of his travel books that were more profitable than novels and less likely to fall foul of Franco's censors, expressed this: "Most of the art treasures that used to belong to the villages where God put them are now in Barcelona, embalmed and bureaucratized in the bone yard."

Though Cela liked to rail against bureaucrats (he had been one himself—a censor), he was not particularly interested in the churches themselves. He preferred describing the huge and delicious meals he ate, the people he talked to and the mountain women he ogled. This may in fact be many men's real ideal of tourism, a view supported by the big sales of Cela's travel books. Cela was writing forty years before the churches of the Boí Valley had become so fashionable that they were made a World Heritage Site in 2000. Ideally, of course, the frescoes should have been left in the churches and the churches restored, protected and secured, but the money was not there for that to happen. If they had been left there, it is probable they would have been stolen or spoiled.

The Boí Valley
After seeing the frescoes at Barcelona, it is worth visiting the Boí Valley itself, from which three of the six naves reproduced in the National Palace museum and several frescoes came. The valley lies well west of Ripoll, and access is from Lleida and Pont de Suert. John Payne caught its character, similar to many of the narrow valleys running up from the foothills into the high Pyrenees: "First impressions are of rushing water, pine and oak woods and high pastures with limestone outcrops... over the hedge as full of brambles and old man's beard as any in England, is a field with a haystack... The trees in the valley are lime, ash, pine, hazel and walnut."

There are seven hamlets running up the valley, each with a slate-roofed stone church with imitation replacement murals. These churches are aligned with each other along the length of the valley. Each church has a stylized tower several storeys high, whose windows dominate the country around. These pierced, slender towers, reminiscent of Italian campaniles, are exactly the same size on each storey, but the window-space grows larger on each ascending level. The secret of their beauty lies in this tension between the simple square symmetry of the structure, solid on the valley floor, and the expanding spaces that pull the eye toward the sky.

At the top of the valley, the village of Taüll now doubles as a ski resort. It has two churches, Santa Maria in its old centre and Sant Climent on the old outskirts, now swallowed up among the resort buildings. Sant Climent has a six-storey tower, the highest village tower in Catalonia. The cathedral at Vic has seven storeys, but Sant Climent's position at the head of the valley makes it more striking. Facing Taüll is the church of Erill-la-Vall, with five storeys. Local rivalry pushed these churches up towards God.

The top of the Boí Valley leads into the Aigüestortes (Tumbling Waters) National Park, with its fifty-odd still, sky-blue lakes and numerous, twisting streams. It is possible to drive to the Llebreta lake and either walk on from there or take one of the park's own white 4-wheel drives up to the highest lakes. Aigüestortes' lakes and pools give evidence of the action of glaciers, now noticeably receding with global warming. The top of the world, ferocious and lethal to humans in winter blizzards, is silent and extraordinarily beautiful in summer. The loose boulders and bare cliffs, scarred by the action of ice, are softened by the still water, turf and fir-trees. The time to visit the Pyrenees is spring, but spring comes late at these altitudes (Taüll is at over 5,000 feet). Late April or May gives that special high-mountain experience of warm sun beating down while snow still chills your feet.

For mountain walkers, botanists or bird-watchers, this is paradise. The air is clean. The "Alpine" flowers, untouched by herbicides, fill the meadows. Purple gentian, maiden pink, carline, foxglove, rhododendron, willow-herb, sempervivum, yellow *lilium pyrenaicum*, orchids, all covered with butterflies. Capercaillie scurry into forests of fir, silver birch and beech. Chamois deer jump across the hills. Lammergeier, griffon vulture, golden eagle can be spotted above the glacier-eroded cirques with their screes of loose stones and snowy peaks.

Access to the higher Pyrenees is up a series of narrow valleys, like the Vall de Boí itself or that of the railway up to Ripoll. Few roads get over the ridges between them. You can walk across in summer: now there are various trans-Pyrenean routes for back-packers to savour the high lakes and spring flowers. These are still wild-looking lands, though not unchanged. Skiers in the winter and walkers in spring and summer can lead to serious traffic jams and constant pressure on the land. Even fifty years ago, John Langdon-Davies, who lived in Catalonia most of his life and in Ripoll in 1921 when he was 24, wrote that many upper reaches of the valleys had been denuded of trees and the rivers dirtied by industry. He describes the Pyrenees in his racy *Gatherings from Catalonia* (1953):

> A series of narrow plains broken by hills in all directions, and surrounded by range after range of tree-covered mountains with bare rocky bluffs rising to distant grassy or granite peaks—here indeed is what our eighteenth century epicures of scenery would have called the picturesque, the sublime, the horrific. Wild gorges with thunderous waterfalls, rocky limbos crowned with a ruined castle or hermitage, sombre woods, barren wastes, lost and forgotten hamlets...

The Spanish Pyrenees below their highest points are fertile, with many shades of green pasture and forest, and cows on the high meadows in summer, whose bells ring across the valleys. In the higher valleys, Langdon-Davies' "lost and forgotten hamlets" have become re-inhabited by city-dwellers' second homes. Often the grandchildren of those who migrated to Barcelona fifty years ago have returned to the village, to do up the family house. If you go to one of these villages on an autumn or spring weekday (in winter it would be snow-bound, in summer bustling), you find it deserted, but many of the houses have been renovated. Shuttered, they await their weekend and summer proprietor. With the coast successfully ruined, for the last twenty years the mountain villages have become second-home preferences. Prices have soared like the lammergeiers and this means young villagers cannot stay even if they want to. These are no longer abandoned villages, but increasingly ghost villages out of season.

Besalú and Girona: the Jewish Tragedy

Besalú, at only about 600 feet in the pre-Pyrenean foothills, is everything Ripoll fails to be: a small, compact medieval town, untouched by industry and so not surrounded by tower-blocks to house workers. Wilfred the Hairy was count here, too. On the River Fluvià, about thirty miles upcountry from Catalonia's northern capital, Girona, Besalú is something of a dream museum piece for rich second home-owners and middle-class tourists. The bland hand of reform and repair has touched most of the town, though this is a hundred times better than tearing it all down. I talked there to Josep, a shopkeeper awaiting custom in the street. He lamented change, nostalgic for twenty years before, when sheep and cows were still driven through the streets and the ground floors of the houses were byres and pens instead of today's gift shops and garages. Josep's were perhaps crocodile tears, for he is no retired cowherd, but an incomer from Badalona and owner of a souvenir-shop by the bridge.

On the austere façade of the Romanesque church in the main square, once part of a Benedictine monastery, two lions face each other, a monkey (the devil) beneath one lion, a serpent (evil) under the other. This tale of good triumphing over bad is still understandable, unlike the frieze at Ripoll, which could be read by illiterate peasants 800 years ago but is a closed book to us book-readers today. Christian iconography is lost to us, with just some stray traces of knowledge remaining like the memory of a foreign language once studied at school.

Besalú's bridge, not straight but built on a dog-leg, with a portcullis gate in the middle to repel the hostile and collect taxes, is the town's pride and justly one of the most famous sites in Catalonia. Destroyed several times over the centuries by thaw waters and most recently in 1939 during the Republican retreat at the end of the Civil War, its line is handsome, the change of direction in the middle rare (it was perhaps to prevent cavalry charges, or perhaps to withstand better the sudden rises in the river), and its setting before wooded hills and the small grey-stone town, idyllic.

In 1964 the owner of a dry-cleaning business was forbidden by the town council to keep taking water from the river. He began to dig a well to find an alternative supply and broke through the roof of an underground chamber. Experts were called to examine a quite large and deep

Besalú: two lions triumphing over evil

room. It was found to be a *mikwah*, a Jewish ritual bath. This was confirmed by the Rabbi of Perpignan, in French Catalonia, for in Spain there were no rabbis. They had all left, been forcibly converted or been expelled in the fourteenth and fifteenth centuries. The Grand Rabbi of Paris came too and certified that this was indeed a *mikwah*, and the only one in Spain. The fact that Besalú, a city of a similar size to Girona in the Middle Ages, has hardly grown since meant that the land had not been continually built on and so the *mikwah* had been conserved. The considerable Jewish community of Besalú had left in 1436. Hoping to return, they sealed the entrance to the *mikwah*.

Steep steps lead down into the chamber. There is then a platform and further steps down to the river water that still circulates through the bathing area, as it did six centuries ago. The walls made of small, square stones are intact, with the lines that flood-waters reached visible. It is clear where the dry-cleaner made his hole in the roof, for the stone of the modern repair is lighter.

These baths confront the visitor with the tragedy of Spain's Jews. If they continued their religious practices in secret after forcible conversion, as a great many probably did, they often betrayed themselves because they did not stink. The rarely-washing Christians smelled like clothed dogs, while the Jews, though their bathing was ritual in purpose, nevertheless removed much sweat and grime when they submerged themselves in flowing water. Urban Romans, too, had washed most days: the bath-houses at imperial Tarraco and elsewhere were centres of social life. Medieval Christians, however, exalted the spirit and disdained the body. People who scourged their wicked bodies were not likely to worry about hygiene or the comfort of a washed body. Indeed, medieval Christian rejection of washing may have contributed to the pandemics—even the Black Death—which the Romans, with their great care in water supply, had never suffered.

The Besalú *mikwah* is a poignant place, evoking the unfulfilled hope of return, the injustice never remedied, the memory of the reasons the Jews left. Jews in twelfth- and thirteenth-century Spain were relatively stable, in Besalú living freely in any part of town and working in many different jobs. As conflict between Church and State or between the nobles and the populace increased, Jews became common scapegoats. After the Black Death in the middle of the fourteenth century killed about one-third of the population of Catalonia, the anger and shock of a traumatized populace could easily be turned against the Jews. They were forbidden certain jobs and driven to live in ghettos. In Besalú the ghetto was the area just by the river where the baths were discovered. In the ghetto, it was no longer possible to work as a doctor, as several Jews had, because it was forbidden to travel round town to visit Christian patients. Blamed for not just Jesus' death but for any murder or death that might occur, they were eventually expropriated, expelled or murdered by those very monks who had built the great Romanesque churches we admire. The Jews were an integral part of that medieval society, but in 1436 they upped and left Besalú, sealing the baths behind them.

There are many traces of that lost Jewish society in Catalonia. The *call*—the Catalan word for ghetto—in Barcelona is a network of the most attractive, twisting streets of the Old City, between the Ramblas and the Plaça Sant Jaume. In recent years the old main synagogue has been found and restored: it is thought to be 1,800 years old, making it, if so, the oldest surviving Jewish building in Western Europe. It can be visited at c/ Marlet 5. It is in Girona, though, that the most extensive memorial of Jewish life in Catalonia is found. The Bonastruc ça Porta centre was opened in 1992, after restoration (still going on) of its crumbling houses and twisting alleys. This complex, on the Carrer de la Força running parallel to the river, is a museum of the city's Jewish life at the heart of the city's medieval quarter. It illustrates the claustrophobic life shut into the ghetto, without windows onto the outside streets or the river.

Girona has a remarkably beautiful, walled old quarter, built up the side of a hill by the River Onyar. Tourists can easily miss it, for until ten years ago there were no buses from the airport eight miles out of town, only the coaches running straight down to the Costa Brava resorts. The Bonastruc ça Porta centre is, aptly given the history, overshadowed by the cathedral just down the street. The cathedral's baroque façade with a non-baroque rose window stands at the top of a triple flight of 86 steps, covered in summer by tourists and students from the nearby university like the Spanish Steps in Rome. Inside, the cathedral is Gothic and is famous for its single nave with a 75-foot span, the widest Gothic nave in Christendom. "Its spacious breadth makes a remarkable effect of tranquil strength and lack of fuss," wrote Rose Macaulay. When Guillem Bofill presented the project to the chapter in 1416, they doubted it could be built. The project only went ahead after a committee of seven architects had studied it.

Girona is to my mind two cities, or a city of two moods: the severe city of the cathedral on the hill dominating the Jewish quarter and the Arab baths. On a grey January day, when temperatures can drop to below freezing, it is grim and thoughts turn to the 25 sieges the city has suffered and how in 1391 the Jews had to take refuge in the Galligants Tower and emerged 17 weeks later to find their houses destroyed.

And then the light, warm mood of Girona's most beautiful feature: the soft-coloured houses in ochre, beige and pink that line the river and are reflected in it. One finds these houses with their ground floors hanging out over the water in several Pyrenean towns: Camprodón is a good example, but only in Girona is there the warmth of these colours. The pedestrian iron bridge over the pebbly river from the bank just by the elegant, arcaded Plaça de la Independència is the best approach to this long row of houses. The Plaça de la Independència and the modern city around it recall that Girona is Spain's wealthiest province and the city's prosperity shows in its conservation, restorations and shops.

Catalonia and Spain have not fully acknowledged their Jewish history. Though nowadays the *mikwah* at Besalú or the Girona centre are major tourist attractions and the latter in particular has been developed accordingly, there is almost total ignorance of this history. Who knows that, between 1492 and 1966, no legal Jewish religious service was held in Spain? One has to conclude that the attractions have only been developed for the tourist market. Even the helpful and well-informed tourist office at Besalú insisted that no Jews were actually killed in Besalú, a curious kind of centuries-old comfort, which shows failure to grasp the terror that made them leave. Even in the unlikely circumstance that no Jews had been killed in Besalú, many Jews had been killed elsewhere. The Jews of Besalú left in fear.

Lucky for the Jews, one might think, there are few left in Spain, for in everyday language, in both Spanish and Catalan, terms such as *marrano* or *marrà* (filthy pig), originally meaning Jews forced to convert, or (in Castilian) *una judiada* to describe a dirty deed, stemming from *judío* (Jew), are commonly used. Most telling was the 2003 campaign for the presidency of Barcelona Football Club. Almost as much media attention is paid to this election as to the campaign for the presidency of the Generalitat. One of the two main candidates, Lluís Bassat, was attacked by another of the candidates as "not being a proper Catalan." His Jewishness was highlighted and linked to his business wealth and support for Israel. Joan Laporta, the winner of the election, was not responsible for this smear campaign, but nor did he speak out against it. On election day a group of *boixos nois* (the "wild boys", fanatical supporters infiltrated by ultra-right political groups) spray-painted anti-Semitic slogans around the ground and heckled Bassat with racist chants. The press reported this, but made no specific criticism. It is unthinkable that this could occur in a high-profile election campaign in Britain or the United States. What does it show? Not that people are more or less racist than elsewhere, but that the Jews are long gone and their absence has created ignorance about anti-Semitism. It is undeniably good to have parties of Brooklyn tourists visiting the *mikwah* at Besalú, but the modern house needs to be put in order.

Chapter Four

Glory and Rapine: Poblet and Athens

"A great feudal monastery"

Well south of Ripoll, the Boí Valley and Besalú, in shallow, fertile valleys between inland Lleida and coastal Tarragona near the towns of Montblanc and Valls, two enormous monasteries and a convent, built a century later than the Pyrenean churches and forming another centre of Romanesque architecture, still stand: Santes Creus, Poblet and the convent of Vallbona.

After the sacking of Barcelona in 985, the threat of Moorish invasion receded through the eleventh and twelfth centuries. Catalonia became consolidated as a political entity, as did its Romance language that was very close to Provençal. In the eleventh century territories towards the south were conquered from the Moors, an area which became known as New Catalonia, distinguishing it from the Old Catalonia of Barcelona, Girona and the Pyrenees.

Meanwhile, the Cistercian order had split off from the powerful Burgundian abbey of Cluny. Whereas the early Romanesque churches in Spain were secluded in out-of-the-way places like the Vall de Boí, where they were safer from Moorish invasion, the three abbeys of the plain were founded in places from which the Moors had just been expelled. The Cistercians exhibited a feature that is characteristic of religious splits: the new order was sterner and more "orthodox" than the Cluniacs they split from. They rebuked the Cluny monks, with some reason, for feasting, complacency and growing lazy and fat. The Cistercians did not believe in founding monasteries in protected places, but in proselytizing and pushing forward the frontiers of Christianity. The dormitory at Poblet makes you think of this militant austerity: it is high, vast, unheatable, cool today even in high summer. Here the monks slept in rows on straw on the ground, like cows in a manger.

Poblet' empty cloisters

At Poblet, the biggest monastery complex in Catalonia, visitors are obliged to take a guided tour, for monks are "still" in residence. Sacheverell Sitwell saw them as indispensable to the full beauty of Poblet:

> The Cistercian monks in their white robes and pointed hoods, so subtly differenced from the white Carthusians—and so much resembling the moors of Fez, for theirs too is a costume that has come down, unaltered from the twelfth century—are in entire harmony with the pointed arches of the abbey church.

"Still" is in inverted commas because there are indeed monks in residence now, but for a long period Poblet was empty. In 1835 the monastic life which had lasted with little change for 682 years was suddenly ended by the convulsive dissolution of the monasteries. Poblet was sacked and its monks fled or were killed. Widespread church-burnings took place in Barcelona the same year, clearing land for industrial development, as Chapter Six describes.

Poblet, despite its foundation by a "purer" order, became a manorial village, in Rose Macaulay's words "girt by its great wall—monastery, church and chapels, cloister, chapter house, orchards and gardens, huge wine cellars, granaries, store-houses, stables, hostels, domestic offices for servants, all the dependencies of a great feudal monastery." The 1835 sacking was not the work of French troops, who had plundered the monastery in 1812, nor of forerunners of the anarchists of 1936. It was the work of local peasants who seized the opportunity to destroy their hated landlords. The monks' feudal powers included imprisonment (and torture), serfdom and the rights to the bridal night—though this last was traditionally bought off by a payment.

The sheer immobility of Spanish history, untouched at Poblet as elsewhere by the development of capitalism, led to the violence of change when it came. One can see in this anti-clerical, anti-feudal uprising of 1835 that Spain was ready for Bakunin's violent form of anarchism, brought into Barcelona a generation later by his Italian agent Fanelli (see Chapter Sixteen). If there is no evolution, no possibility of gradual change at all, then the conditions are ripe for violent action to change everything overnight.

Later Poblet was reclaimed as a National Monument, but left to moulder in its ruins, "an abomination of desolation... the most utterly ruined ruin that can exist. Violence and vengeance are written on every stone... as if the shock of a terrible earthquake had passed over them," wrote Augustus Hare, always good value in his vehemence, in 1871. What we see today is a huge restoration, as at Ripoll.

The impressive alabaster royal tombs of Poblet hang in a double row above head height in the cool gloom of the church, where Hare found donkeys tied up. Eight counts of Barcelona, the Catalan monarchs, are buried at Poblet, including Pere el Gran (The Great), who conquered Sicily in the thirteenth century. Several of the monarchs' tombs have two effigies: one of the monarch as soldier-king, one of him as monk. Richard Ford, who found the monastery "in a deplorable state of neglect" in 1843, commented: "...this is truly characteristic of the medieval Spaniard, half soldier, half monk, a crusading knight of Santiago; his manhood spent in combating for the cross, his declining years dedicated to religion."

The tombs, too, are restored, for the anarchists who came a hundred years later, in 1936, to further sack the monastery broke them open. Today's guide says that they were ignorant people hunting for treasure. "They didn't know," she told us, "that, unlike Muslims, Christian Kings were not buried with jewels." This may be so, but the real motive was not robbery, but militant atheism. The anarchists broke open coffins to demonstrate that there was nothing sacred about monarchs. Kings were flesh and blood decayed to dust, like everyone else. Breaking open monarchs' tombs and dragging out their corpses were dramatic visual gestures, not unlike the drama of the Bible stories told on the Ripoll frieze or on the Pyrenean frescoes. In Barcelona, in that same 1936 revolution, they broke open tombs of nuns and priests and exhibited the remains for similar educational reasons: to show that the corpses were human, not incorrupt as the Church asserted.

All the sacking does not alter the beauty of Poblet, at the entrance of a fertile valley. Indeed the violence adds to its beauty by dragging into turbulent history this pastoral spot surrounded by vineyards and low, rolling hills. Otherwise, the idyllic feel of its landscape would be false. While the medieval monks prayed, the lay brothers and peasants toiled in the fields or in the huge now-empty wine-store, with its runnels cut into the stone for the liquid. Cees Nooteboom caught the essence of its architecture:

> A Romanesque gate and Gothic arch usher me into the Church. "It is with landscapes as with architecture," Unamuno said, "nakedness is the last aspect you learn to appreciate." The interior is bare, austere, light, the walls high and undecorated... functional forthrightness of the unadorned Cistercian style... renunciation of superfluity.

The style has nothing to do with the over-wrought gold and silver ornamentation found in later Spanish and Italian churches. There is no stained glass, no adorned capitals, no ornate chapels, no distractions. As at nearby Tarragona, the soft-looking local sandstone is not harsh. The unadorned space in the Poblet church makes one think of infinity, of emptiness.

Santes Creus (Holy Crosses), nearby, is in a similar setting, but with a village around it, whose houses have the air of a cathedral close like Salisbury's. There are no monks here, so no guide to prevent vis-

Embroidered stones, Santes Creus

itors from wandering in and out of chapels, living-quarters and into some unrestored, crumbling areas. One door-less door-space is closed by brambles growing back over the worn and cracked stones. The cemetery has no crosses or tombs: monks were buried unmarked in the ground for their remains to mingle, as used to happen in Spanish villages.

Santes Creus' church is even more austere than Poblet's. In the middle, though, hangs a large, greenish, modern candelabra. It makes you wonder whether modern priests have any sense of the awe of God. The cloister at Santes Creus is later, in the Gothic style, which means that its capitals are beautifully carved with figures of animals—bats, lions, donkeys—and monks working. Alastair Boyd in *The Essence of Catalonia* (1988) says that part of this cloister was designed in the 1330s by the English master, Reinard Fonoll. If so, this is a rare example of an early medieval artist being named. Influence was from both North and South, for the cloister is full of orange trees and the sound of water, Arab features you do not find in France or Italy.

49

Peace and Conquest

The grandiose tombs of the great kings and their queens at Poblet remind us of the complex early history of Catalonia. By the twelfth century Catalonia was well established both north and south of the current France-Spain border. With some reason, nationalists like to recall the *Usatges* of Barcelona, composed first in about 1060 under Ramon Berenguer I (there were four successive counts with this name; and for good measure Ramon Berenguer I's father was called Berenguer Ramon). Like Oliva's *Pau i Treva de Déu*, the *Usatges* was a stepping-stone towards the rule of law. It was a constitutional charter that limited the absolute powers of the feudal monarch, not of course in favour of the peasantry, but to the advantage of the counts and burghers in exchange for their allegiance. The *Usatges* predates Britain's *Magna Carta*, a similar contract between barons and king, by 150 years. It and the *Treva* are often cited as showing that Catalonia was more freedom-loving from its earliest days than absolutist France and Castile. It was the first democracy in Europe, claimed Pau Casals. It certainly introduced the idea of "pacting", dear to Catalans' self-image to this day. And negotiated pacts are clearly more desirable than violent conquest.

In a tone somewhat different from the *Usatges*, more consonant with Catalonia's growing imperial ambition, Ramon Berenguer IV explained why he continued to call himself Count of Barcelona, even after he had united the houses of Catalonia and Aragon by marrying Petronella of Aragon in 1137. He boasted: "Because I would be the least of Kings, but am the greatest of Counts".

With the death at the Battle of Muret in 1213 of King Pere (Peter) the Catholic, the aspirations of Catalonia towards what is now southern France were violently curtailed. The united Aragonese and Catalan crowns turned their attentions to the Mediterranean. They conquered and colonized the Balearic Islands, Catalan-speaking to this day, apart from the hordes of German and British immigrants and tourists. They expanded south, expelling the Moors from Valencia. This is why today Catalan (or Valencian: it is the same language) is spoken right down to the south of Alacant (or Alicante in Castilian) province and into the edge of Murcia. It gives rise to the fancy entertained by the most expansion-minded nationalists today of creating a Greater Catalonia from the Roussillon to Murcia.

Francis Drake is known as an admiral in English history and a pirate in Spanish school-books. Similarly, Roger de Llúria who led the conquest of the western Mediterranean at the end of the thirteenth century, establishing Catalan power in Sardinia, Naples and Sicily, is a Great Admiral in Catalonia and a pirate-tyrant in Italy. It is Roger de Llúria's statue, already noted, that dominates the Balcony of the Mediterranean at Tarragona. Curiously with his back to the sea, the admiral's statue gazes inland, towards peaceful Santes Creus monastery, where he is buried.

Catalonia's imperial expansion produced one of medieval Europe's greatest minds, Ramon Llull or Raymond Lully (1232-1316). Brought up in Mallorca after the island's conquest, Llull wrote over 200 books and travelled throughout the Christian and Arab worlds. Llull was the first European philosopher to write treatises in the vernacular; in doing so, he expanded the range of Catalan. Recognized as their precursor by Descartes and Leibniz, Llull attempted to systematize all human knowledge. As the American philosopher Anthony Bonner wrote: "[Llull] hardly ever treats a concept in isolation, but presents it as part of a group of concepts, where what matters is... its relationship with adjoining concepts."

His motives were Christian. A mystic, his was yet the dream of reason: that if only Christianity was expressed with sufficient clarity and logic, the Muslims would not be able to resist the true word of God. Llull learned Arabic to spread his ideas in Islamic countries and advised popes to spread Christianity by word not sword. It is probable that he died at the hands of an enraged crowd while preaching outside a mosque in Tunisia.

The greatest material glory of this imperial conquest eastwards came at the over-ripe end of the Catalan empire: the reign of Alfons the Magnanimous, King of Naples ("Naples" meant then the whole of southern Italy) from 1435 to 1458, renowned for his patronage of the arts, his extravagance and his alleviation of taxes on the poor. The contradiction between the last two points led to his extorting money from the Jews and eventually his court's bankruptcy, but has not tarnished his reputation. Jacob Burckhardt wrote of this Aragonese-Catalan, in the nineteenth-century classic *The Civilisation of the Renaissance in Italy*.

The great Alfonso... Brilliant in his whole existence, fearless in mixing
with his people, mild and generous towards his enemies, dignified and
affable in intercourse, modest notwithstanding his legitimate royal
descent... Alfonso was able to entertain distinguished guests with unri-
valled splendour; he found pleasure in ceaseless expense, even for the
benefit of his enemies, and in rewarding literary work knew absolutely no measure. Poggio received 500 pieces of gold for translating
Xenophon's *Cyropaedia.*

Imperial Rapine

Whereas Alfons created at Naples the most glittering Catalan court ever
seen, within Catalonia more lasting fame has been reserved for another
Italian Catalan. We have to step back 150 years to the short life of the
warrior Roger de Flor, born in Brindisi in 1266 and murdered in
Adrianopolis in 1306.

A curious event took place in October 2005. Joaquim Nadal, prominent socialist and Minister for Public Works in the Catalan government,
went to Greece on behalf of the Generalitat. His purpose was to visit the
Athos peninsula and apologize for the sacking of the monasteries there
700 years earlier. Nadal was seeking to make amends for a historic injustice, but also taking the political high-ground in long-running,
smouldering differences with the Spanish government. The sub-text of
his visit could be: if we Catalans are disposed to apologize for errors
(showing our most "pacting" and democratic face), then the Madrid government is exposed as narrow-minded and rancorous for refusing to
apologize for frequent offences to Catalonia, such as in 1518 (banning
of American trade), 1641 (War of the Reapers), 1714 (suppression of all
national rights) or 1939 (ditto 1714).

The sub-text is not just historical: it refers to current events, such as
the wave of hysteria whipped up by nationalist-centralist Spain in
2005/2006 against the proposal for a new Catalan Statute of Autonomy.
The Spanish Right exceeded all normal bounds of parliamentary dis-
course; even to suggest, as the Catalan parliament did, the inclusion in
the preamble to the statute of "Catalonia is a nation" was habitually
referred to as an insult. Within some echelons of the COPE, the
Catholic Church's radio station, and of the opposition Partido Popular,
the Catalan government was referred to as Nazi, because it was based on

an alliance between nationalists and socialists.

In his visit to Greece, Nadal was following in Pope John Paul II's footsteps. When Wojtyla visited Athens in 2001, he apologized for the abuses of the Catholic Church in its wars against the Greek Orthodox schism. What is known in Greece as "the Catalan revenge" was the part of these wars for which Nadal was apologizing. This takes us to the story of the Catalans in what today is Greece and Turkey. Whatever had the Catalans done, to warrant an apology 700 years later?

Roger de Flor was an impoverished son of a German nobleman. A terrible situation: impoverished, he had nothing to eat, but as a nobleman he was not prepared to work like anyone else. His skill with arms, ruthlessness and leadership qualities took him from poverty to wealth and European notoriety in just fifteen years. In Gibbon's words, "Roger was successively a templar, an apostate, a pirate, and at length the richest and most powerful admiral of the Mediterranean." At the same time as Llull's impeccable logic was failing to convert Muslims, Roger set out on a more conventional career of conversion by terror. Roger started by joining the Knights Templar, with whom he went on the last crusade in 1291. Accused, however, of robbing treasure from the Christians under his protection during their evacuation from Acre in Palestine, he was expelled from the order. He became a mercenary, a word which sounds worse now than then, when most armies were raised by paying a general who would pay his army. There were no professional, standing armies. Federic II, the Catalan King of Sicily, son of the Pere el Gran buried at Poblet, named him head of the companies of *almogàvers*. These were companies that had fought for the Catalan crown throughout the thirteenth-century expansion. In 1282 some 15,000 *almogàvers* spearheaded the Catalan conquest of Sicily, but with the peace treaty signed in 1302 these warriors were unemployed.

The emperor of Byzantium, Andronicus II, sought their help against the Turks. Federic was only too glad to pay the passage out of Sicily of 4,000 restless *almogàvers* on 39 ships under the command of Roger de Flor. In Asia Minor, what is today western Turkey, Roger, with his "Great Catalan Company", triumphed against the Muslims—unlike the defeat at Acre. Andronicus named Roger grand-duke and offered him his niece Maria in marriage. Yet Roger de Flor was not content with enjoying his triumph in peace and prosperity. Ambition gnawed his soul and he demanded to be named King of Asia Minor. The emperor, weak in arms but not in the head, perceived Roger's ambition and negotiated with him. He named Roger "Caesar" and ceded him part of the territory he had conquered. Invited then to a banquet at Adrianopolis—some say to celebrate the accord; others say, to negotiate outstanding payments to the *almogàvers*—Roger de Flor and 130 of his commanders were plied with fine manners, food and wine and then murdered at the table on 4 April 1306.

Andronicus had been more astute than wise. He beheaded the *almogàvers*, but had underestimated the body. The dead Roger de Flor's army attacked the empire head-on, burning and pillaging their way round the coast of modern Greece and Turkey to Constantinople itself. This became known as the "Catalan vengeance". As a result two Catalan states were founded in Greece, at Neopatria and Athens, ruled by the Catalans for seventy years. It led the Count of Barcelona, Pere the Ceremonious, to boast: "There is no jewel in the world more beautiful than the Parthenon." The Catalan flag flew on the Acropolis, but at least the Catalans did not remove the marbles, unlike Lord Elgin 500 years later.

Catalonia's imperial exploits were reflected in the literature of the period. "Since literature follows political power, a Catalan literature became inevitable," as Gerald Brenan put it. There were four great Catalan "chronicles" written in the thirteenth and fourteenth centuries. Two of these were written by Counts of Barcelona themselves, royal autobiographies. (One might wish British monarchs had been cultured enough to write books.) One of the other two, Ramon Muntaner, wrote contemporary history: Muntaner was an administrator in Sicily for Roger de Flor and later commander of the garrison at Gallipoli on the Constantinople expedition. He is a unique witness of the events he is describing, though this does not make him always reliable. His objective was to glorify his commander Roger de Flor, the great warrior infamously murdered, and he glosses over episodes of rape and pillage that reflect poorly on his *almogàvers*. Muntaner's chronicle made the German-Italian Roger de Flor a folk hero throughout Catalonia. Muntaner was both a magnificent contemporary source and the creator of imperial myth.

More concerned with facts although less vivid, a Thucydides to

Muntaner's Herodotus, the fourth chronicler Bernard Desclot described the *almogàvers* as follows:

> These men called almogàvers live only from carrying arms. They do not inhabit the cities, but the mountains and forests, and wage war without truce against the Saracens, entering their territory for a day or two to steal and take prisoners. They live from these earnings. Few people could support their lives. They can go two days without eating if need be or eating grasses from the fields... Each one is armed with a good knife, a good spear and two darts. On their backs they carry a leather bag with food for two or three days. They are very strong men and light for hunting and fleeing. They are Catalan and Aragonese.

In Catalonia's later three-century decline, the mountainous countryside was rife with bandits. In the *almogàvers*, prototype guerrilla fighters, one can see where they came from. The word *almogàver* is of Arab origin, like nearly all words in Spanish and Catalan beginning with "al". It probably comes from *al-mughânir*, meaning "raider". Without armour, on foot, strong and fast, the *almogàvers* were fearsome raiders. They inspired enormous fear in the more conventional armies they faced. Muntaner writes that before battle they banged their short swords on the ground, shouting "Wake up, iron!" (*Desperta ferro*) until the sparks flew. Desclot says that, unlike the neat French troops (whom both he and Muntaner despised for being too well-dressed to fight properly), the Catalans were filthy, long-haired and half-naked: "[the almogàver] wore only an animal-skin tunic tied with a cord, without a shirt, he was black from the heat of the sun, his beard was very long, his hair black and long..."

As well as filling the Chronicles of Muntaner and Desclot, the raids of this legendary imperialist strike-force became the subject matter of what is generally considered the first modern novel, *Tirant lo Blanch* by the Valencian Joanot Martorell, published in 1490. The eponymous Tirant is a Breton knight who starts his adventures by becoming champion of England, reminding readers of one of Europe's main sources of chivalric legend: King Arthur and his Round Table. Then Tirant changes worlds. As the novel bridges the chivalric Middle Ages with modern irony and realism, so Tirant moves from England to Constantinople, where he meets the Princess Carmesina.

Cervantes' view of Tirant is famous. He has the priest tell the barber in a discussion of literature at the start of *Don Quixote*: "...because of its style, [*Tirant lo Blanch*] is the best book in the world: in it knights eat, and sleep, and die in their beds, and make a will before they die, and do everything else that all the other books of this sort leave out."

As Cervantes suggests, its greatness as a novel is how it combines the knightly tradition, which despite the artifice of its manners nevertheless was the life led at the courts of the time, with realism—what other chivalric books left out. Martorell describes the history and customs of the places Tirant visits in detail, giving a clear picture of the court—though this is more like Barcelona's than Constantinople's. It is also an erotic and psychological book in its description of the relationship of the two lovers. Indeed, its freedom in talking of sex and its author's lack of moralizing commentary are features marking Tirant's originality. The style of stories prior to Tirant was to draw out an explicitly religious and conventional moral. Plaerdemavida (Pleasureofmylife), the lady-in-waiting, is like Chaucer's bawdy women. Free in sexual discussion, she smuggles Tirant into the princess' bed. With Tirant, the modern novel is born. Not only history—the public affairs recounted in the Chronicles—fills its pages, but it does what the novel uniquely does: it explores the contradictions between people's formal public face and conventional morality, and their private desires and practice.

The hero Tirant lo Blanch ("the White") is based on Roger de Flor, but ironically. Tirant, like Roger, is a triumphant warrior. The Emperor crowns Tirant Caesar, yet Tirant's fate is not to be treacherously murdered at Adrianopolis, but in the same city to catch a chill while walking by the river and die of pneumonia. Irony, the deflation of claims to glory, flowers at the dawn of the novel.

The history of Roger de Flor and his brave, fearsome and filthy *almogàvers* should make us think. They were, of course, not kindly visitors to Greece and Asia Minor. They did not practise Catalan "pacting": imperialists do not pact with the people they conquer. Still today, in some parts of coastal Sicily, when parents want to frighten their children into behaving, they hiss: "The Catalans are coming, the Catalans are coming." The Catalans were the bogey-men. Modern Catalan nationalists are proud that Catalan is spoken in four states: France, Spain, Andorra and Italy. However, nationalist pride should be nuanced; as John Payne points out in his *Catalonia*, it is only spoken in L'Alguer (on Sardinia and thus part of Italy) because conquering Catalans threatened with prison or death those who refused to speak it. This mirror-image of Franco's 1940s insistence that only Castilian Spanish be used should make Catalans reflect before rushing to celebrate the geographical range of their language. Joaquim Nadal's apology at Athos may seem an exaggerated gesture, but there is no doubt that Catalans have not always been peaceful pacters, nor only victims squeezed between French and Spanish expansion. They too had their moment of imperial glory and rapine. There was good cause behind Nadal's apology for the "Catalan vengeance".

Jacint Verdaguer, Catalonia's national poet

Chapter Five

The Poet-Priest and the Indiano:
Verdaguer and Antonio López

Catalonia's long decline from the splendour of the art of the Vall de Boí, Poblet, Llull and *Tirant lo Blanch* and from the riches of its medieval empire was gradual, often hardly noticed at the time, because it lasted several centuries. Castilian power and language slowly became prominent. From today's vantage-point we can see the union of Aragon and Castile in a new Spanish state in 1492 as a fateful moment, but in April 1493 when the new monarchs Ferdinand of Aragon and Isabel of Castile received Christopher Columbus in Barcelona's Plaça del Rei on his first return from the Americas, who could have imagined that Catalonia was going to be marginalized? To the marvel of the crowds, Columbus brought to Europe fabulous animals such as parrots, unknown plants such as bananas, and the "Indians" themselves, who were baptized in the font of Barcelona's cathedral. But Columbus' voyage was to open up wealth for the Atlantic ports of Cádiz and Sevilla, and bring the 1518 prohibition of Catalan trade with America, for the centralizing Spanish monarchs feared Catalan marine mercantile power.

The two most dramatic events of the centuries that followed were the War of the Reapers, which lasted from 1640 to 1652, and the 1714 summer siege of Barcelona. In the middle of the Thirty Years War the Catalans rose against the Spanish King Philip IV and his minister, the Count-Duke Olivares, at Corpus Christi 1640. The rising was an explosion of peasant rage against years of having Spanish troops billeted on them, with all the abuses and extra expense that entailed, combined with increased taxation from an impoverished monarchy. The Spanish Viceroy was killed in the reapers' uprising and Catalonia declared its independence. Olivares sent an army, forcing the Catalan leader Pau Claris to seek protection from the King of France. After Olivares' fall in 1643 Philip IV, overstretched in the imperial war in Flanders, pursued a softer policy, but by 1651 Catalonia surrendered. Its autonomy was restricted further, but preserved. The main effects of the War of the Reapers were two: Portugal regained its independence (Philip could not keep a third war front open) and in 1659 Roussillon and Cerdanya, Catalonia's territories north of the Pyrenees, were annexed by France.

The end of the seventeenth century was a tough period for Catalonia: it was invaded three times by France, which occupied Barcelona in 1697. Weakened in relation to both Spain and France, Catalonia's leaders took the wrong side in the War of the Spanish Succession. It seemed a good bet to ally themselves with England and Holland against the absolutist Bourbon monarchy in Madrid. Yet when the pretender to the Spanish throne, Archduke Charles, became the German Emperor in 1711, England and Holland changed tack. They did not want the same person on the German and Spanish thrones and ceased supporting Archduke Charles' claim to Spain. Catalonia was left high and dry and, after a ten-week siege, Barcelona fell to Philip V's army on 11 September 1714.

This latter defeat led to the formal dismantling of all Catalan rights in the judiciary, education and government. Martial law, with its executions and terror, was imposed. The Generalitat was disbanded, Catalan autonomy was removed, the university was closed, citadels were built to control Lleida and Barcelona, the Catalan language was forbidden. Catalonia had lost. The year 1714 meant that it had failed to become a small trading nation like Holland and was to be another exploited province of the backward, poverty-stricken Spanish monarchy. This is not a history book as such, but the subjection of Catalonia to Spain's central monarchs has to be grasped if the subsequent renaissance of the nineteenth and twentieth centuries—and the great art it threw up—is to be appreciated. In a nation without a state, the defeats underlining that statelessness chafe at the mind like blisters under a coarse vest chafe the skin.

A long historical view might say that Catalonia was only treated in 1714 the same as it had treated Sicilians and Greeks in the thirteenth and fourteenth centuries. This is clearly true, but one historical injustice suffered—slaughter, rapine, poverty—is not offset because the victims' ancestors had done the same several hundred years before. Yet the same applies the other way round: arguments that Catalans are intrinsically democratic because of their medieval institutions are specious. They are reminiscent of British claims to superiority because of their democratic institutions, or the American spirit of justice and equality wielded to justify foreign invasion.

The Renaissance

History often needs high theatre to fix a change in people's minds. The *Jocs Florals* (Floral Games) of 1866 saw such a dramatization of the Catalan renaissance. A twenty-year old young seminarist from Vic won two of the main prizes. The unknown poet caused a sensation at the awards ceremony in the Saló de Cent, the Room of the Hundred, Barcelona City Hall's council chamber: he dressed not in the clothes of the ecclesiastical student he was, but in the traditional peasant clothing of rough cord trousers and shirt, with a loose, red cap, called the *barretina*—or the cap of liberty as this floppy long cap, not unlike a Dickensian bed cap, was sometimes called.

The *Jocs Florals* had been set up in 1859, in recovery of a medieval tradition. The early poets of the renaissance had idealized in their archaic language a Catalan peasantry. Here, from the very heart of the country, appeared ready-made a peasant who yet spoke a modern, musical and elegant Catalan. Moreover, one of his winning poems was an "Ode to Rafael Casanovas", the hero of the ten-week siege and defeat of 1714. The young man's name was Jacint Verdaguer. Do not be misled by his name, Hyacinth in English, which sounds as if his parents were pushing him towards nature poetry from the baptismal font: in Catalonia it was an authentic enough country name.

Verdaguer's career illustrates particularly well the complexity and conflicts of the Catalan *renaixença*, the renaissance that burst into Catalan life in the mid-nineteenth century. Verdaguer's life describes an arc from birth in poverty and obscurity to the summit of fame and social success, then tragedy and disgrace in his final years. Throughout, the poet himself was acting on a stage, his chin thrust forward in challenge, his eyes burning with noble passion, his pen producing poetry of rare intensity. Verdaguer had an unusual awareness of his country's history and his own poetic destiny, combined with extraordinary blindness about the society he lived in.

The suburban train that runs from Barcelona's Plaça de Catalunya towards Sant Cugat has its first stop outside the city at Baixador de Vallvidrera. The funicular takes you from there up to the wealthy, fresh-air village of Vallvidrera on top of the Collserola hills, with a magnificent view over Barcelona. Instead of taking the funicular, follow the signs and path through the woods. Only fifteen minutes uphill, you come to the Vil·la Joana, or Quinta Juana as it proclaims in Castilian on large tiles high on the façade beside the sun-dial. The Vil·la Joana is where the Miralles family gave Verdaguer refuge in the weeks before his death from tuberculosis in June 1902. Now converted into a museum to the poet, it is reminiscent of a similar museum of romantic pilgrimage, the Keats house by the Spanish Steps in Rome: not the poet's own house, but where, homeless and moneyless, he was brought by friends to die.

The Vil·la Joana is a mix of a country house for the wealthy and an eighteenth-century working farmhouse, with a tower rising from the middle of the roof. In the Catalan countryside, whether in the Empordà round Girona or near inland Lleida, you often see fortified, thick-walled farmhouses with few outside windows and a tower to watch for the bandits who roamed the countryside during the several centuries of Catalonia's decline (the unemployed no longer had the possibility of joining up as *almogàvers*). In a famous passage of Cervantes' novel, Don Quixote tells the frightened Sancho Panza that men they found hanging from trees are bandits: "...in this region the law usually hangs them... in groups of twenty or thirty, which leads me to think I must be close to Barcelona." The Vil·la Joana preserves the tower; it also has covered galleries front and back on the first floor where the owners lived, with wooden slatted blinds knocking lightly in the breeze. Downstairs was the working part of the farmhouse: the kitchen, the stores for crops and vegetables, animals perhaps; and upstairs, the servants' quarters, as owners have never liked to climb too many stairs. In Mediterranean mansions, as in Catalan apartment blocks, it is the first floor that is the noble floor.

The Vil·la Joana is today a beautiful house. The front yard holds four classic Mediterranean trees: the cracked trunks of two wisteria twisted with age that squeeze like anacondas the stone columns marking the entrance, their scent pervading the Spring air, thin tall cypresses, a purple-flowering Judas tree (known in Spanish as "tree of love") and a big, round-topped Mediterranean pine. Inside, the wide and high, well-lit rooms have cool earth-coloured tiles, polished

The Vil·la Joana, where Verdaguer died in 1902

wooden beams across the ceiling and tall windows. From one of the first-floor windows the mountain of Montserrat is visible through a dip in the forest. The house is surrounded by thick woods of pines, oak and wild-strawberry trees, draped with lianas and the dense undergrowth of the coastal ranges that gives the name *selva*, jungle, to this kind of vegetation. Here, wild boar thrive, snuffling out of a jungle-filled ravine at dusk to turn over dustbins: it is hard to believe we are just four miles from downtown Barcelona. It was a better place for the peasant-poet to die than the room on Barcelona's Carrer Aragó where he had been living in penury.

The Vil·la Joana (entrance free) has various relics of the poet's life: his work table, the bed he died in—not, apparently, burned on his death due to fear of infection, as Keats' was—the wooden chaise-longue like a dentist's chair he rested in and the altar where he prayed, as brightly vulgar and garishly tiled as a fun-fair. And through the rooms of the museum you can follow the majestic rise, triumph and fall of Verdaguer's life.

Peasant Son and Poet

He was born in 1845 to a peasant family in Folgueroles, a village three miles from Vic. Out of nine children only he and three others reached adulthood. At the age of ten he was sent to the seminary at Vic, walking there and back every day. This was no indication of religious vocation: indeed, at fourteen Verdaguer ran away to be a soldier, though he got no further than Figueres. Being sent to the seminary was common among younger sons of the poor, if they showed signs of intelligence. It was the only way of educating them for a job with a certain social status; it meant a mouth less to feed, and it was very important for the Catalan inheritance system. This worked (and works) on the basis that smallholdings or farms were not subdivided among all the children on a peasant-proprietor's death, but were inherited whole by the eldest son. When Verdaguer was young, this system contributed to mass emigration into the newly industrializing cities and to Spanish America. Economically, it was important, because it kept the Catalan farm as a viable unit and avoided the impoverishment that affected a region like Galicia in northwest Spain, where endless sub-division of the land led to hunger.

At Vic, Verdaguer studied, moved in intellectual circles and began to write. Romanticism came late to Catalonia, but when it arrived in Verdaguer's youth, it was entwined with the assertion of Catalonia's nationhood, the rebirth of its culture which many of Verdaguer's generation hoped would lead to a new nation. Forty years earlier, Byron's romantic idealism had found a similar outlet in the cause of Greece. This movement of young intellectuals was radical in several ways. It insisted on the use of Catalan against the Spanish state's desires. It reclaimed the countryside, starting the cult of *excursionisme* or rambling, so that Catalans could get to know their own country. Even today this ideal is strong and there are few mountains you walk up without finding Catalan flags on the top or meeting groups of nationalist ramblers. In 1940s Franco-controlled Barcelona people resorted to the roof-tops to speak in Catalan or with a certain freedom; perhaps for the same reason, Catalans of different generations, like Verdaguer's, took to the mountain-tops.

At the same time, Catalanism was a reactionary movement, imbued with strong fundamentalist traits and based on a profoundly traditionalist view of the peasantry as the core of the nation, and the *casa pairal*—literally, the patriarchal house—as the backbone of the peasantry. The country priest watched over this structure, helping it survive against the godless anarchism that was beginning to gain a hold among the workers in the new factories and the city poor.

Despite failing his theological exams several times and earning the displeasure of his teachers at Vic for writing non-religious poetry, it would seem that Verdaguer grew into a serious religious vocation. He was ordained at the age of 25 and sent to be a country priest near Vic.

In 1874 Verdaguer suffered an unspecified medical crisis, brought on perhaps by self-neglect. He was prescribed gymnastics, sea-bathing and tobacco as a cure. He took at least the sea component seriously and found a job as ship's chaplain with the Transatlántica shipping company. His first ship was named *Antonio López* after its owner, with whose family Verdaguer's fortunes were to be entwined for the rest of his life. He made nine trips—eighteen crossings in all—between Cádiz and Havana, Cuba, ministering to the numerous Andalusian and Galician emigrants fleeing impoverishment to the New World, just as people from Latin America migrate to Spain today. At this period he wrote the poem "L'emigrant", quite simply the best-known Catalan poem in Catalonia:

> Beautiful valley, cradle of my childhood,
> white Pyrenees
> Banks and streams, hermitage hanging in the sky,
> Good-bye for ever!
> Harps of the forest, gold-finches,
> Sing, sing.
> In tears, I tell woods and valleys:
> Farewell.
>
> Where will I find your healthy airs,
> your golden sky?
> But oh, oh, where will I find your peaks,
> beautiful Montserrat?...
>
> Good-bye brothers, good-bye my father,
> I will see you no more!
> Oh, if I had my bed in the grave

Where my sweet mother lies!

...

I am ill, but oh! Take me back to land,

There I want to die!

Montserrat Caballé, modern Catalonia's most famous soprano, told Robert Hughes on BBC TV in 1991: "When I hear L'emigrant, tears come to my eyes." When tenor Josep Carreras sang it at the official celebration of Catalonia's National Day, on 11 September 2005, even such a hardened politician as Pasqual Maragall, the president of the Generalitat, wiped away a tear.

Even in this short extract (about half the poem), characteristic features of Verdaguer's writing can be drawn out. In my doggerel translation the musical rhythm of the words does not come across, so you will have to take that on credit. Even so, his tendency to morbid sentimentalism combined with a grandiose vision is clear. The evocation of nature, the identification of Catalonia with mountains, the directness of the language can all be seen. Ernest Hemingway and the twentieth century in English have made us accustomed to find virtue in directness of expression. Latin-derived, Romance languages tend towards the more ornate, still discernible in literature, official forms and letters and political speeches. Here is Josep Pla, talking of the preachers of his youth at the start of the twentieth century: "There was a tendency, held as highly respectable, to say things in the most back-to-front way possible, long-winded and confused."

In addition to the rhetorical style, nineteenth-century Catalan was an extraordinarily straitjacketed literary language, with little connection to the popular Catalan spoken. Verdaguer brought that popular Catalan, with its directness, its abrupt consonants, hissing "s's" and short one-syllable words, onto the page. He cut through the ornateness while keeping the grandiose sentiments—to us perhaps ridiculous-sounding, as in the extract from "L'emigrant"—of his romantic-religious identification with Catalonia. This combination of directness and lofty patriotic feeling made him revered by his contemporaries.

Triumph and Fall

After two years crossing the Atlantic, in 1876 Verdaguer's prodigious decade opened. López, one of the richest men in Spain, hired him as household chaplain and he went to live with the family at the Palau Moja, the Moja Mansion, on the corner of Barcelona's Ramblas and Carrer Portaferrissa (Iron Gate Street). Today the mansion, large though not remarkable for its beauty, is used for offices of the Generalitat and exhibitions. A private chaplain, and especially a famous poet, was a trophy for a *nouveau riche* like López. For the first time in his life Verdaguer had servants to make sure he lived well, and he had nothing to complain of in the López family's treatment. When Antonio died in 1883, having been created Marquis of Comillas, his son Claudio maintained Verdaguer in the household.

In 1877 Verdaguer became the most famous writer in the land when his epic *Atlàntida* (Atlantis) won the special prize at the Floral Games; and López financed its publication. In 1881, to celebrate the millennium of the supposed finding of the Black Virgin of Montserrat in its cave on the saw-toothed mountain Verdaguer could see from his window at the Vil·la Joana while he was dying, extensive religious-patriotic celebrations were held. In these celebrations the founding of Catalonia by Wilfred the Hairy was closely linked to the rebirth of Christianity as the Muslims were expelled (the War on Islam is nothing new). Verdaguer won the literary contest. In 1885 he reached his creative peak with *Canigó*, another epic poem, this time about the founding of Catalonia itself. The Canigó is the great mountain just to the north of the Pyrenees, inland from Perpignan. Though its snowy cap is visible from many parts of Spanish Catalonia, it stands in French Roussillon, part of what is known to Catalan nationalists as *Catalunya nord*, North Catalonia. Verdaguer's choice of the Canigó as the symbol of Catalonia would not have failed to move the nationalists of the *renaixença*. Its message was that Catalonia is greater than the borders in which the modern Spanish and French states have confined it.

Verdaguer is not only the national poet, but was widely read, too: his 1883 *Oda a Barcelona* was published by the City Council in an edition of 100,000 that sold out. He scaled the heights of literary recognition in 1886 when proclaimed "poet of Catalonia" by the Bishop of Vic in a ceremony in the Abbey of Ripoll. Verdaguer was crowned with a laurel wreath from the tree he himself had planted at Vinyoles, his first parish. He was Catalonia's poet laureate.

Few people today read epic poems about the founding of a nation. Even in Catalonia, Verdaguer is undoubtedly not read outside school syllabuses. He is best known for his hunched figure on an enormous, rather ugly column in Barcelona's Passeig de Sant Joan, beside the underground station that bears his name. Yet his poetry is nonetheless known: through songs like the "Virolai" or "L'emigrant". And for anyone who can read Catalan and opens the *Canigó*, his direct, colloquial and descriptive voice is a happy surprise. As Arthur Terry put it in his summary of Catalan literature, Verdaguer has "a visionary sweep which at the same time is rooted in direct observation." Of course, Verdaguer is a religious poet, with mystic, exalted tones and an unnuanced sense of good and evil, but religion for him—as for his near-contemporary Gaudí—was to be seen everywhere in nature. This is the sort of religion that delights in God's creations. Verdaguer described this nature in lyrical detail: the birds, flowers and landscapes of the Pyrenees, in particular. Thus, generations of Catalans since have found enormous pleasure in walking the magic mountains of Verdaguer's poetry, feeling the heady mix of fresh air, patriotism and religious passion that the young seminarist had felt when he walked in the 1860s.

In his time, so great was Verdaguer's fame that his poetry had practical effect, something all writers dream of but almost none achieve. The restoration of the Abbey of Ripoll and other Pyrenean churches is directly attributable to his epilogue to *Canigó*, called "The Two Bell-Towers", in which silent, empty towers of abandoned churches bemoan their fate. It was not, of course, the poet's fault that Ripoll was restored so badly. Here are some lines from this epilogue, which is calling on Catalans in the richest language simultaneously to restore their ruined churches and rebuild their oppressed country:

Of the Romanesque altars no trace remains,
of the Byzantine cloister there is nothing left:
the alabaster images have fallen
and their lamps gone out, like a star
that will shine on Canigó no more.

Like two giants of a sacred legion
only two bell-towers still stand.

Verdaguer led a worldly life in the years of his glory. Summering in 1881 with the López family in fashionable Comillas near Santander in northern Spain, he met the royal family, government ministers and famous writers. He travelled, too, with the López entourage, in all the luxury with which the wealthy travelled in those days, to North Africa, Russia and Palestine. He wrote successful travel books, especially his *Diary of a Pilgrim to the Holy Land*.

Yet in his worldly success squirmed a worm of discontent. Verdaguer's book on the Holy Land showed how he was searching for a more spiritual path. In the late 1880s he became almoner for the López family and began to distribute money and spiritual advice to the poor from his office by the back door of the Palau Moja. There was no shortage of customers. These were years in which, within a hundred yards of the palace where the López family lived, families of numerous unemployed factory workers were dying of hunger. Cross the Ramblas even today from the Palau Moja and you enter dark, dank streets, stinking of urine and the special tang of re-heated cheap cooking oil, with tiny decaying apartments crowding over the street. Built in the 1840s at the start of industrialization, these tenements were among the worst slums in Europe.

For many years Claudio López, the second Marquis, accepted Verdaguer's charitable work. López was himself deeply religious as well as prosperous, and it was prestigious to have his own priest dispensing charity. In 1893, however, Verdaguer was effectively sacked when López's accountants found huge holes in his ledgers. Verdaguer had gone beyond the accepted ideas of Christian charity and was supporting long-term some 300 families with López's money. Under pressure from López, the Bishop of Vic banished Verdaguer to a lonely sanctuary at Gleva, on the left of the road from Vic up to Ripoll. Here, suddenly out of the city's bustle and with time to ruminate on his life, Verdaguer took to writing again.

The financial scandal was intertwined with a theological scandal. Verdaguer had come to believe that illness was caused by diabolical possession. He rented an apartment near the Palau Moja, where he practised exorcisms with various other equally fanatical priests and a woman medium. Later, he performed his exorcisms in the Palau Moja itself. He was falling into heresy. There is a third element in Verdaguer's downfall:

the whiff of sexual scandal. Verdaguer was urging Claudio López's wife to come back to Barcelona from Madrid where she was living with her husband and become more involved in charity work. López was not pleased at his priest exerting his considerable charisma to persuade his wife to (more or less) leave him. In the great houses where young priests were hired and wives and daughters had nothing to do, sexual scandal was plausibly in the air. It is a theme in several well-known novels, among them, the most famous Spanish novel of the 1880s, Emilia Pardo Bazán's *The Manor House at Ulloa* (1886) and Stendhal's earlier *The Red and the Black* (1830). Even if nothing happened, the suspicion was there. In Verdaguer's case almost certainly nothing happened. He suffered from ingenuousness in not covering his back, but was both genuinely religious and completely frank.

The last period of Verdaguer's life, the years of polemic, opens in 1895. He left the sanctuary of Gleva without his bishop's permission to go to Madrid and try and sort things out with Claudio López. Unsuccessful and penniless—he had not just spent López's money, but also his own—he returned to Barcelona to live in poverty in the flat of a widow and her two daughters. They were a family he had provided for previously. No-one believes that he had any sexual relation with his land-lady, but his choice of residence fuelled the scandal-mongers' imaginations. He was suspended from the priesthood and ostracized by both the Church and upper-class society. Against friends' advice, Verdaguer wrote a series of articles in his own defence. These articles are embarrassingly insistent and shrill on the correctness of his views and actions. His very naïveté led to his depth of indignation that his accusers could sink so low. The articles polarized society further. The anti-Verdaguerians found evidence of fanaticism, even madness in them; his supporters saw how he had been persecuted by the rich because he was a true Catalanist, a man of the people not just in word but in deed.

In 1898 he was reinstated as a priest and sent as an assistant to the Belem (Bethlehem) Church, a huge windowless building, black with dirt, still to be seen squat and ugly on the Ramblas just opposite the Palau Moja. Verdaguer's fall was summed up by humorists: he moved thirty yards from one side of the Rambla to the other. That move, of course, was from a mansion to the slums.

When Verdaguer died at the Vil·la Joana, in 1902, he had the greatest funeral procession ever seen in Barcelona. Some 100,000 people followed his coffin in homage, though it was pouring with rain. Agustí Calvet, later a well-known journalist though only fourteen at the time, followed the hearse to the Montjuïc Cemetery. He wrote:

> When at last we reached the cemetery, dusk was falling. My feet were aching, but we still had to climb to the top of the mountain. The tomb—a great hole opened in the bare rock—was high up. In the delicate glow of late afternoon, the site of the tomb was shown by flaring torches above us.

So the people of Barcelona buried Verdaguer, under pouring rain and burning torches. In front of the Vil·la Joana there is a simple and beautiful sculpture to the poet-priest: a book opened beyond 180 degrees, a broken-backed book.

Two contradictory strands of public opinion came together at Verdaguer's death to honour his qualities of leadership, honesty and lack of compromise. Conservative, religious Catalonia saw in his genius the expression of a Catholic nation with deep roots. The anti-clerical Republican tradition identified with a later Verdaguer, who was rejected by both Church and aristocracy because he gave money to the poor. This latter tradition could find in his writing the popular, down-to-earth descriptions of nature. Both views responded to the physical detail of his poetry and to his epic vision. Verdaguer's poetry expressed the founding myths of a nation in modern language.

The Slave-Trading Philanthropist

Depending on your outlook, Verdaguer's patron Antonio López was either a slave-trader or a philanthropist. He has been dead for 125 years, but his name still arouses passion. A square, at the bottom of Barcelona's Via Laietana and opposite the main post office (built as in all Spanish cities like a baroque palace), was named after him. The political left today is clamouring for the square to be renamed and his statue removed, for the commemoration of a slave-trader is inappropriate in these days of immigration from Africa. The left is undoubtedly correct, but names should celebrate history as it was. His statue could be left there, but, beside its plaque that proclaims "Spain has lost one of the men who lent it greatest service," one could add the words of Cuban historian Aurea Fernández: "A business-man who enriched himself in Santiago de Cuba through the trafficking of slaves."

López's statue has always been controversial. After Verdaguer's death the Gràcia radical paper *La Campana*, "The Bell", called for it to be melted down into coins to be distributed among the poor and for a statue of Verdaguer to be put up in its place. The proposal did not prosper, but in the 1936 Revolution the City Council withdrew the statue under popular demand. In 1939 it was recovered from municipal stores and reinstated by Franco's dictatorship. And there the grimy figure of López still stands, looking across the road at Roy Lichtenstein's multi-coloured pop sculpture *Head of Barcelona* and Xavier Mariscal's giant *Prawn*. The French writer André Pieyre de Mandiargues, noting in his novel *La marge* that López's statue was on top of a pillar nearly one hundred feet high (though it is not as tall as Verdaguer's column), added: "There are no other cities where the statues are placed so high as in Barcelona, as if there was fear of leaving them within the reach of men."

Antonio López is one of Walter Benjamin's "barbarians" who financed our civilization. He is an archetype of the *indianos*, not Indians, but people who went from Spain to the Americas and returned with fortunes. Many of them were central to the investment that developed Catalonia's industrial revolution. As Marx wrote—and he could have been thinking of his almost exact contemporary López: "It is slavery that has given value to the American colonies. It is the colonies that have created world trade and world trade is the necessary condition for big industry in the modern world."

López was not actually Catalan. Born in 1817 in Comillas near Santander on Spain's north Coast, at the age of nine he left his widowed mother, who was a fishmonger, and several brothers and sisters, to work in a relative's shop in Andalusia. He left for Cuba at fourteen and opened a shop in Santiago. Lacking capital, he borrowed money from a Catalan, whose daughter he then married in 1848 (he would not need to pay back the loan). He expanded his business into land and slave trafficking. Land meant slaves on sugar plantations: one of López's colleagues was the Catalan Facundo Bacardí, founder of the famous white rum firm and remembered in the name of a pretty square in the outlying Barcelona quarter of Horta.

By 1853, when López and his young family left Cuba for Barcelona to escape a cholera epidemic, he had made his fortune. Settled in Barcelona, he founded three major businesses: the Banco (Bank) Hispano-Colonial, which ended up lending money to the government and to King Alfonso XII (in return, López was made Marquis of Comillas in 1878); and Tabacos de Filipinas (the Philippine Tobacco Company), with its headquarters on the Ramblas, opposite and just up from the Palau Moja. The ugly cigar-coloured building has recently been converted into a no-smoking hotel. López would have approved; business changes its forms, he would have known, because of his own transformation from slaver to philanthropic Marquis, but remains business. The third company was the Transatlántica Shipping Company, set up in 1859, which, as well as its regular Atlantic run, provided steamships for the government to transport troops in its colonial wars in Morocco in 1859 and in Cuba from 1868-78.

The services López "lent" to the state fully justified the words placed on his statue when he died in an odour of sanctity in 1883. Anxiety about his destiny after death led him in his final years not only to finance the publication of Verdaguer's poems, but to endow a religious university in Comillas. He may thus have bought the salvation of his soul, just as he had bought his position in society and marquisate. Despite posthumous praise from Pope Leo X himself, it is as a Maecenas that López achieved immortality. The richest man in Spain is remembered not for his God or his money, but for his sponsorship of that intense poet-priest who was driven by the demon of art and had no money or business sense at all.

The Casa Casaramona, Barcelona

Chapter Six

The Lancashire of Spain: Gaudí and Güell

In 1871 Antonio López paid for the society wedding of the year. His eldest daughter Isabel married Eusebi Güell, thus joining two of the richest families in Catalonia. Like Antonio López, Eusebi's father Joan Güell had made his money from slave trading and sugar plantations in Cuba. The children of these uneducated, self-made men had every advantage money could buy, and became connoisseurs and patrons of the arts. Eusebi's hobbies were to draw, paint and play music. On his tours of Europe he visited not just industrial fairs, but museums. Eusebi Güell had better luck in his posthumous fame than Antonio López and his son Claudio, for Güell's protégé was the architect Antoni Gaudí (1852-1926), now a world-renowned figure and Barcelona's main tourist attraction. The money made from the sweat of slaves was converted into beautiful houses, parks and chapels. Güell's name became identified with great art, like Maecenas in Ancient Rome or the Medicis in Florence. The money's origins were forgotten, but spare a thought, as you gaze on Gaudí's wonderful buildings, for the Africans who died to create Barcelona's booming tourism industry.

Whereas the last chapter told the story of Jacint Verdaguer, the great poet of the Catalan renaissance, this chapter looks at the development of Catalonia's industrial revolution. It ends on the industrial village that Eusebi Güell's workers built at Santa Coloma de Cervelló, whose chapel is often cited as Gaudí's masterpiece. In the figure of Eusebi Güell and this village the industrial revolution and the nationalist renaissance intertwine.

Putting out the Fires of Revolt

The poorest part of the *Ciutat vella* or Old City of Barcelona was and is the Raval (see Chapter Twelve). This *barri* or neighbourhood on the right of the Ramblas, as you walk from the Plaça de Catalunya towards the sea, still had vacant land in the early nineteenth century. The year 1833 saw the installation of the first steam-driven looms in Catalonia, at Josep Bonaplata's new textile factory in the Carrer Tallers. In the following years Barcelona's Raval became packed with workshops and factories; coal to run them came in through the nearby port. After Richard Ford visited the city in the 1840s, he wrote: "Barcelona is one of the finest and certainly the most manufacturing city of Spain. It is the Manchester of Catalonia, which is the Lancashire of the Peninsula."

With his customary mix of passion and disdain for all things Spanish, Ford added: "compared, however, to the mighty hives of English industry and skill, everything is petty." This was true, in that space was at a premium. The city was confined within its walls, with the First Carlist War raging outside in the 1830s. The Carlists, supporters of the pretender to absolute monarchy, Don Carlos, had a big following in rural Catalonia. Despite these handicaps, by 1850 Catalonia's cotton industry was the third in Europe after England and France.

In the 1840s steam-driven factories known as *vapors* (literally "steams") started to be built on the plain beyond Barcelona's city walls, in the nearby village of Sants and the coastal swamps now known as Poble Nou (New Town). Despite the changes in Barcelona since the end of the dictatorship in 1977—the urban renewal and the closure of factories—remains of old industrial buildings are dotted all over the city. The Sants public library is a magnificent conversion of the first factory of Joan Güell, with its high, iron roof girders over the book-lined shelves and huge chimney soaring above it. Nearby, beside Barcelona's main railway station, which bears the name of Sants, the fascinating Parc de l'Espanya Industrial is built on the site of the old factory of the same name, in the nineteenth century the biggest factory in Spain. Its workforce, as in most of the big textiles factories, consisted mainly of women. In Poble Nou, overhauled for the 1992 Olympic Village and under constant redevelopment ever since, several chimneys still stand. The most impressive is that of the textile factory Can Saladrigas, in the Carrer Joncar, though its boiler and entrance were destroyed by municipal-speculator vandalism. Can Saladrigas has gone the way of most factories preserved in the middle of a redevelopment area: it has become a community centre.

On the flanks of Montjuïc the recently restored Casa Casaramona (Plaça de Espanya subway station) was originally built as a textile factory in 1911. After becoming stables for the police, it is now a museum owned by Catalonia's biggest bank, La Caixa, which has stinted nothing on its restoration. Designed by Puig i Cadafalch, it is entirely in brick but for the cast-iron beams and pillars that support the vaults and the scrolled iron that guards the windows. The low, repeated sheds of the factory are crowned by two elegant, ornate water-towers. One tower is a thin, square Moorish construction; the other, rounded and blue-tiled at the top, like a lighthouse or ship's mast of fantasy. The whole building is light, despite its battlements. This is perhaps because the brick is scrubbed clean, but also because of the width of windows, the lowness of the roof, the shallow curve of the eaves and the unthreatening pointed battlements that soften it. La Caixa hired Arata Isozaki to build onto the front a multi-level entrance in shining white slabs of stone, with a bandstand-style cover of steel and glass. The white clashes against the brick—or highlights it. The boldness of Isozaki's design makes the Casa Casaramona triumphantly modern, as well as a jewel of Art Nouveau.

Catalonia's industrial revolution was not confined to Barcelona. It spread to the nearby cities of Terrassa and Sabadell, on the plain behind the slim coastal range of hills, and up the coast to Mataró, connected to Barcelona in 1848 by Spain's first railway. Development was hampered, though, by the lack of coal to run the automated factories. Coal imports were dear, the mines in southern Aragon were not close and there was only one mine in Catalonia, at Fígols, and its coal was low-quality. This was to be a major stimulus to the building of textile mills along the Ter and Llobregat rivers, to use the power of the water flowing fast and tempestuously off the Pyrenees.

The industrial revolution was hampered, too, by the rebellion of the new working class against appalling conditions of work and accommodation. Pulled off the land by economic necessity, as in the rest of Europe and the United States, the industrial proletariat found twelve-hour days the norm. Lay-offs and wage cuts were common. Unions were banned and retaliation was crude; Bonaplata's 600-worker factory, for example, was burnt down on 6 August 1835. The bosses' reprisals were ruthless: four workers were executed for this sabotage. This first steam factory became known as *el vapor cremat*, the "burnt steam factory".

For those who like to reflect on such events, 1835 in Barcelona gives a wonderful example of the compression of historical processes in Spain. The struggle of a nascent capitalism against feudal restrictions was occurring at the same time as the fight between these first capitalists and their workers. The next year saw the disestablishment of the monasteries in Spain under the (relatively) liberal regime of Mendizábal. This was, to some degree, rubber-stamping what had already happened. 1835 witnessed numerous convents and monasteries in the city burnt and Church land thus freed up for factories and workers' housing. The Liceu opera house on the Ramblas was also built at this time on the site of a burnt-down convent. The new industrialists in Barcelona delighted in turning the anger of its people against the Church, but were not so pleased when the rage of this new working class formed by their factories turned against them, with the burning of Bonaplata's *vapor*.

There was not just a shortage of space for industry: Barcelona was bursting. About 200,000 people lived in the walled city in 1850. Yet as many of the buildings were the spacious mansions of merchants, convents with gardens, factories or government buildings, one can imagine the accumulation of the poor in the instant slums, the Raval tenements built to house the industrial workers. The historian Montse Armengol summarizes the situation:

> The workers of the first factories within Barcelona's city walls lived on top of each other in disease-filled flats in the damp, narrow streets of an over-populated city. They occupied attics and pigeon-lofts when the miserable flats without ventilation could be sub-divided no further. They ate sardines and dry bread. They worked thirteen-hour days in unhealthy factories. They died of tuberculosis on breathing all day the dust of the fibres and chimney-smoke...

Ildefons Cerdà, utopian socialist and author of the plan eventually accepted for the Eixample, the expansion beyond the Old City walls, calculated that the average life expectancy of a textile worker in 1850 was 44 years. All sectors of society—the rich because they wanted space and were scared of the multiple cholera epidemics of the period—wanted to see the city walls come down. Finally, in 1859 the Madrid government agreed to let the city expand over the plain.

Barcelona's first general strike took place in 1855. It was a reaction to the arrival in 1854 of the latest generation of mule jennies, imported from England. These were known in Catalan as *selfactines*, a word derived from the English "self-acting" machine, and caused widespread lay-offs. The newly founded unions called for a ten-hour day and marched through the city under the dramatic banners of "Bread and Jobs" and "Unions or Death". The latter slogan was quite literal. As usual, the army was sent in to dismantle barricades and protect strike-breakers. Dozens of strikers died and the managing director of Joan Güell's El Vapor Vell factory in Sants (the one that is now the library) was shot dead in retaliation. This and subsequent violent fights for unionization led to the Manchester industrialist Frederick Engels writing in the 1880s that Barcelona was "the city whose history records more struggle on the barricades than that of any other city in the world." In later years it became known as the Rosa del foc, the Rose of Fire, as revolutionary trade unionism led by anarchists became dominant in its working class between the 1880s and 1937.

Factory owners and the upper class reacted in a number of ways to the threat of living cheek by jowl with their impoverished workers. One was to flee the Old City from the 1860s onwards, to live in the newly developing Eixample (Extension), built on a grid system. "The city began to spread towards the hills, it advanced like golden lava across the plain, it flooded the market gardens," wrote Ignacio Agustí in his classic novel of late nineteenth-century Barcelona, *Mariona Rebull* (1944). Or "it leapt over its stone enclosure like a lion," in Verdaguer's *Oda a Barcelona*.

The other reaction was to give serious thought as to how to dampen the fires of workers' radicalism. One successful solution was the construction of workers' villages, "colonies" they were called in Spanish and Catalan, along the Ter and Llobregat rivers. The fast-flowing rivers were suitable for driving the turbines and distances were short, allowing communications to be opened up to the factory-colonies by road or rail.

Industrial villages were common enough in nineteenth-century Europe and the United States, but Catalonia had a uniquely high concentration of them on these two rivers: some seventy-five. The problems of lack of coal and surfeit of rebellious workers could be solved together. The colonies were safely outside the Rosa de foc and the equally militant industrial towns of Terrassa and Sabadell in Barcelona's hinterland. In some of these colonies conditions were probably little better than on the Cuban slave plantations they resembled, and with which many of the new industrialists would be familiar because they had made their money there. In others a genuine paternalism was practised. In all of them, workers, educated in religion and subservience in isolated villages, were conveniently dependent on their employers for both job and home. The colonies were expensive to build, but guaranteed relatively low wages and a docile workforce for decades. Indeed, some plants, such as the Fabra i Coats cotton plant at Torelló, on the Ter between Vic and Ripoll, were still running until just a few years ago.

The densest number of colonies lies on the upper Llobregat river downstream from Berga, where there were fourteen textile factories with their villages on a fifteen-mile stretch. A "river park" has now been laid out and the whole distance can be walked. For the less energetic, starting at L'Ametlla de Merola, a two-to-three-hour river path leads to the village of Puig-reig. L'Ametlla itself is a place of fantasy, the workers' houses designed like seaside cottages and painted white, to represent the colour of cotton and, it was hoped, of social harmony. The canal cut from the river to drive the turbine was also used to irrigate market gardens. Use of water power meant that no chimney was necessary, so only the church stands out, right in the middle of the colony and raised in stone high above the cottages like a threat or a promise.

The river path runs lightly upstream through the characteristic pre-Pyrenean landscape of tall pines, poplars, box and ash, quite different from the Mediterranean jungle at Tarragona's Pont del Diable or Portbou's low pines and prickly pear. Ducks land on the water and kingfishers flash through the trees. It is more reminiscent of northern scenery than either the coastal or high-mountain country. At the Cal Riera plant (*Cal* or *Can* is like *chez* in French, "house of"), the waterfall was used originally by a medieval mill and then to drive the factory turbines. Slightly higher up, Can Vidal has been converted into an industrial museum, which tells the story of the *colonies* along the river.

Indianos

Despite Catalonia's decline and defeat in 1714, it had maintained its trading tradition, which was then re-stimulated when the 262-year prohibition on trade with the Americas was lifted in 1780. The money that came back from Cuba was vital to Catalonia's industrial revolution. All over the region there are big country houses, known as *masies*, each shaded by a tall palm rising by its front door and curling its fronds over the roof. The palm is not indigenous to Catalonia: only the scrubby small palm, the *margalló* or palmetto, whose hearts are served in restaurants, is native. The tall palm tree is the symbol of the successful *indiano*, the poor boy who fled poverty as a teenager and returned from the Indies in triumph. Some of them are the legendary founders of Catalan business dynasties.

Joan Güell was born in Torredembarra, near Tarragona, in 1800, and as a child looked after his family's sheep on the hills. After twenty years in Cuba, he returned in the 1830s to open a textile factory, first in Barcelona's Old City, then the one in Sants mentioned above. In the 1840s he married. His Italian wife died in childbirth. A practical man, he married her sister. In 1871 he married his eldest son to a daughter of Antonio López and then died, dynasty and wealth assured, in 1872.

This shepherd-boy, then slave-owner, was a passionate innovator. Not only was he one of the first industrialists to move his factory out onto the plain, but he also diversified, setting up in 1855 La Maquinista, in Barceloneta, to manufacture railway carriages. (In 1920 La Maquinista moved to the Barcelona *barri* of Sant Andreu. The factory is now a shopping mall and cinema complex in this attractive outlying quarter.) He was also a leader of Catalan business, arguing strongly for protectionism to defend Catalan textiles from French and English competition in the Spanish market.

Eusebi, son of this fabulously rich self-made man, was sent by his father in the 1860s to study law and economics in France and England. Connoisseur of art and touched by the breeze of the Catalan *Renaixença*, Eusebi visited Paris for the 1878 Universal Exhibition. It was there that he fell in love with an exhibit that was to change his life and make his name world-famous. It was a cabinet for exhibiting gloves, carved in oak, with slim cast iron supporting strangely-shaped glass windows. The strange shapes were not only eccentric, but were designed to show off the exhibits to best effect. He asked who had designed this showcase that was at the same time both exotic and practical and was told that the author of the glove cabinet came from a workshop in Barcelona. On returning home, Güell visited the workshop and was introduced to the recently qualified architect Gaudí.

Gaudí and Güell hit it off. They became friends and remained so until Güell's death in 1918. They were both conservative Catalan nationalists. Just as Verdaguer had a mystic vision of the rebirth of Catalonia that he expressed in his poetry, so Gaudí saw his buildings as part of the recovery of the lost past. Güell's view was undoubtedly more worldly and practical, but he financed much of Gaudí's work, famously giving him a free hand to spend as much as he wanted. Catalan *modernisme* was financed by private capital, not by public commissions as is the norm today. All the new wealth was trying to build a new country. The Catalan bourgeoisie, frustrated at not holding political power in Madrid, poured their energy and spare cash into art.

Santa Coloma Colony

Due to labour problems, Eusebi Güell was toying with the idea of relocating his main textile factory at Sants to a site outside the city. He owned some land by the Llobregat river that his father had bought decades earlier. A particular incident finally decided him; a few days before Christmas 1889 Ferran Alsina, the technical manager of El Vapor Vell, was walking home through the Eixample after work when he was fired on from the dark. Though Alsina escaped uninjured, within two years a new factory had been built on the Llobregat river site, the huge boiler had been transferred there from Sants, the Sants factory was closed and most of its workers were sacked.

Güell would have been aware of the murder of his father's manager in 1855 and had the money to attempt a unique project. Anyone who has been to Saltaire, the village of Sir Titus Salt near Bradford in West Yorkshire, will recognize the mix of religious benevolence and of worry about profits (and life) in Güell's project. Jack Reynolds, biographer of Salt, wrote of Saltaire:

> ... [Salt] decided to build a new model village, in which a somewhat old-fashioned paternalism would be the guiding principle. He hoped that it would offer an example of happy labour relations free from class conflict and demonstrate the possibilities of improvement and change in the lives of working people. It was the product both of decent

humanity and an understandable concern with his business and his family.

Add to Saltaire the greater militancy of the workers' movement in Barcelona, and replace dissenting religion with Catholic, Catalan-nationalist consciousness, and you have Santa Coloma. The paternalism and the employer's intelligent attempt to douse class conflict by concession and education were the same.

School, nursery, choral society, football team, shops, café... Santa Coloma was a complete village. So well did the workers live that they were known as toffs by other factory workers. For the boss, the business was perfect; not only could salaries be lower, but he could also earn from the shops, house rentals and café. And he could mould his workers from the cradle through all their schooling (Catalan and religious with separation of sexes) and social activities.

Güell's village was not typical of the dozens of other colonies on the Llobregat in three aspects: it did not use the river water to drive the looms; it is very close to Barcelona, only a few miles from the mouth of the Llobregat; and its lay-out and buildings are of extraordinary quality. Santa Coloma is not just the Gaudí chapel or the museum behind the ticket office. The whole village is worth walking round, to appreciate the unity of its concept and the dozens of artistic details on the buildings, designed by artisans and architects chosen by Gaudí.

Houses were built of brick, with small gardens. The smallest measured 600 square feet, a standard living space for most families today and a vast improvement for workers' families moving from a single room in the Old City slums. Bricks in Santa Coloma were not just placed one on top of the other: there are salients, bricks that protrude for decoration, a mix of vertical and horizontal brickwork. In some houses brick walls are mixed with stone. There are numerous *modernista* details on the buildings, for these architects were building to make their houses beautiful not just functional. They were not socialists like William Morris, but Morris' Arts and Crafts movement was present in their minds.

Among these exceptional and ordinary terraced houses, quite a step up on Saltaire's, are a number of fine bigger buildings: the school, connected by a bridge to the teacher's house, the store, and the factory manager's and foreman's houses. The manager's house Ca l'Espinal, designed by Rubió i Bellver, is the colony's noblest dwelling. Its bricks, thin windows and triangular shapes above the door give it the look of a Moorish keep, but the effect is lightened by the asymmetry of the decorative brickwork and the bulging cylindrical corner with an open balcony. The walls are in stone, but all the decoration is in brick, characteristic of many *modernista* buildings and reaching back to Spain's Arab tradition.

At the centre of the village, in the Plaça Joan Güell, stands the Ateneu, the Atheneum, the cultural centre that most Catalan towns possess. Here evening classes, meetings of the choir and amateur dramatics or lectures on science and art were held. The rest of the village runs out from this square. The factory itself, now converted into several industrial units, had 1,000 workers, nearly all women. The cotton-drying part is a curious building, with slats in it for ventilating recently dyed cloth. The huge, now smokeless chimney speaks of the glorious industrial past. We may yearn after this lost solidity, but even for the toffs of Santa Coloma the chimney was the symbol of pollution and exploitation.

The Chapel in the Woods
Experts agree that Gaudí's chapel at Santa Coloma de Cervelló is his greatest work. It is not his most visited, since it is not in Barcelona, where tourists flock to the Casa Milà ("la Pedrera"), the Sagrada Família and the Park Güell. At first sight it is not easy to see why the chapel is thought so outstanding. It does not have the shattering impact of the Casa Milà on Barcelona's Passeig de Gràcia. Before this apartment block's rippling, plastic stone that looks like molten lava or the waves of the sea, tourists' mouths drop open. In the square-grid Eixample of Barcelona's wealthy business-people, the Casa Milà looks like the drunken uncle at a formal wedding. Then again, his Sagrada Família cathedral, with the endless stairs criss-crossing the towers, is unlike any other cathedral in the world. The chapel at Santa Coloma, in comparison, seems to be just a smallish, odd but not particularly spectacular building in the woods.

Unlike the church right in the middle of L'Ametlla de Merola, Gaudí's chapel is on an adjacent low hill in a pine wood. As Gaudí drew his inspiration from the forms of nature, he liked God's temple to be surrounded by trees. And he was subtle: he drew attention to the chapel not

Gaudí's chapel at Santa Coloma de Cervelló

by placing it unavoidably in the middle of the village, but by hiding it. It is an intimate chapel, its interior lay-out wholly visible from the door. This is unusual for churches, if you think of it. Even small ones usually have side-altars or sections concealed by pillars or screens. Here, all the seats are positioned with a view of the altar, making it rather like a theatre-in-the-round, an impression accentuated by the passage-way round the back of the altar and two aisles through the seats. Though unusual, Gaudí was following a certain tendency in Catalan medieval churches. Alastair Boyd cites as examples the Gothic churches at Ulldecona and La Sénia, on the southern frontier of Catalonia, and remarks suggestively: "In all these buildings there is evidence of the democratic Catalan urge to suppress the recesses and shadows and mysteries associated with earlier church architecture by creating a type of hall church without barriers between the priesthood and the people." It brings to mind, too, at the other end of the size scale, Girona's mightiest Gothic nave in Europe, creating a huge open space without pillars or secret corners.

Few drawings for the chapel survive, and it is hard to see how drawings could have been made, as there is such a riot of bricks running in all directions. Here we can see Gaudí in close-up, for the chapel is smaller and lower than any of his other buildings. We can also see his passion for asymmetry, as fragments of stone burst through straight lines. And the curved arches are not real arches, but alarmingly askew elongated curves.

Gaudí invented here his famous method of using leaning columns without any counter-weight. He worked out the loads by hanging lead-filled bags from a cord suspended between two hooks. If the bag is in the middle of the cord, the bag hangs straight down with equal lengths of cord on each side. But as you move the bag along the cord, not only is there more cord on one side of the bag than on the other, but the loop of the cord changes its form. Gaudí then inverted the string and placed the column in the precise angle indicated to him by the position of the bag on the string. The column's leaning position supported the vault of the roof naturally, creating his famous parabolic arches which seem to defy gravity. It was the method he was to use in much greater scale on the Sagrada Família.

The chapel at Santa Coloma contains no images or sculpture. The decoration is reserved for the windows of stained glass and cast iron, some of them in the colour and shape of a butterfly. In a fabulous imaginative stroke Gaudí thus joins the external space full of butterflies in the wood and the internal. Constantly fluttering coloured light pours through the stained glass into the chapel and provides all the decoration needed. Many of the external supports of the chapel resemble tree trunks, once again merging the building into its surrounding nature, as he later did in the Park Güell. The yellowish stone follows Gaudí's desire to use always local stone, so that the building fits better into its setting.

In front of the chapel, as a sort of extension to it, connected by a covered walkway is a large stone "porch", with a bench running all round its inside. This lay shelter outside the church proper is a traditional feature of Mediterranean churches. It was a place where worshippers' animals could wait, tramps sleep at night or men sit and chat. It is an area between the church and the factory housing, another of the subtle gradations between inside and outside, like the tree-shaped columns and the butterfly windows.

The porch pays tribute to the realities of life, not just Gaudí's religious desires. At packed masses on feast days in Spain the women fill the pews, but men often smoke by the open door. Their buzz of conversation competes with the priest's sing-song. Though strange to Protestants, in Catholic countries this is part of the way that daily and religious life are not so separated.

There is a certain parallel with his near-contemporary Verdaguer in the arc of Gaudí's life. As young men they were both good-looking, quite worldly and glamorous figures in high society before they began to be dominated by religious passion. Gaudí in the 1880s was even known as something of a dandy, though forty years later, in 1926, he looked so poor that he was taken to the charity ward to die after being run over by a tram. Like Jacint Verdaguer, Gaudí died in poverty, amidst controversy and surrounded by an odour of sanctity. Since 2000 he is being processed for sainthood by the Church. Just as tens of thousands had followed Verdaguer's funeral cortège, so a huge crowd followed Gaudí's. Unlike the poet, though, Gaudí suffered no financial, religious or sexual scandals. Unlike the poet too, Gaudí today is world-famous, though this reflects nothing on their respective geniuses. It is only to say that architecture's rough stones can be caressed more readily than poetry.

Part Two

Geniuses

The Casa Navàs, Reus

Chapter Seven
Fleeing the Straight and Narrow: Gaudí and Reus

Chapter Six explained how Catalan Art Nouveau, or *modernisme*, was the spoilt child of Catalonia's industrial revolution. The newly wealthy magnates paid for Art Nouveau as the style of their houses. These barbarians, to recall Walter Benjamin's phrase, gave confidence to the *renaixença*, the cultural and political renaissance that motivated the desire to show in stone and brick the rebirth of Catalonia as a nation. In his book on Prague, Richard Burton maintains: "Art Nouveau seems most to have thrived in marginalized political and cultural entities (Scotland, Catalonia, Belgium, and Bohemia/Moravia) and may be seen as a protest against provincialization by a dominant metropolis (London, Madrid, Paris and Vienna respectively) formulated in an international rather than a national style."

This is certainly so with Catalonia, the "marginalized political and cultural entity" with the greatest amount of Art Nouveau architecture in Europe. Art Nouveau was a protest of a frustrated bourgeoisie that was the wealthiest in a more backward Spanish state, but was excluded from political power. This chapter looks further at this wide-ranging movement; first at other buildings in the style, then returning to its genius, Gaudí.

Reus: Wealth in Stone

The city of Reus is best known outside Catalonia as the site of the region's third commercial airport, after Barcelona and Girona. Most people landing on holiday flights are bussed straight from the airport to resorts like Salou on the Costa Daurada. Few tourists venture into Reus itself, less well-known than Roman Tarragona, its twin and rival city only seven miles away across the plain known as the Baix Camp, the Low Country. In the Baix Camp the mountains recede from the coast, as they do in the Empordà, creating a coastal plain.

Reus in the nineteenth century was a thriving commercial and industrial centre, the second city of Catalonia after Barcelona. In 1820 its census gave it 25,500 inhabitants. "This modern busy manufacturing town is in perfect contrast with desolate decaying Tarragona," wrote Richard Ford. *Aguardiente*, "fire-water", distilled from the lees of the grape juice used to make wine, was Reus' most famous product, exported through the port of Salou all over Europe and to America. Reus exported wine and olive oil, too. Later, hazelnuts replaced the wine after the phylloxera epidemic that destroyed Bordeaux wines in the 1870s reached Catalonia. The destruction of the French wine industry by the vine-loving phylloxera aphid had led at first to a boom in the Catalan wine industry. The Spanish government was not unaware that the phylloxera fly could cross the Pyrenees, though its range was not large, and decreed the destruction of all vines within ten miles of the border. It is said that Catalan peasants, unwilling to comply (it would have meant their ruin), thus allowed the fly to spread into Spain.

Salou became Reus' main port because the Archbishopric of Tarragona levied too heavy taxes on the Reus burghers' *aguardiente*. Now Salou's golden sands, from which comes the name Costa Daurada, Gold Coast, given to this part of the Mediterranean shore, have made it southern Catalonia's main beach resort. The Universal Studios theme park Port Aventura, the biggest in Spain, has crowned Salou's reputation as a family holiday destination. It could have been different: two hundred years ago there was a plan to build a canal from Salou to give Reus its own harbour. In 1804 the central government granted permission, as long as Reus paid for it. Local business collected the money, but Napoleon's invasion meant the money was confiscated by the government for military purposes.

Reus has always been more self-consciously and assertively Catalan than Tarragona. Its nineteenth-century business wealth and Spain's appropriation of its canal cash meant that it felt keenly, and before other parts of Catalonia, the negative effects of an impoverished central state. Reus was a modern, commercial city, fed up with both the Carlist strongholds that waged trade-damaging war in the hills behind it and a Madrid without the money to develop infrastructures.

The city has none of the ancient history of Barcelona or Tarragona. It was before 1750 just another small market town dealing in the agricultural produce of its hinterland. Unlike Barcelona whose newly rich burghers were industrialists and *indianos*, Reus produced a class of farmer-merchants. However, just as in Barcelona (though in Reus this occurred rather later, at the start of the twentieth century), its bourgeoisie built extravagant houses to show off its wealth in stone. The tourist attraction of Reus today is these 100-odd *modernista* buildings scattered round the city's relatively small centre, easy to walk round in half a day. Reus offers a condensed introduction to the varied styles of Catalan Art Nouveau.

The centre of Reus is prosperous, its shops elegant. It has no rickety medieval quarter to worry about, quarters that in Catalan cities such as Lleida, Manresa or Barcelona are falling apart. These medieval city centres need massive renovation, even though they are their cities' major tourist attractions. Reus is different. Not an especially beautiful city, it is interesting for the middle-class financial solidity expressed in its prosperous town houses, combined with the flaring fantasy of *modernisme*. These provincial farmers, turned into olive oil and *aguardiente* exporters, allowed their artists free rein.

Reus' *modernista* houses run the whole range from Gothic revival to neoclassical *noucentista* (see below) buildings with barely a touch of *modernisme* (most notably, Pere Domènech's beautiful 1926 Casa Marcò on the Raval de Santa Anna). Reus shows how *modernisme* in Catalonia was often just a swirl of plaster, twisting metalwork or disordered bricks above a balcony, tacked on as adornment to a house and quite distant from the fusion of style and function in the most famous *modernista* buildings.

Reus turns around two squares, Prim and Mercadal. The former is the smaller and is dominated by an enormous, energetic equestrian statue of General Prim, sabre stretched towards the sky. The general, responsible for the coup that ushered in Spain's First Republic in 1868, became prime minister, only to be assassinated in Madrid on the snowy night of 27 December 1870. Given Reus' business prowess and its bitterness that Madrid had robbed it of the money for its canal, it is no accident that it was a *reussenc*, a man from Reus, who was central in this attempt to modernize Spain's economy and political structures.

The Mercadal Square is the more elegant, apart from a hideous 1960s extension to the Town Hall, curiously the site of the house where Prim was born. A row of nineteenth-century houses, with arcades below, forms the best side of the square. All the houses in the row are of slightly different heights, with the huge *modernista* Casa Navàs at one end. Designed by a famous architect, Lluís Domènech i Montaner, the Casa Navàs (finished 1907) is the most imposing house in the city. The ground floor houses a draper's shop with all the original decoration. On the middle floor are the tall windows and rooms of the owners' accommodation; and above, the wider but flattened windows of the servants' floor. The flat façade is adorned with shallow-pyramid bumps. These castle-like bumps, the house's stained-glass windows and the brown of the wall give the house a medieval severity. The side giving onto the square is much fancier, with the delight in rounded balconies and columns on its corner that is typical of the *modernista* style.

Domènech's finest Reus building is outside the town, the mental asylum, Institut Pere Matas. It was his first commission of the five buildings he designed in Reus. The Pere Matas broke new ground in concepts of mental health care, notably the idea that beautiful surroundings improve people's health. Its several pavilions are set on a low hill among olive and almond groves. A stroll from the Plaça Prim across the railway line and out through these Baix Camp orchards takes only thirty minutes. All the rooms are sun-lit and well-ventilated, each pavilion surrounded by gardens. The grounds are landscaped with a raised area before a ditch, known as the *salt del llop* (wolf's leap), so that the patients have a view of the country beyond the walls, but do not see the perimeter wall itself. Blue tiles, light, space in the grounds for strolling, and fertile country all round: you could ask for no better setting for a mental asylum. The VIPs' pavilion (tourist visits can be pre-booked) is the most luxuriously decorated, though even a VIP would not have liked being locked away in this somewhat sinister (despite all its provisions) mansion on a low hill on the edge of town. The VIP rooms have a servant's room attached; the sane servant had to live in the asylum alongside his/her mad but rich employer. The Pere Matas is the precursor of Domènech's work in Barcelona on the Sant Pau Hospital, discussed at the end of this chapter as the counterpoint to Gaudí's Sagrada Família.

Gaudí

Antoni Gaudí was born in 1852 either in Reus itself or in Riudoms, a village fifteen miles south of Reus. No-one knows which: his parents had a copper workshop in the city of Reus, and a house where they lived as much of the time as they could in Riudoms. If you look for Gaudí in Reus, there is no trace of him except the tourist office assertion that he was indeed born in Reus and a pretty statue put up to him in 2002 on the 150th anniversary of his birth. The statue, of the adolescent Gaudí playing marbles with a pose between melancholy and concentration, is said to be in front of his family house. Which house this is, though, is not clear, for there is no plaque or sign. Despite Gaudí now surpassing Prim as Reus' most famous son (art usually defeats politics in history, though not of course during life), his great work is in Barcelona. He built nothing at all in Reus, even though the style he made so famous pervades the city.

Gaudí grew up in a family of prosperous artisans making copper pots, boilers and stills. He was fascinated by the working of metal and knew its techniques. His father's particular branch of metalwork dealt in the conversion of flat metal into curved, three-dimensional forms. It was an abiding influence; Gaudí was unique among architects of his time for working alongside the artisans making the balconies, window-frames, doors or furniture of the houses he designed. He knew how to work metals. He often impressed artisans by showing them in practice, not just on paper or in words, what he wanted. Gaudí had a "total concept" of architecture. He did not want to design only the walls and roof, but everything in the house. The butterfly forms of the windows at his Santa Coloma chapel bear witness to his integration of artisan techniques into his architectural designs.

This background explains why Gaudí, before and after qualifying as an architect in 1878, was working in Eudald Puntí's arts-and-crafts iron, wood and glass workshop in Barcelona. It was here that he built the glove cabinet exhibited in Paris that Eusebi Güell saw. It was to this workshop that Güell came to find Gaudí and start the famous patronage that Gaudí needed. Even then, Gaudí must have known he would need a Maecenas. His idea of building was not going to be cheap. Cheap houses are built square. Gaudí was seeking his main inspiration in God's work, i.e. nature—and nature comes in all shapes and sizes, anything but square. "Straight lines belong to men; curves, to God," said Gaudí, who had a good stock of highly quotable remarks.

The architect's ambitions and influences can be discerned in two stories of his early years. When he was in his teens, like most nation-conscious Catalans of the *Renaixença* period and like Verdaguer in the same decade, he went rambling all over Catalonia, climbing its many mountains and exploring its myriad ruins. He and two school-friends discovered the monastery of Poblet, not so far from Reus. Poblet, sacked in 1835, had sunk further into ruin, to the desolation described by Augustus Hare (see p.47). Gaudí and his friends formulated the enormous project of rebuilding and repopulating Poblet as an ideal community. They were following the spirit of the times in reaching deep back into Catalonia's medieval greatness to find its roots and formulating utopias of how its future could be. The teenagers' drawings and writings on Poblet survive and illustrate both the fantasy and the obsessive detail that were to characterize Gaudí's later work.

The three schoolboys projected in detail rail and road communications, and planned for Poblet a museum (exhibits specified), an art gallery, a souvenir shop and a café with a billiards table. They calculated the water needed, the quarries for the stone and the workers required. They showed their youthful yearning for adventure in the fabulous project of sending a ship to Asia to return with precious woods and ebony. This was not quite as far-fetched as it sounds; ships already plied back and forth between Barcelona or Salou and Egypt, bringing raw cotton for the textiles industry. Gaudí never became involved in the subsequent actual restoration of Poblet, but one of the three friends, Eduard Toda, became the director of the foundation in charge of the restoration of the monastery.

The other story concerns Gaudí's university studies. His family was well enough off to send him to Barcelona to the School of Architecture. There, he neglected his course-work to spend hours in the library immersed in books on Moorish or Indian architecture. Here too, Gaudí came across the books and articles of the French architect Viollet-le-Duc and of Ruskin and Morris' Arts and Crafts movement. Already, one discerns an architect deeply rooted in his own land's traditions, but with huge curiosity for other cultures and styles. The stubborn student Gaudí educated himself in his own way, running the risk of failing his course.

His teachers, recognizing his talents, bent the rules to allow him to submit a special project to a jury. It was a design of an ornamental fountain. It is not clear what this had to do with architecture, but it allowed his teachers to pass him. Elías Rogent, the director of the School, is said to have made the famous comment at Gaudí's graduation: "Gentlemen, today we are in the presence of either a genius or a madman," to which Gaudí replied: "Well, now I'd say I was an architect."

Gaudí's Reputation

If the chapel at Santa Coloma is considered Gaudí's most exquisite work, even though it is unfinished, his fame rests on the great houses he built in Barcelona. Twelve of his eighteen buildings are in the city. They have not always been highly regarded. By the time he died, his reputation was eclipsed by new styles. He was thought out of date, working in old-fashioned stone, too influenced by the medieval, spending far too much money and overloading his buildings with fantasy adornment and excessive religious and nationalist symbolism.

There is a particular moment when one can say that Gaudí's star set. In 1912 he handed over the Casa Milà (known also as the Pedrera, the Quarry), his block of flats on the Passeig de Gràcia, to the Milà family. The Milà family had refused to allow him to place an enormous statue of the Virgin on the roof. On occupying their own flat on the first floor, the Milàs at once had the inside stripped out and straight rectangular walls put in. Legend has it that the Senyora de Milà lamented to Gaudí, on first seeing the rippling walls of her new flat, "Where can I put my dog kennel?" The lofty, ageing architect, by now beyond caring, replied: "Buy yourself a snake, Madam."

Neoclassicism came into fashion as a reaction against the "drunkenness of forms... architecture of ice-cream cornet sellers", as *L'architecture*, a leading Paris magazine, described Gaudí in 1910. *Noucentisme*, named after the new century, was the movement of straight walls, lines without fancy adornment and economic shapes that became fashionable in the 1910s and 1920s. In contrast, Gaudí and his overloaded, romantic, harking-back-to-the-past buildings seemed passé. Gaudí's star did not rise again until the 1960s, when foreigners began to visit Barcelona to hunt out *modernisme*. Earlier, George Orwell's 1937 philistine comment on the Sagrada Família stood for a standard view:

...a modern cathedral, and one of the most hideous buildings in the world. It has four crenellated spires exactly the shape of hock bottles. Unlike most of the churches in Barcelona it was not damaged during the revolution—it was spared because of its "artistic value", people said. I think the Anarchists showed bad taste in not blowing it up when they had the chance.

This was a political reaction, rather than an artistic one. Orwell's view was shared by Picasso, himself an artistic revolutionary who one might have expected would enjoy Gaudí's free artistic spirit. Orwell and Picasso were reacting to Gaudí's fundamentalist Catholicism and to comments such as the words of the papal nuncio Ragonesi in 1915, addressing Gaudí on behalf of the Vatican: "You are the Dante of architecture. Your magnificent work is a Christian poem carved in stone."

Under Franco, several *modernista* buildings were knocked down, so little were they appreciated, including the Gaudí-designed Café Torino—now rebuilt on the Passeig de Gràcia to original designs and reopened in 1995. As recently as 1980 the Casa Milà was shabby and in urgent need of restoration. It was not until one of the two big savings banks of Catalonia, the Caixa de Catalunya, bought it in 1986 that it was properly restored.

Even in his eclipse Gaudí had his supporters, and not just among the religious and Catalanist right who in 1952 restarted work on the Sagrada Família halted in 1926. The architect Louis Sullivan pronounced that Gaudí was "spirit symbolized in stone". Le Corbusier himself, whose rationalist, square-lined architecture might seem the diametric opposite of Gaudí, affirmed that Gaudí was "the creator of modern, organic architecture". In 1928, after first visiting Barcelona, Le Corbusier wrote with prescience:

Gaudí is the builder of the twentieth century, the craftsman, builder in brick, iron and stone... Gaudí was a great artist; only those who touch the sensitive part of men's hearts will last. In the medium term, though, they will be mistreated, misunderstood or accused of the sin of being fashionable at the time.

In the last twenty years Gaudí has become Barcelona's greatest money-spinner. An ironic destiny for an architect who cared nothing for clothes, food or tourism and who did not even build himself a house. In 1984 the Park Güell, the Casa Milà and the Palau Güell were named UNESCO World Heritage Sites and in 2005 five other buildings, including the chapel at Santa Coloma and the Sagrada Família, were added to the list. There is no other single artist with eight World Heritage Sites.

Palau Güell

It is worth looking at one of these in detail, the Palau Güell, the first work of Gaudí's artistic maturity. It was started in 1885, commissioned by Eusebi Güell, who wanted a mighty palace to show off his wealth and to purchase a title. He succeeded, in that the Queen Regent María Cristina was persuaded to lodge there during her visit to the 1889 Universal Exhibition and must have enjoyed herself enough for Güell to be named a count in 1908. No expense was spared on the Palau Güell: this was the period of Barcelona's stock market fever, when everyone was gambling and money spilled from the pockets of the wealthy.

The Palau Güell is one of few *modernista* houses in the Old City of Barcelona. The other main ones are Domènech's Palau de la Música Catalana and the Quatre gats café (see Chapter Eight). The Hotel Europa on Carrer Sant Pau, the London Bar on Nou de la Rambla and the Escribà cake-shop on the Ramblas are decorated in a *modernista* style, but Barcelona's *modernisme* is basically in the Eixample, as it was there that the wealthy industrialists like Milà and Batlló built their houses after the 1859 demolition of the city walls.

Unlike many of Gaudí's works, the Palau Güell was completed. The architect himself was responsible for the structure and every item of decoration. Because the Palau Güell is in the narrow Nou de la Rambla, it is impossible to see it as a whole from a distance (the same happens with the Palau de la Música). Not only tourists, but Güell and Gaudí were confined by the narrowness of the site. Because of this the building turns in on itself, around its central dome. Yet lack of space does not fully explain the severity of the outside of this urban palace. Great arched doors are filled with decorative iron and between them a standard clings to the wall like a great beast from Hell. The ironwork constantly turns and twists round itself, imitating the build-

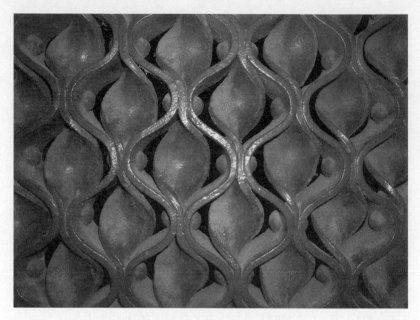

Detail from the main door of the Palau Güell

ing itself; the bars fold over the cross-bars in molten flaps. The façade is flat, unlike most Art Nouveau buildings. Its severity, we come to see, is the result of its design as a rich man's palace in the medieval sense: it was built for defensive purposes against the local population, the poor who surround it. Alastair Boyd associated such a medieval fortress with the later colony at Santa Coloma, both examples of "industrial feudalism": "This brilliantly executed but frankly sinister building is an extraordinary statement of the architect's view of the industrial magnate."

The inside contains a magnificent surprise. The frankly sinister building on a narrow, dirty street explodes on the first floor into a huge hall soaring towards the light. The straight lines and fortress style melt into warm, curving refinement. Unlike Gaudí's later Casa Milà or Casa Batlló, whose interior entirely reflects the outside, the Palau Güell's severe medieval facade and entrance conceal the modern luxury of the magnate. The palace thus becomes both a forbidding public statement of Güell's wealth, imposing itself on the city centre, and a private lair of luxury hidden from the masses. Heavy severity turns to light and grace.

Earlier than Gaudí's other famous buildings, the neo-Gothic influence of Viollet-le-Duc, the designer of the citadel at Carcassonne, is clearer. As well as Gothic, Arab traces are evident, too. Yet the other elements of Gaudí's later style are already in place, only seven years after his qualification as an architect: the plasticity of the iron-work, wood and stone. The greatest feature is this central salon that, like a cathedral, rises right up to the upper storey where its dome bursts through the roof, which is a cornucopia of multi-shaped and multi-coloured chimneys. The huge room, lit from above and by galleries opening at different levels, is the equal of anything Gaudí did later. Here Güell entertained his guests with concerts, poetry readings and exhibitions; this was a formal, high-bourgeois art salon, not at all bohemian or avant-garde, as Rusiñol's at Sitges was (see Chapter Eight).

In this building, Gaudí first surrounded himself with his team, the stone-masons, tile-designers and -firers, jewellers, carpenters, woodworkers, metal-workers and glaziers with whom he was to work for the next twenty years. The house was designed in its entirety—glass, furniture, doors, tiles, colours of the walls—with Gaudí like the player-manager of a football team, not just telling people what to do, but showing them. It was the attempt, in Eduardo and Cristina Mendoza's phrase, "to fuse all the arts, decisive for the splendour of *modernista* architecture."

Today, the Palau Güell, refurbished, is one of the city's great tourist attractions. The neighbourhood outside, though, is still the barrio chino, Chinatown, and at night young African prostitutes hang out in front of the great iron doors. In the block between the palace and the Ramblas the old and the new Raval meet: a traditional furrier's, Finn Macool's Irish pub, a 24-hour Spar supermarket (called inevitably the Spar Gaudí), a cheap hostel, an Indian restaurant (Rajah), a Turkish restaurant (La Turca), a cheap watch bazaar and a bank. This is the mix of traditional business and the new worlds brought together by globalization: through it all, the vibrant and lively yet poor and sordid nature of the Raval has persisted in the century plus since the palace was built.

Sant Pau and the Sagrada Família

Just as Domènech's Palace of Music in its grandeur faces Gaudí's Palau Güell on the opposite side of the Old City, so his Hospital de Sant Pau also faces Gaudí's Sagrada Família, on the edge of the Eixample. The hospital and the cathedral are joined or separated by the Avinguda de Gaudí, a rare diagonal cutting through the Eixample's rectangular blocks.

The Sagrada Família, Catalonia's most famous building, was started in 1882 and Gaudí took it on in 1883. It was conceived from the start as an Expiatory Temple. The idea was to build an offering to the glory of God to expiate the sins of Barcelona. These sins were not, of course, of the city's slave-trading or barbarian industrial magnates, but rather of the godless workers and their revolutionary ideologies. From the start, the cathedral was an ideological counter-attack on revolutionary Barcelona.

Gaudí, the bright, inquiring school and university student, the dapper young man of his early work, became gradually possessed by religious passion. He neglected clothing, appearance and nutrition for this spiritual project. By 1912 he abandoned all other work for the Sagrada Família. There he worked non-stop and almost lived, sleeping on a cot in the workshop; religious mania had gripped him. The spires that already soar above the bourgeois Eixample were to be exceeded by a central tower reaching 500 feet, higher than St. Peter's in Rome. Whether this will ever be built is uncertain. Since the early 1980s, though, work has continued apace, mainly financed by donations from Japanese tourists.

The best part of the Sagrada Família is the Nativity façade, seen from the street outside and completed in Gaudí's lifetime. The Baroque façade with three portals is carved in great detail, so needs time (and binoculars) to observe not just the Nativity story, but plants and animals—Gaudí's religious passion was all-embracing, including all the wonders of the natural world. The towers are worth climbing, for the space you find within them. They look narrow, but inside the climber finds that they criss-cross from one to the other, creating a sudden window, a vision of coloured tiles at the top of the lollipop-like towers or little vantage-points, where often young lovers are wedged together above the void. From the towers, you can look out over the inventiveness of people living in bee-hive apartment blocks, unlike the spread of detached houses in British and American suburbs. Roof-top gardens are everywhere, often with big trees in little pots.

Along the pedestrian-only Avinguda de Gaudí, its fast-food shops growing out from the permanent tourist market round the Sagrada Família, stands the great main gate of Domènech's Sant Pau Hospital, physically the largest *modernista* complex in Catalonia (the site covers 360 acres). Sant Pau, like the Pere Matas Hospital at Reus, was quite the reverse of Gaudí's response to the poor. Like the Pere Matas, Sant Pau was the work of an enlightened bourgeoisie, moving the medieval hospital out from the Old City (still there in the Carrer Hospital, now Catalonia's National Library) to a green-field site on the slopes of a hill on the edge of the Eixample. To their credit, the Barcelona ruling-class and authorities paid for the hospital, while they abandoned the church to its fate. They were, of course, keen to end the epidemics—not least cholera—that flayed the poor, but also touched the rich.

Sant Pau's 48 domed pavilions in red and green tiles are connected by underground passages and divided by gardens. These were measures against infection, but also what Domènech called "the tyranny of the straight line" in characteristic conservative rejection of the Eixample's rational blocks. Just as the buildings are rounded, its internal roads twist, too. Domènech fled, in the words of Robert Hughes, from the "depressing, labyrinthine character that big general hospitals share with prisons." Domènech's light-filled vision was the opposite of Gaudí's morbid obsession with death and suffering, with expiation of sins. "He thought that everything that could give a form of well-being to the sick was also a form of therapy," said Pere, his son, who completed the project. Thus the main gate is open, grandiose and rich in stained glass and mosaic; and pavilions for patients tend to the intimate with varied and fascinating ceramics—of lizards, doctors, flowers. Domènech's asylum at Reus and hospital in Barcelona are among the finest examples of art at the service of humanity.

Sitges

Chapter Eight

The Birth of Modern Painting: Rusiñol at Sitges, Casas and Pablo Picasso

Modernisme was not just an architectural movement. The same conditions of industrial revolution and *renaixença* that combined to produce such exotic architecture underlay similar movements in sculpture, jewellery, tiling, music, literature and painting. Whereas the *renaixença* signalled the rebirth of the use of Catalan in cultured circles and writing and a boost in national consciousness, *modernisme* connected Catalonia's young artists, architects and writers with vanguards throughout Europe. Symbolism, art for art's sake and the cult of individualism marked the Art Nouveau of Paris and Vienna. In Catalonia there was a conscious effort to integrate this innovative movement into Catalonia's reborn traditions and to make it part of a new, national culture.

Modernisme in painting, after initial doubts, very rapidly burst the bounds of the small artistic avant-garde and became mainstream in Catalonia. By 1898, for instance, the painter Ramon Casas won the public competition to design the Anís del mono advertising poster in a thoroughly *modernista* style, unthinkable a decade earlier.

This new painting movement did not just spring out of the stateless nation's impulse to modernity. Catalonia had had its painters throughout the ages. Marià Fortuny from Reus was prominent in the nineteenth century, but Catalonia was not a great centre of European painting as the Madrid court had been, drawing to it artists of the stature of El Greco, Ribera, Velázquez, Murillo, the Venetian Tiepolo and Goya.

At the end of the nineteenth century, however, an important generation of painters arose in Catalonia. These precursors were led by Casas and his lifelong friend Santiago Rusiñol. Following them came Nonell and Picasso; and then a third generation, led by Dalí and Miró. By the mid-twentieth century, they had placed Catalonia in the forefront of modern art.

The Iron Burrow

This story of the birth of modern painting in Catalonia starts at Sitges, a seaside town some 25 miles south of Barcelona. The great sight at Sitges is its church (see this book's cover), magnificently silhouetted at dusk on the cliff above the mile-long curving beach and esplanade. The church has two belfries, one open with the bell enclosed in cast iron, the other concealed in stone, and a façade of pale limestone from the Garraf hills behind pitted by the salt. Below the church stands a statue of the painter Domenicos Theotocopouli, El Greco. Among the jumble of lanes behind the church is a small museum with two paintings by this painter from Crete who settled in Toledo, Spain. El Greco never visited Sitges. How then have his statue and paintings come to be there?

Sitges is one of Catalonia's most elegant seaside resorts, connected to Barcelona's main station at Sants by a rapid train service. On the Sitges line many of the trains are double-deckers: sit upstairs for the views. The train runs out through the high-rise working-class suburbs of Barcelona, then the abandoned factories round the airport and the new roll-up factories and warehouses encroaching onto the Llobregat river's loamy coastal plain. There are still farmhouses, wells and fields among the rampant new building: artichokes and lettuces for the city are grown among the motorway intersections. Horses graze alongside hypermarkets.

It is a spectacular train, with views of the wild Garraf range of hills that reach right down to the sea and contain, in hidden valleys, cement works dusting the scrub white and Barcelona's now-closed rubbish dump. As the train runs into the tunnelled cliffs beyond Castelldefels it passes the wine vaults designed by Gaudí in the village of Garraf, where Le Corbusier, taken on this route by Sert in 1928 (see Chapter Ten), had his first glimpse of Gaudí's work. After Garraf, a pretty village with multi-coloured bathing huts along its beach, the track runs along the edge of the cliffs in and out of several tunnels with glimpses of the sea breaking on the rocks.

Beyond the Garraf range, the heart and the sea-front of Sitges have been particularly well preserved, without high-rise blocks, unlike most other towns on the coast. Sitges was a place where, a century ago, many *indiano*-owned mansions with their palm trees and *modernista* houses were built. The influence of their owners has helped conserve the town. This said, the 1970s Aiguadolç harbour and apartments at its northern end are decidedly ugly. In the last two decades, too, villas have straggled up the dry hills behind Sitges like bindweed, and that plague of modern Catalonia, the golf course whose greens gulp down water, has been laid out beside the pretty coastal walk from Sitges to the next town south, Vilanova i la Geltrú. This is despite a chronic water shortage at Sitges: until the early 1990s the old town had only sea-water in the taps.

The town has two beaches, the small and intimate Platja Sant Sebastià, ringed by a line of classic Mediterranean balconied blue and white-painted houses, and the longer beach to the south that stretches away, first to the bar and club area round the "Street of Sin" and then to the huge beach homes of the Barcelona bourgeoisie. Many of these bars and clubs have a gay clientele, and Sitges has become one of Europe's great gay holiday resorts.

On the headland between the beaches lies the old village, a network of winding streets on different levels. The white houses are shuttered, and one glimpses palms and bougainvillea that hint at gardens behind the walls. On a stormy day the sea crashes against the rocks below the weather-beaten church and pours over the wide steps. At the top of these steps an ancient cannon points out to sea and an inscription explains how, in an action in 1797, six such cannon drove off two English frigates in a four-hour engagement.

On this headland the painter Santiago Rusiñol inherited two ruined fishermen's houses in 1891. He liked the soft light at Sitges. He liked the temperature, too: it is a couple of degrees warmer than Barcelona, out of reach of the *tramuntana* north wind. He had the houses rebuilt and established residence there when he was not on his long stays in Paris. Rusiñol's house, Cau ferrat, "Iron Burrow" in Catalan, is now a cluttered, fascinating, small museum, the walls packed with paintings and the shelves with the old iron-work that fascinated him just as it did Gaudí.

Santiago Rusiñol has a special place in the history of Catalan art. A great painter himself, though many say he did not fulfil his potential, he became the showman who created an ambience for art to flourish in Catalonia and also a precursor, the person whose organizational and theoretical skills unlocked the doors that Picasso, Nonell, Miró and Dalí later pushed open.

Rusiñol was born in 1861 into a prosperous textile family, owners of a plant at Manlleu on the Ter river. His father died young, but his mother and grandfather forced him into the family firm up to the age of 27. The heir would escape from the Barcelona office to draw and paint on the docks. It was not until his grandfather's death that he finally pressured his mother into allowing him to become a painter.

Rusiñol later became as successful a writer as painter. His most famous work, *L'auca del senyor Esteve* (The *Auca* of Mr. Stephen), was written as an autobiographical novel in 1907 with drawings by Casas. In 1917 he adapted it for the theatre: the play is still performed in Catalonia. An *auca* is a sort of saga, written often in pictures and in rhyme. Rusiñol's *auca* deals precisely with the conflict between a life dedicated to art and Catalan business. Senyor Esteve, owner of a textiles business, wants his idealistic and artistic grandson to work in the family firm. Though treated ironically by Rusiñol, Senyor Esteve is not seen just in negative terms; Rusiñol could by this later stage of his life portray his grandfather with sympathy. The conflict ends in a pact, adding to the literature on how Catalans like to resolve conflicts by pacting.

Like Esteve's grandson, Rusiñol did not have to break with his family and live in a garret. His style of artistic bohemianism was wealthy. From 1888 he spent long periods in Paris, which had displaced Rome— where Fortuny had died a decade earlier—as the capital of European art. Paris was also the model for bohemian lives, and Rusiñol for a period shared with Ramon Casas a flat over the Moulin de la Galette in still semi-rural Montmartre. When he returned from the metropolis to a provincial Barcelona, he brought with him all the authority of a man who had drunk from the well of modern art in Paris. It was an epoch when the whole Catalan upper class forgot that France has been as oppressive towards Catalonia as Spain. *Afrancesada* or Francophile, the local elite reacted to Madrid's backwardness by mimicking everything

French. Posh restaurants had their menus in French, while sophisticated women dressed in Parisian styles. Rich young men like Rusiñol escaped there from provincial boredom.

The fishing village of Sitges was home to a number of landscape and seascape painters in the 1870s and 1880s. These were good regional painters, exploiting the light to paint realistic rows of cottages or boats drawn up on the sand. Rusiñol's work imitated their light and realism, but gave it a twist. Many of his paintings from the 1890s, his best period, are preoccupied with long entrances leading into rooms, lit from a garden glimpsed behind. In this relation between indoors and out, in a realistic, urban setting, lie hints of privacy half seen. His painting is often said to be second-rate, a mere fusion of the Sitges painters drawing together scenes full of light and the work of Whistler, Renoir and Degas. It has weathered well, though, and if the same paintings had been done by a Paris Impressionist rather than a Catalan equivalent, one wonders whether critics, connoisseurs or public would notice the difference.

It was, however, as a promoter of the arts that Rusiñol broke new ground. In 1892 he organized a fine arts exhibition in Sitges, showing the work of local painters of shifting light and weather and some of his own paintings. The following year he put on a second festival, which smashed the conventional bounds of Catalan, or European, art. *Modernisme* sought to integrate all the arts and, as well as an exhibition, Rusiñol organized the first performance in Spain of the Belgian Maurice Maeterlinck's symbolist play, *The Intruder*. Rusiñol himself read a polemic against "insincere art, written with rhetorical sighs and borrowed tears." The *modernistes* were against "speeches inflated with words that fall like oratorical waterfalls" and "shouted monologues." Most guilty though Rusiñol himself was of inflated speeches, the point was made. It was the cry against cosy drawing-room art that is repeated from generation to generation.

The third festival took place on 4 November 1894, *modernista* painting's coming of age. By now Rusiñol had become a master of publicity. He announced in advance that he had bought in Paris two paintings by El Greco. El Greco (1541-1614) was an Old Master fallen, unusually for old masters, into a certain disregard in the nineteenth century, but even so his paintings did not come cheap. The recovery of El Greco was part of the *modernistes'* opposition to nineteenth-century academic painting by numbers. They emphasized El Greco's heightened colouring, realistic and anguished faces, and flowing clothes.

A brass band greeted a special train laid on from Barcelona. A huge crowd assembled. Rusiñol had organized a magnificent procession: a local artist on horseback, the band, two giant iron candelabras, and then the two El Greco canvases borne shoulder-high marched through Sitges to the newly refurbished Cau ferrat. There they still are, along with Rusiñol's brasses and paintings by him, Casas, Miquel Utrillo (the leading Catalan art critic and father of the painter Maurice Utrillo) and his most famous protégé, Pablo Picasso. People threw flowers out of their windows onto the art procession. "Everyone", as they say, was there: Casas, Utrillo, the poet Joan Maragall, the architect Puig i Cadafalch. Gaudí and Verdaguer were absent. They belonged to the religious right and had nothing to do with these bohemian, godless drunkards.

That evening Puig i Cadafalch spoke at the party held on the rocks beside Rusiñol's new house in favour of "art in shirt-sleeves, in favour of that modern art that wants no ornaments, however old they are, since they always turn out ridiculous." This young searcher after the new became later a leading conservative politician, as well as the famous architect who led the cataloguing of the Romanesque treasures in the Pyrenees.

Rusiñol spoke of the need to look beyond the boundaries of Catalonia. In his words, one can see his conscious desire to bind together a movement, as he endows it with a sense of those present being special, being in the know:

> Here we can let off steam and shout what we often do not dare to say when we are surrounded by the flock: that we want to be poets and that we look down on and pity those who do not feel the poetry; that we prefer a Leonardo or a Dante to a province or a village; that we would rather be symbolists and unbalanced, even mad and decadent, than debased and cowardly; common sense strangles us...

The next day the artists rowed out in boats at dusk, rigged up lights behind them and danced in silhouette in the boats on the fortuitously calm sea. Crowds on the seafront drank in the spectacle. One can imagine the locals watching these artists at play, just as today they sit at the café tables and watch benevolently the gay and the young on Sin Street. Colm Tóibín caught the mood:

> [Sitges] retains something of its turn-of-the-century glamour... The sun-tanned young wander the streets, watching and waiting, the bars throb with fast music, the discos are full of people gathered for the holy sacrament of sex. The mad and decadent world that Santiago Rusiñol proposed in 1894 goes on in Sitges until the dawn.

Sitges 1894 was something never seen before in Spain. Despite the elitist, art-for-art's-sake tones of Rusiñol's diatribe, the festival was popular with the council, press and, judging by the crowds, the local populace. This says something about the nature of Catalonia at the time. Its rulers lusted to break out of the Spanish straitjacket into the colourful freedoms of the rest of Europe. These were the years after the tremendous collective effort that it took to organize Barcelona's Universal Exhibition of 1889. Just as people had been enthused by the exhibition's conscious bid to put Catalan business on the international map, so they were excited by Rusiñol's efforts to bring international art to Sitges and Barcelona. *Modernisme* was the attempt to modernize the country through culture. All the above explains why there is a statue of El Greco on the front at Sitges. On the small, prettier beach, only a hundred yards from his house, there is one of Rusiñol, too.

Darwin's Monkey
After 1894 there were two more *festes modernistes* at Sitges, in 1897 and 1899. By then, the movement was fully consolidated. Big business advertised its wares with Art Nouveau posters. Barcelona's fashionable society flocked to its shows. All sorts of magazines were founded and traditional ones were revamped with the wavy lines and straight-gazing yet languid girls of Art Nouveau motifs. The new industrialists were competing with each other to build the most fantastical houses in the Eixample.

In 1897 Ramon Casas financed the opening of the Quatre gats café. This imitation of Le chat noir in Paris lasted only six years, but it was crucial in bringing onto the stage the next generation of artists. The Quatre gats—Four Cats—is on a narrow street, just off the Portal de l'Àngel, the broad, short street in Barcelona's Old City whose shops now pay the highest commercial rentals in Spain. The café was not just a meeting-place, but published a magazine and put on exhibitions, theatre shows, concerts and poetry readings. It is in a building designed by Puig i Cadafalch in his mock medieval-fortress style. Today it is again a café and one of the great pleasures of having a drink or a meal there is that its decor is much as it was from 1897 to 1903. Attractively decorated in a *modernista* style, with a delicate wooden gallery with small tables round the inner room, it has the added excitement of being a place that marked the history of modern art. Its menu, on a stand in the street, was designed by Picasso; the pictures on the walls are photographs or repro-ductions of pictures by people now famous.

Paris or Vienna had hit Barcelona. For a few short years this arts café became the centre of the Catalan art world.

Ramon Casas, the greatest painter of Catalan *modernisme*, left school at the age of twelve in 1878. This was not because of poverty, for his parents were archetypical *nouveaux riches* of the period, a successful *indiano* and a textiles heiress. His family, though, accepted that Casas was a bad student and wanted to paint, and let him attend a painting and crafts workshop. In his lack of schooling Casas was like Picasso a gener-ation later. They both lacked the general culture and breadth of knowledge with which Rusiñol overflowed.

At fifteen, Casas was in Paris, while the five years-older Rusiñol was still fighting with his grandfather to escape the family business. Casas' most famous picture of this Paris period is his 1892 *Au Moulin de la Galette*. A young woman is looking directly at someone out of the picture while sitting alone at a table, smoking a cigar and with a glass of spirits before her. In the mirror, a full bar is reflected. Its theme is very much like similar pictures by Degas, Manet or other Impressionists. The theme of a "fallen" or modern woman was mildly scandalous at the time, though today what stands out is the quality of Casas' painting of her. His lines are sharper than the above-mentioned Impressionists' and his ability to draw a face greater.

Like Toulouse-Lautrec, Casas' ability with line, taste for colour, and bold simplified shapes found its greatest outlet in advertising posters. He blazed a new trail for artists in the commercial art that was to become one of the twentieth century's dominant art forms. Casas sold his talents to big business, as mass consumer production got off the ground in the 1890s. He did not need to hang his work in academies or museums. The new techniques of mass reproduction in colour meant that he could hang his work on street walls.

Casas' most famous posters were for Anís del mono, "Monkey anisette", a sticky, sweet alcoholic drink made by a Badalona drinks company and popular throughout Europe at the time. The proprietor Vicente Bosch owned a monkey, which roamed his factory. Casas' monkey is said to have had Bosch's face in the posters, reflecting the debate raging at the time about whether or not humans were descended from apes. The poster and subsequent similar ones were so successful that Casas' image is still popular today. There is an original design still in place on the outside wall of the delicatessen Can Murrià, on the corner of Carrers València and Roger de Llúria in Barcelona's Eixample.

The use of "Darwin's monkey" and "advanced" pretty young women smoking and drinking anisette were tantalizingly modern. Casas, rich already, made a lot more money as his epoch's leading poster designer. He even did one for the rival drinks firm of Anís del Tigre (Tiger Anisette), which showed a tiger eating the monkey. The *cava* firm Codorniu, whose cellars were designed in a neo-Gothic Art Nouveau style by Puig i Cadafalch, also employed Casas for its posters. Later in life he designed a stunning poster calling on people to seek medical help for tuberculosis. After his death in 1932, this poster's haggard figures were re-used in Civil War propaganda appealing for help for the hungry.

Around 1907 Casas fused his easy dominance of line with raw passion to paint *La Sargantain*, a portrait of enormous sensual power: much more so than the rather awkward nudes, like still lives, he had painted in the naughty nineties. *La Sargantain* is fully dressed in a crinkly yellow dress shading off into green that recalls the colouring of El Greco, one of whose paintings Casas had carried through the streets of Sitges at the third *modernista* festival. Her long, strong fingers grip the arm of her chair and she stares, smouldering, at the painter. The model was Júlia Peraire, a young eighteen-year-old lottery-seller Casas met in the Ramblas in 1905. This was a love match against his family's wishes: it was not till 1922 that he eventually married Júlia. Alas, in Casas, there was nothing else as raw and felt as *La Sargantain*: for the rest of his career he used his gift to reproduce faces to paint fine but conventional portraits of rich women.

Before that, in late 1890s Barcelona, Casas caused a sensation with three canvases of social scenes: a public garrotting outside the Cordellers prison in the Raval, the moment before the bombing of the Corpus Christi procession (1896) and a police charge against strikers in 1899. This latter he re-dated to 1902 to coincide with the general strike of that year. The Corpus Christi procession was an annual popular procession from the Santa Maria de Mar church (see Chapter Twelve): the people killed in the attack were workers and children. The 1893 Liceu opera house bombing became more famous because of its fulfilment of the new bourgeoisie's wildest fears of anarchism. Santiago Salvador, the Liceu bomber, dropped his bomb from the fifth storey, the "gods", onto the stalls, killing twenty people. At the time, though, the Corpus Christi attack had even more impact, precisely because its victims were the poor. Indeed, it was widely rumoured that the bombers were police provocateurs, causing outrage in order to justify the repression of the anarchists that followed. This is certainly possible, but has never been proved one way or the other.

These political paintings and what right-wingers like Gaudí considered the decadent internationalism (women smoking cigars and drinking etc.) of *modernista* painting did not mean that Rusiñol or Casas were left-wing. It was the next generation, that of Pablo Picasso (1881-1973) and Isidre Nonell (1873-1911), which went a step further in their denunciation of social injustice. The realism introduced by Casas and Rusiñol at times aroused controversy, but was basically as amiable as Rusiñol's personality. Picasso and Nonell, their younger protégés at the Quatre gats, were well aware that very few people lived in the luxury enjoyed by Casas and Rusiñol and the people they painted.

While Casas' studio was in his house on the Passeig de Gràcia, one house away from the Casa Milà, the huge block of apartments Gaudí was to build between 1906 and 1912, Picasso painted in a series of rented rooms in the Old City. Casas' luxury flat and garden can still be seen today, on the first floor of the Vinçon department store (open the same hours that the shop is open).

As Picasso could not afford furniture, in one of his studios he painted a table and chair on the walls. It was a representation of poverty rather than real suffering; he went off to eat with his parents every lunch-time. The intent, though, was clear: to take painting out of the drawing-rooms into the slums.

The Vertical Invader

Pablo Picasso was not Catalan. He came from another great Mediterranean sea-port, Malaga in Andalusia. However, his best (not at all his most comprehensive) museum is in Barcelona. Although he spent under a decade in Catalonia (1895-1904), he identified with it. It is where he spent his adolescence and early adulthood, learned his craft, formed his personality and developed his left-wing politics. He mar-velled at Barcelona, with its modern industry, its medieval streets, its great bourgeoisie and its powerful revolutionary movement. In Barcelona, Pablo Ruiz became "Picasso", the most famous painter and great art revolutionary of the twentieth century. That is why sixty years later he chose Barcelona for his museum.

Picasso lived in Barcelona when the anarchist movement was renowned for its terrorist phase, "propaganda by deed", such as the bombing of the Liceu or the Corpus Christi procession. Their argument was that exemplary, individual action could arouse the working masses. Picasso was in no way an active supporter of the anarchists, but he breathed the air that gave rise to their actions. His anarchism, like that of the other young artists who gathered at the Quatre gats, was a general anti-authoritarianism, a dislike of the same things that the anarchists hated. In terms of political activism, throughout his life he was extreme-ly cautious: nothing interrupted his painting.

His father, José Ruiz, was a failed painter but good painting teacher, though his melancholy suggests that the latter was little consolation. He moved to Barcelona for a job in 1895, when Pablo was fourteen. The school was in the Llotja (Stock Exchange) building near the harbour in the Old City, and the Picasso family lived nearby. With his friends Manuel Pallarès and Carlos Casagemas, who was to shoot himself over disappointed love in a Paris café in 1902 (bohemian melodrama becom-ing real tragedy), Picasso spent his adolescence traipsing these chaotic, filthy, bustling streets. He drew and painted the figures he saw, and espe-cially hands, numerous hands. He went too to the Quatre gats. By all accounts, he was a silent participant at the long, brilliant, rambling conversations led by Rusiñol. His education was uneven, he was very young, he did not speak Catalan well.

In November 1899 Picasso saw Casas' exhibition of charcoal drawings at the Quatre gats, mainly of other *modernista* artists. Impressed and inspired by them, and encouraged by Casas himself (Picasso's later kindness towards painters such as Miró was learned from the generosity of Rusiñol and Casas), he set to doing a series, and in spring 1900 had his first exhibition of some 100 charcoal drawings, also at the Quatre gats. With this initial success, Picasso made his first visit to Paris, where that October Casas drew him.

The Ribera part of Barcelona is the quarter most closely associated with Picasso, though he roamed across the whole Old City. It is in the Ribera that Picasso attended the art school where his father worked, where his family lived and he had studios, and where his museum was opened in the 1960s. Today the Ribera is changing rapidly, but it costs little imagination to see some of these streets with their medieval lay-out as Picasso found them. To imagine Picasso's city, walk from Domènech's Palau down Verdaguer i Callís. The street is narrow, cobbled and dark, without a pavement. The buildings are five storeys high, with damp blocks of stone at their base. Washing hangs out over the street. There is no piped gas in this area: it is delivered by Pakistani or Moroccan *butaners* who cart the orange butane-gas cylinders up the narrow, uneven stairs to the poor living in tiny flats. Still-malodorous drains recall why the bourgeoisie was desperate to break out of this TB- and cholera-ridden place in the mid-nineteenth century.

In the National Museum of Catalan Art on Montjuïc there are several paintings by the gifted Isidre Nonell. Fascinated with the downtrodden and outcast, Nonell started his career in the 1890s drawing deformed, goitred people at the spa town of Caldes de Boí, up above the Romanesque churches of the Boí Valley. Later, till his sudden death at the age of 38, he painted gypsies and the poor from these Barcelona slums. Nonell was little recognized in his day: he broke the bourgeois consensus within which Rusiñol and Casas, even with the latter's three political canvases, had remained. Nonell's dark paintings, in blacks, browns and reds, of the poor, sick and deformed, are the kind of art that is more appreciated by later generations than his own, which was unwilling to be too closely reminded of the harsh reality of the city it lived in.

Barcelona's Old City

Picasso was strongly influenced by Nonell in what is known as his "Blue Period", because of the dark shades of blue and black, which immediately preceded his Cubism. Blue was the tone of sadness. In these years Picasso's bearded, drawn features in photos and portraits could have meant that he was heading for a death as early as Nonell's. The sights of the Ribera in Barcelona, the poverty of his first years in Paris, fear of his great eyes being blinded by venereal disease, and the effect of the suicide of his friend Casagemas all combined to make the Blue Period.

Picasso's museum in Barcelona's Carrer Montcada, one of five in the world devoted to the painter, is mainly a record of his early days in Barcelona and the Blue Period. It is enhanced by his own gifts in the late 1960s, including his *Meninas* series after Velázquez. It has been for two decades the most popular museum in Barcelona, explained perhaps by the romance of the young Picasso in this city and the museum's magnificent setting in a series of merchants' mansions, or *palaus* (palaces) as they are called in Catalan. Several of these mansions are works of art in their own right: the Aguilar and Finestres palaces have rare painted ceilings from the fourteenth century of animals and scenes from daily life—rare because most surviving paintings of the period are religious.

When the museum opened in 1963 it was called the Sabartés Foundation, its stock was small and, up to Picasso's death on 8 April, 1973, was considered an embarrassing failure. The rise of the Picasso Museum has been intimately connected with Barcelona's remarkable transformation from a slum city in the 1960s, in which the barely changed Old City would have been instantly recognized by Picasso, to a world-renowned tourist city. The post-Franco city authorities understood the attraction of its association with Picasso. They liked him, too. He was not just the artist who had found himself in Barcelona, but he hated Franco and supported Catalan independence.

More than anything, for Catalans, squeezed throughout their history between Paris and Madrid, Picasso came from the Spanish provinces to Barcelona, educated himself there in the new artistic trends brought back from Paris by Rusiñol and Casas, then himself went to Paris and conquered what was then the art capital of the world. He entered Paris like a "vertical invader", in the beautiful phrase John Berger appropriates from the Spanish philosopher Ortega y Gasset. Berger explains Picasso in terms of how Spain had not experienced a bourgeois revolution, of the type that the rest of Europe saw in the nineteenth century. This meant that Catalonia, despite being the most developed part of Spain, was "stretched on the rack" of history. He means by this that different historical periods co-existed there, leading to the extraordinary violence of Barcelona's labour relations and political protests. The vertical invader Picasso, coming up through successive and coexisting stages of history, brought revolutionary Barcelona, in paint of course not bombs, into the Parisian drawing-rooms. "A painting," said Picasso, in an utterance worthy of the anarchists, "is a sum of destruction." On Barcelona's Passeig de Picasso, beside the Ciutadella Park, is a pile of rubbish in a glass cube. This work by Antoni Tàpies is titled "Homage to Picasso". I do not think that Tàpies believes Picasso is rubbish, but that Tàpies is showing that Picasso thought that capitalist society was rubbish.

Picasso had not just urban Catalan roots, but spent nine months in 1898 recovering from scarlet fever at Horta de Sant Joan, the home village of his fellow-student Manuel Pallarès. Though Horta, in the limestone hills on the southern edge of Catalonia, known as the *Terra Alta*, the High Country, is today accustomed to Picasso fans, it is still at the back of beyond. Here with Pallarès' family, he worked on the land, picking grapes and olives and making wine and oil, painted and learned Catalan. He was wont to say of this idyll in later years: "Everything I learned, I learned at Horta."

While Picasso revolutionized world painting, his sponsors Casas and Rusiñol were left behind. In middle age, Casas took to painting rich women for large fees and Rusiñol became well-known for his paintings of the gardens of Spain, in which he indulged his love of complicated perspectives.

Rusiñol and Casas had paved the way for Nonell and Picasso, then for Dalí and Miró. They themselves had not walked down this path of modern, revolutionary art, but veered away into gardens and society salons. Rusiñol lived his last years in Aranjuez where he died at seventy, while painting in a garden, in June 1931.

The Dalí Theatre-Museum, Figueres

Chapter Nine
The Terminal Beach: Salvador Dalí

Salvador Dalí, who at the age of seven wanted to be Napoleon and "from then on my ambition grew without stopping," would adore his native Figueres today. Nearly twenty years after his death in 1989, the Dalí industry dominates the centre of this small town just twelve miles from the French border. Here the visitor can buy in shop after shop the normal calendars, books, postcards and reproductions of an artist become big business. In addition, Dalí's work allows for all sorts of arte-facts: melting watches, crutches (Dalí's symbol of impotence), floppy pencils (which make you think of impotence too, but also how firm and clear Dalí's real pencil was), locusts (of which he was terrified), ants, severed hands, eggs or beautiful white masks cracked nearly in two. There lies a clue to some of his popularity. You can take home a Dalí object from the Dalí museum, something you cannot do from a Velázquez or Vermeer exhibition. And his popularity, boosted by his cen-tenary in 2004, is still growing. The highly competitive Dalí would be ecstatic that his museum now has more visitors than Barcelona's Picasso museum. Whereas the Picasso museum is the most visited art museum in Barcelona, Dalí's at Figueres is the most visited in Catalonia. Unlike most other sites, it draws Catalonia's two kinds of foreign tourist: the "culture long-weekenders" who take the train up for a day from Barcelona, and the Costa Brava sand-and-sun visitor.

Castle and Theatre: Figueres
Before plunging into the depths of the Dalí museum, walk up the hill to the eighteenth-century castle built to protect the rich Empordà plain from French invasion. "It is pentagonal, cut out of the rock... It is of truly Roman magnificence and solidity, and as far as art can go, it ought to be impregnable," wrote Richard Ford in the 1840s. Sixteen thousand men could be quartered there. It fell, though, to French invasion in 1794 and 1808, due to its "miserable governor" and "astounding cowardice",

thunders Ford, who wrote well but had never been in a war in his life.

One who did volunteer for a war was the writer Laurie Lee, who wrote: "On a bleak naked hill above the town, Figueres castle stood like a white acropolis." After crossing the Pyrenees to fight in the Civil War, Laurie Lee spent three weeks here alongside other bedraggled latecomers waiting to be sent south. This was before the castle was partially blown up at the end of the war (on 8 February 1939) after the last meeting of the Republican Spanish Cortes was held there on 1 February: for a week Figueres was effectively capital of the dying Spanish Republic. The castle's position not only commands the plain, but gives it a panoramic view of the Pyrenees, with Verdaguer's snow-covered Canigó "like an immense magnolia" towering behind the front range. The castle's best feature is not at once obvious, but should not be missed. Underneath the main buildings runs a 400 yard-long curving eighteenth-century stable, constructed entirely of small red bricks, with a drain down the middle, stalls on one side and a yard on the other. They are beautiful now, empty and cool. They give you a sense of the huge numbers of cavalry and riders the castle held in its prime.

The other great building of Figueres also looks like a fortress. Iron grilles protect tall windows and its long severe reddish wall is dotted symmetrically with bumps like metal studs. A closer look reveals that these studs, reminiscent of Domènech i Montaner's triangular bumps on the "castle" wall of the Casa Navàs in Reus, are croissants in ochre plaster. As your eyes sweep up the wall, they meet a jumble of huge white eggs adorning the roof. On a winter's day these fade into the low cloud scudding off the Pyrenees. In sun they glisten in the clear sky, the fantasy of art at the heart of this practical Catalan market town.

This wall is the back of the Salvador Dalí Theatre-Museum, called "theatre" because it used to be one and not just because its contents are more theatrical than museum exhibits are wont to be. Unusually, the artist himself designed both building and contents for its opening in 1974, which suggests how consciously Dalí planned for immortality. Uniquely, the artist is buried in the museum. His tomb is another exhibit, in the basement and "next to the loos", as his biographer, Ian Gibson, comments with apt irreverence. Dalí himself had seen it more grandly: "The spiritual centre of Europe... is situated in the perpendicular centre of the cupola of the museum."

On the front of the museum and in the square outside Dalí let himself go with all his delight in the bizarre. His motifs abound: deep-sea divers ("plumbing the surrealist depths," he said), stomachless women bearing tridents and bread, tyres and TV sets piled high. Gilded women signalling in what might be Morse line the roof in a parody of medieval gargoyles. The museum is fun inside too, with its wet Cadillac (you press a button and rain soaks its eternally patient occupants) and Mae West room. This has the red sofa shaped like lips, with which he conquered New York in the late 1930s.

Ambivalent Legacy

Despite his prestige as a money-earner and his status as "universal genius", much of Catalonia is ambivalent about Dalí because he was an ardent supporter of the Franco dictatorship. Dalí affirmed in a 1951 lecture that Franco "imposed clarity, truth and order on the country at a time when the world was experiencing its greatest anarchy." This was not just some isolated, perhaps surrealist, comment, but a systematic, oft-repeated view. Even in 1975, at the end of Franco's life, Dalí praised him for the executions of ETA activists. Even so, right-wingers are not par-ticularly comfortable with Dalí, either; his surrealist stunts and sexually explicit paintings hardly endeared him to Catholic Spain.

The Pianist, one of the best novels of the Barcelona writer Manuel Vázquez Montalbán (1939-2003), contains the portrait of a musician who is famous as a young man in Paris for his revolutionary *boutades*, adored as an icon of Spain by Franco and then revered as a Grand Old Man by the socialists in the new 1980s democracy. I do not know if this opportunist musician, called in the novel Luis Doria, was consciously based on Dalí, but he could well have been. In the moment that, in the novel, Doria's girlfriend perceives the hollowness at the centre of the musician, she replies to his logorrhea, "Bla, bla, bla". It would be a not undeserved epithet for Dalí.

Unfortunately, it was not just Dalí's political views that stank. After his expulsion from the Surrealist movement in 1937 for "white suprema-cism", André Breton dubbed him "Avida Dollars", an anagram of Salvador Dalí. The name stuck, precisely because his lust for money was so evident. Not only did he bend his talent in the 1940s and 1950s towards churning out repetitive work for the US market, but by the

1960s he was signing reproductions of his paintings to increase their value, and then signing and selling blank sheets of paper. Commentators often shift the blame onto his wife Gala for this greed and these frauds. The truth was that neither he nor Gala had any business or artistic ethics at all. She would demand payment in cash for Dalí's paintings and cart suitcases stuffed with dollar bills back to Port Lligat. Dalí loved money almost as much as painting and masturbation.

For the Catalan nationalist burghers of Figueres, a great deal of squaring of circles has been required to turn Dalí into a "universal Catalan genius". The squaring was eased along, of course, by the ringing of cash registers. Not only was he a supporter of a fascist dictatorship that suppressed all rights of his own people, but he maintained his anti-Catalanism even after his death in January 1989. Despite his promises to the contrary, he left his paintings not to Catalonia, but to the Spanish state in Madrid. Some of the best Dalís are now on exhibit in the Reina Sofía Museum near Atocha in that city.

Dalí's father was a notary in Figueres. A notary in Spain is a prominent figure, able to charge fat fees for processing official papers. The Dalí family lived in some style, in large town-houses and summering at a house they owned on the coast at nearby Cadaqués. Dalí's mother died when he was sixteen. His father became for Dalí a daunting figure and appears in numerous paintings threatening him with castration. Despite the role he played in Dalí's imagination, Dalí senior was indulgent with him at several points of his life: for example, when he was expelled from art school in Madrid for refusing to take his final exams controlled by "inferior artists". In the famous blow-up between them in 1929, when Dalí's father threw him out of the house, Dalí senior seems entirely justified. The cause was that Dalí had written "I spit for pleasure on the portrait of my mother" on a publicly exhibited painting. Even then, on throwing him out, Dalí's father let him go to the house at Cadaqués with Buñuel, where they worked out their second film *L'age d'or*. It was not an isolated instance of Dalí's impulse to gratuitous cruelty. Later, Buñuel himself was to become a victim.

A few years ago the Gala and Salvador Dalí Foundation organized "Dalí year 2004" to celebrate the centenary of Dalí's birth in Figueres on 11 May 1904. Over and above the obvious aim of fomenting tourism, the purpose of Dalí year's special events, exhibitions and publications was to resurrect Dalí as a great painter. It aimed to rescue the artist from the ruins of his personal reputation.

This was, and is, a complicated job, because Dalí's fame is due partly, even mainly some argue, to his image. Everyone agrees the man was a genius, but was he a painting genius or was his just a genius for publicity? He was a flamboyant showman, heir of medieval jesters and nineteenth-century circus performers, precursor of rock stars. His waxed moustache, staring eyes, long hair and head thrown back in defiance make his image as recognizable as Chaplin's. His showmanship, Ian Gibson argues, was a strategy to conceal his deep sexual shame and embarrassment. In implicit rebuke of Gibson's view, the guide at Dalí's Port Lligat house (as at the Besalú *mikwah* and Poblet monastery, you are obliged to go round Port Lligat with a guide) told me: "He was not a buffoon; it was to provoke people." In his beginnings, when he was a left-winger and even imprisoned for two weeks under the 1920s dictatorship of Primo de Rivera, surreal acts might have been intended to provoke the bourgeoisie. In later years they became a publicity strategy in themselves. Dalí and Gala understood how to become famous and sell pictures in the modern world of art as a mass commodity.

The handsome young Salvador Dalí left Figueres in 1922 for art school in Madrid. Here he met Lorca and Buñuel at the celebrated Students' Residence and became one of a legendary artistic generation. In the 1920s his restless creativity drove him through a whole gamut of styles, in all of which he showed himself a master. Pointillism, Impressionism, Expressionism, Cubism preceded his famous surrealist style. In the realist *Figure at a Window* (1925) and *Girl from Figueres* (1926), the clarity of light and intensity of detail convey already a dream-like quality. In 1929 he and Buñuel made the short dream-film *Un chien andalou*, which contains the definitive image of the searing impact of cinema: the eye held open and sliced suddenly by a razor. Freud readers, as Dalí was, will recognize in blinding the image of castration, too.

The early 1930s saw Dalí's artistic prime. The Surrealists gave him the language and film rounded off Dalí's development. Really, he was the only one of all the Surrealists to mould that idea and movement into great art. Whereas his exhibitionism in life served to conceal his privacy, on canvas he found the freedom to explore with extraordinary bold-ness—honesty even—his deepest obsessions, contradictions and desires.

From film he took its ability to show a rapid sequence of images, as in automatic thinking or a dream. Many of his paintings, such as *The Great Masturbator* (1929) on his sexual impotence or *William Tell* (1930) on his father, can be read back and forth across the canvas as a series of film stills. The absolutely realist detail heightens the super-realist effect of strange shapes and startling juxtapositions.

Some of this can be seen in the Theatre-Museum, beyond or behind Dalí's exhibitionist face. The greatest painting at Figueres (most of Dalí's best-known paintings are scattered across America, exchanged for Gala's suitcases of dollar bills) can easily be missed. It is the remarkable minia-ture, no more than five by six inches, *The Spectre of Sex Appeal* (1932). This is an entirely realistic landscape, with an exquisitely drawn small boy (a feature of many of his paintings: the painter, one assumes) looking anxiously up at a huge surreal rotting headless woman, supported by crutches. The boy, carrying a hoop, wears a sailor-suit typical of middle-class Spanish boys in both Dalí's time and later generations. The boy's fixed stare, the grotesqueness of the putrid woman and the impossibility of contact have produced a masterpiece about male fear of women.

Cadaqués

The landscape in *The Spectre of Sex Appeal* is that of the rocks of Cap (Cape) de Creus and the beach at nearby Cadaqués, where from child-hood Dalí spent his summer holidays. Though only 25 miles from Figueres, Cadaqués is remote, due to the pointed, arid peaks rising to over 2,000 feet that separate it from the lush farmland of the Empordà. Its remoteness is not just physical, but emotional. The rolling fertile farming landscape, interspersed with woodland and low hills, runs onto a harsh, arid promontory. Even today there is just one steep and winding road across the moor into Cadaqués. The road twists and turns, passing occasional abandoned farmhouses and sparse grape-vines on plots cleared from the splintered rock. Military communications saucers and masts cap the highest peak on the cape, like one of Dalí's fantasies.

Cadaqués today is still the jewel of the Costa Brava. There is no high-rise building. It is like Sitges, but more remote (no railway) and more refined. There are no tourist packages, there is no Street of Sin. The front, dominated by a statue of Dalí, is lined by the whitewashed three- and four-storey houses of the wealthy, but they are not ostentatious. In

Cadaqués the real rich, who do not need to show off with fancy mansions, have their second homes. The salt-weathered semi-hippies smoking joints in the waterfront cafés are likely to be the heirs and heiresses of Catalan business.

The conservation of Cadaqués is normally attributed to the building controls that the rich were able to exert to keep their remote refuge intact. That is true enough, but not the whole truth, for in the 1950s Dalí sought direct intervention from General Franco for the protection of the coastline. Franco responded, with a decree protecting Cap de Creus. Indeed, under today's democracy free enterprise is building apace around Port Lligat and invading some of the remoter parts of the Cape (ignoring its status as a National Park). We owe the conservation of the headland not just to its remoteness, and not to an enlightened bourgeoisie, but rather to the Dictator himself and the only great Spanish artist who could stomach him.

It was to the family home on the beach at Cadaqués that Dalí brought the poet Federico García Lorca in the mid-1920s. Lorca was dazzled by this isolated coast, with its vineyards, the murmur of the waves and, in a characteristic Lorquian phrase, "the silver fishes that come out to take the moon." Lorca had met Dalí in the Students' Residence in Madrid and in these summers at Cadaqués the two developed their intense and famous friendship.

In 1930 Dalí bought a fisherman's hut on the beach at Port Lligat. Port Lligat is a mile along the coast from Cadaqués and on the other side of the village from his father's house. He had begun to earn real money as a painter and had just met Gala. In the five decades until Gala's death in 1982, this was their base. It is easy to leave the Figueres Theatre-Museum with the view that Dalí was little more than a talented buffoon and self-publicist. This is what he was in the eight post-Civil War years spent in New York and later winters in Paris. Most of the year, though, he and Gala lived at Port Lligat. Here, he worked in the light-flooded studio overlooking the sea eight or ten hours a day. Gala and he received few visits. It seemed otherwise because, when visitors did come, there were many of them and some were famous. Port Lligat brings out an intensely private Dalí, dedicated to his art. Such public performers as Gala and Dalí needed this refuge. When winter came, they would pack their bags and cavort for a few months on the stages of Paris and London, before returning to paint and read, to be alone.

For many years, when I thought of Dalí, I thought of him as an ostentatious show-off, an eccentric and also a one-off. More recently, reading his contemporary Josep Pla and visiting the landscapes of Dalí's life, I began to realize how, in several ways, Dalí was not so untypical, but was formed in his character and his painting by his culture and his landscape. In his diary-style masterpiece, *The Grey Note-book*, Pla is obsessed by trying to explain the character of his fellow-countrymen:

> ...We have such an exuberant imagination that we confuse flies and eagles... The people of the Empordà are perhaps the most absolutely elemental and enthusiastic types of Catalan... In this country, a man seen as picturesque by the majority can do, literally, exactly what he likes...

This suggests that Dalí should not be seen as a one-off, an outsider in his own society, an extravagant excrescence. His exaggerated behaviour and dress, his "madness" and eccentricity are not so rare in the places where he grew up.

Dalí grew up fearing madness, and it is one of the springs of his talent. This fear led him to explore psychoanalysis and use its language, the language of dreams and unconscious associations, to explore in his painting the landscape of the mind. There is an overwhelming story of the painter's paternal grandfather, Gal Dalí. Gal lived in Cadaqués, but found he could not stand the *tramuntana* north wind. Fearing he might kill himself, he moved his family to Barcelona in 1881. His flight was futile. Five years later he committed suicide by throwing himself from his windless third-floor flat on Barcelona's Rambla de Catalunya. The cause of Dalí's grandfather's death was not revealed to Dalí until he was a young adult. His uncle, too, attempted suicide. The fear of madness was no fantasy, but a real presence for Dalí, who was famous for his saying: "The only difference between a madman and Dalí is that Dalí is not mad."

The *tramuntana* causes depression and prostration. When it blows, it is hard to stand up in the street. The constant noise and banging of shutters keeps your nerves on edge or casts you into lethargy. It is a wind specific to the Empordà and particularly the Alt (Upper) Empordà, the area round Figueres. In his 1982 story of suicide, called simply *Tramontana*, Gabriel García Márquez explains: "In Spring and Autumn, which were the seasons in which Cadaqués was most attractive, no-one could fail to think with apprehension about the tramontana, an inclement and tenacious land wind, that according to the natives and some writers who had learned its lesson, carries with it the germs of madness." As well as being a wind that can form the character of the people, the *tramuntana* changes the character of the air and light. Langdon-Davies explained its effect on Dalí's work:

> Dalí paints as if there were no air between himself and his subjects, as if the Tramuntana were blowing... Even the tricks of perspective by which he introduces infinity into his pictures are suggested by the Tramuntana, the wind that opens up the world for immense distances and draws it all close to the retina.

Whereas the *tramuntana* is the cold wind off the mountains, leaving impossibly clear skies and annihilating distances, the *garbí* is the south wind off the sea, warm and misty. The poet Joan Maragall called the Empordà "the Palace of Wind" because there the two types of wind and mind pulled people one way or another. In late 2006 a new cultural centre was announced for Figueres that brilliantly combines Dalinian imagination and the Empordà's wind. With a forest of 200 165-foot flexible bars on the roof that are swept horizontal when the *tramuntana* roars, this punk building will create electricity. "Instead of standing up to the wind, this building dances with the wind," says its architect, Enric Ruiz-Geli.

Over the years Dalí bought up seven adjoining huts at Port Lligat and linked them to create the labyrinthine house on various levels that is preserved today as it was when Dalí left it on Gala's death. Dalí talked of his house as a living organism: "a true biological structure. Each new pulse in our life has its own cell, a room." It is perhaps morbid to visit the house of dead people. In the case of Dalí, a visit can be justified because at Port Lligat the showman of the Theatre-Museum fades to unimportance as we face the artist in his lair and landscape. If never unmasked, at least the showman-artist's mask slips.

The house strikingly combines several features. It is, first of all, a typical Mediterranean house, not at all flashy, with tiled floors, bright matting and whitewashed shelving and walls. Its wide windows look out over the fishing-boats pulled up on the beach and the beautiful, enclosed bay. Yellow Helychrisum is draped round the windows; chunks of tortured rock brought from nearby Cap de Creus lie about on floors and shelves.

Then the simplicity and beauty of the house clash with numerous kitsch objects: plastic ducks, stuffed animals, Michelin men, cloth snakes, velvet sofas, brightly coloured drapes, bedspreads and cushions... the cheap artefacts of modern life. Here is the pop artist ahead of his time. Classicists lament the Pirelli tires spoiling the thin swimming pool, whose brickwork and fountain are reminiscent of Moorish Granada. Dalí fans revel in the juxtapositions provocatively undermining conventional canons of beauty.

Third, the house reveals Dalí's extraordinary inventiveness. In every room there are details of his ingenuity. There is a fascinating collection of his famous twisted walking-sticks, or a hole in the floor for moving his easel up and down when he was painting a large picture. Dalí positioned a mirror so that from their bedroom he and Gala could watch the dawn. "Each day, I am the first person in Spain to see the sun rise," he would say, for Port Lligat is the easternmost village of mainland Spain. The still heart of the house is the windowless oval room at its centre, built for Gala as her private refuge. Here, the famous exhibitionist would read quietly for hours on end. The room is shaped just like the tiny prickly sea urchins that used to be common on the Costa Brava and are still eaten as a delicacy. When you stand in the middle of this room and speak, you hear an echo.

Near Port Lligat, the first twisted outcrops of the Pyrenees were pushed up from the sea at Cap de Creus. Sun, wind, salt and rain have splintered, worn hollow and tortured the schist rock into weird shapes— the source probably of Dalí's ingenious double images, such as *The Great Paranoiac* (1936) in which a woman's buttocks eloquently transform into the main male figure's nose... and every other character's head hangs in sexual shame. On Cap de Creus you can sit and find multiple forms in its "lizard-ridged rocks" (Ballard), just as a child watches burning coals produce ever-changing shapes in the hearth. Cap de Creus has smooth

Cap de Creus landscape

rocks, wrinkled rocks, cleft rocks and rocks so sharp you cut your hands on them. It has rocks like fingers pointing to the sky, rocks with holes in them like so many of Dalí's figures and melting rocks like paste squeezed from a tube or like the limp, dissolving watches, the most famous icon in his painting.

There is a white lighthouse on the tip of the cape where you can hire rooms and listen at night to the waves crashing against the outcrop. These waves and rocks, bent in anguish like the soul of Dalí, offer a total contrast with the peace of Port Lligat bay. There is another twist, though, to Port Lligat and Cap de Creus. On a grey day Port Lligat is a melancholy, empty place, with the tamed, tideless sea only lapping, never breaking on the gently rotting beach. The smell of stale water, piled weed and fish remains is sweetly decayed and pervasive on such a still day. Against this shut-in water, the wind and wave-battered cape is refreshing and liberating. Lying in bed in the lighthouse-*pensió* you can feel the freedom of snugness among the wildest nature.

I have borrowed a J. G. Ballard title for this chapter, because

Ballard's apocalyptic vision seems so close to Dalí's. Like Dalí, who draws with pin-point detail and draws out from his unconscious monstrous images, Ballard reveals in hypnotically calm prose the wildest yearnings of our secret selves. The beach and the rocks are Dalí's two basic landscapes. They have come to haunt the twentieth-century imagination as images of the mind itself: the nightmare beach, with every figure and object etched in bright *tramuntana* light and stark shadow, and tormented Cap de Creus behind it. Much of what seems most surreal in Dalí's work emerges from the improbable real weather and geology of his childhood.

Chapter Ten
Feet Rooted to the Red Earth: Joan Miró

In 1925 an obscure 26-year-old American journalist bought Joan Miró's *La masia* (The Farm) for 250 dollars. He didn't have the cash, but ran around the expatriate bars of Paris to beg and borrow the asking price off friends. Triumphant, he carried the huge canvas home in an open taxi—measuring 58 by 52 inches, it was too big to fit in a closed car. He had to ask the driver to slow to a crawl as the painting billowed in the wind.

The picture was a present to his wife, who hung it above their bed. Miró came to see it and approved of its new home. The journalist was Ernest Hemingway. When he separated from Hadley, his first wife, in 1927, she sent round a list of goods she wanted him to deliver to her new flat. Among them was *La masia*, which Hemingway histrionically pushed round in a wheelbarrow. On delivering it to Hadley, he burst into tears. Whether this was because the impact of what he had done in leaving Hadley finally hit him at that moment or because he could not bear to part with the painting is not clear. It is clear that Hemingway lusted after *La masia*. In 1934 he asked Hadley to lend him the picture for five years. This she did, but her good faith was ill rewarded. He never returned it to her. It became one of the most valuable of the items squabbled over in unseemly fashion by his heirs after he shot himself in 1961.

In 1929 Hemingway, now a famous novelist, visited Miró at Montroig. The painter spent all his summers there in a house his parents had bought in 1911, the *masia* or farmhouse of the famous painting. Hemingway did not record his emotions at seeing the site portrayed in the painting that he had wheeled away from his happy first marriage just two summers before, but he did write about Montroig. Here he witnessed a bloody and characteristic country scene that fitted perfectly into *Death in the Afternoon*, published in 1932. Though Hemingway was still a young man, towards the end of the book he writes elegiacally of the

"Woman and Bird" in Parc de Joan Miró, Barcelona

places in Spain that he loved, as though he were eighty years old and the places were irrecoverable. This is Hemingway on Montroig ("pronounced Montroych," he noted) in his precise, baroquely stylized, hypnotizing prose:

> ... sitting in the heavy twilight at Miró's; vines as far as you can see, cut by the hedges and the road; the railroad and the sea with pebbly beach and tall papyrus grass. There were earthen jars for the different years of wine, twelve feet high, set side by side in a dark room; a tower on the house to climb to in the evening to see the vines, the villages and the mountains, and to listen and to hear how quiet it was. In front of the barn a woman held a duck whose throat she had cut and stroked her gently while a little girl held up a cup to catch the blood for making gravy. The duck seemed very contented, and when they put her down (the blood all in the cup) she waddled twice and found that she was dead. We ate her later, stuffed and roasted...

Montroig, literally "red hill" from the red earth of its fields, is some ten miles south of Tarragona, four miles back from the sea and on a low hill just in front of stern-looking sheer cliffs which form the edge of the Serra de Siurana, the abrupt escarpment that divides this coastal strip from the Ebro Valley. Miró's *masia* is on the right of the road inland to Montroig that turns off the coastal road south from Cambrils, and today behind a large garden centre just before a bridge over the motorway. Since the death of Dolors, Miró's only child, in December 2004, fearsome notices warning of fierce dogs and privacy adorn the gate of the *masia*, so it is not possible to enter and see if it is still as Hemingway saw it.

The characteristic watchtower of Catalan farmhouses, which Hemingway mentions though it does not appear in the painting (which in fact portrays the out-buildings rather than the house itself) is visible from the road. It reminds us that bandits frequented the land in the seventeenth century, Arab pirates raided the coast right up to the end of the eighteenth century and Carlists, led by the redoubtable Ramon Cabrera, The Tiger of the Maestrazgo, raged through these hills behind Montroig for much of the nineteenth century. One finds these semi-fortified farmhouses throughout Catalonia. The tower remained a stylistic feature even after banditry was over. Many town houses in the wealthier areas of Barcelona have a tower, and in the Catalan language any detached house with a garden, whether it actually has a tower or not, is called a *torre*, a tower.

Surprisingly, Cabrera, famous Carlist general and absolutist Count of Morella, died peacefully at Wentworth, Surrey, in 1877 after putting much of Catalonia to the sword in the name of the divine right of kings in the 1830s and 1840s. His Surrey house, called Tortosa Cottage after his birthplace, is still there. He is the anti-hero of Joan Perucho's curious novel about vampires, *Natural Histories* (1960), one of the few Catalan novels to be included in Harold Bloom's Western Canon.

The friendship between Hemingway the extrovert and Miró, the reserved man, is hard to imagine. Miró used to referee Hemingway's boxing matches, small, silent and punctiliously dressed, with a stop-watch. Sometimes, despite the discrepancy in size, Miró climbed into the ring with Hemingway. Unlike the other great names in Catalan art—Dalí, Picasso or Gaudí—Miró was throughout his life a passionate sportsperson, enthused by running, gymnastics, boxing. In his studio, its smooth whitewashed walls undisturbed by any painting, he hung a boxing poster. Despite his mildness and famous silences, Miró compared the impact of a good picture to a punch on the chin. The viewer, he meant, should experience the picture without having time to think about it. Hemingway, who liked to "knock out" his rivals with his stunning stories, agreed with this violent—or passionate—view of art. One wonders if Miró saw the world heavyweight champion Jack Johnson fight the French poet Arthur Cravan in Barcelona's Monumental bull-ring on St. George's Day, 23 April 1916. Cravan, then boxing instructor at Barcelona's Maritime Club, set this up as a show: "The nephew of Oscar Wilde (i.e. Cravan) will talk, dance and box in a magnificent exhibition of dance-boxing." Johnson's courtesy allowed Cravan to last six rounds. Like Miró later, Cravan, self-styled "boxer-poet", talked of his art in highly aggressive terms.

As well as the vines, the country round Montroig is rich with *garrofers* and olives, portrayed in many of Miró's early landscapes. The first orange groves, prolific in Valencia province a hundred miles south, appear. *Garrofers*—carob trees—have wide-spreading branches and deep-green leaves. Their fruits, used for pig food or flour for biscuits, hang down in clusters like overgrown runner beans. Olive trees' twisted, often cracked trunks make them look their age. In December canvas is still laid out on the ground and the fruit is beaten with sticks out of the trees—today usually by seasonal, African labour.

Spanish writers have, with good reason, waxed lyrical about olive groves. Country-people spend hours wandering through the endless trees. Jean Giono, the poet of Provence, suggested that on Sunday mornings men go to commune with their olive trees, just as women go to mass. In the wind off Montroig beach on a sunny day, the small leaves are tossed up or turned over and the olive trees become silvery as the undersides of the light-green leaves catch the sun, as if the trees were dusted with snow.

The beach here is still recognizably that of Hemingway's memory, beautiful pebbles of all kinds of stone and size, rounded and worn smooth by the action of water and deposited by the currents on this shore. The beaches are full in summer, but there are no high-rise resorts or hotels along this part, south of tourist Salou and Cambrils. It is a scruffy, homely stretch of coast, with gardens running down to the beach, cheap bar-restaurants, campsites and rubbish sprinkled among the papyrus grass and round-topped pines. Curiously, Miró never painted the beach or sea: you would never guess that his inspirational scenes of Montroig and the *masia* were only a few miles from the Mediterranean. Yet often, after a day's painting, he would run or cycle to the beach and enjoy the smell of the Mediterranean and detail of the stones.

The ochre town of Montroig is on a low hill across the valley from Miró's *masia* and now has a Miró museum in the old church. It is a prosperous agricultural town, with the Joan Miró Square by the church irregularly shaped and built on a slope, its perspective foreshortened as if it were modelled on a Miró painting. From his more realistic early phase of highly coloured canvases filled with detail, there are several of Montroig. The best-known, *Montroig, Village and Church*, shows the church and houses from the plain. They form a line along the back of the painting, their photographic detail and shadow in precise outline against the sky of blues. The middle ground consists of bushes and trees painted in the same apparent detail, but grouped together they look quite unrealistic patches of colour. The foreground holds a man working in smallholdings. Each individual plant is drawn, though in a naive style. In many of Miró's paintings of this first period, such tiny plants and insects can be discerned. He explained his minimalist aesthetic:

> ... painting a landscape... I gradually begin to comprehend the enormous wealth of nuances—a concentrated wealth that is a gift from the sun. It is the joy of being outside, in the country, and waiting for an understanding of a blade of grass... People only ever look for and paint masses of trees or mountains, without listening for the music that pours forth from tiny flowers, blades of grass and little stones by the side of one's path.

Miró's attachment to the details of nature stemmed from (or extended to) a profound identification with Catalonia. Like Dalí in the Empordà, Miró was imbued with a fierce sense of belonging to the countryside around Montroig. Unlike Dalí, however, he was a lifelong anti-fascist and Catalan nationalist. Miró painted sometimes in bare feet on the ground to feel nature and, still more specifically, to feel the Catalan earth, a foreshadowing of how President Companys faced the firing squad in his bare feet. Memorably Miró explained: "One has to keep one's feet well rooted to the earth, so as to then jump high in the air, towards the sky."

Miró's attachment to Catalonia meant that he returned from Paris to Montroig every summer of the 1920s and early 1930s. Catalonia for him was closely associated with his beloved mother, who quarrelled with his first fiancée, Pilar, over domestic control and then accepted his second more docile choice, also Pilar, whom he married in 1929. Miró paid the chilling compliment to his wife that she was "without the stain of intellectuality." Miró was looking for someone to cook and care for him in his old age when his mother was dead. Working away obsessively in his studio, he needed a middle-class family and docile women to service him.

Hemingway wrote about his beloved *La masia*: "It has in it all that you feel about Spain when you are there and all that you feel when you are away and cannot go there. No one else has been able to paint these two very opposing things." If we replace "Spain" by "Catalonia", Hemingway's comment makes one think of Miró's coming and going between Paris and Montroig throughout the 1920s and 1930s, drawn always back to his mother and to Catalonia, felt by the painter very probably as one. The success of *La masia*, so detailed yet looking like a colourful cartoon, is based on the intensity of Miró's inner world, highlighted by that burning love and need honed by his removal to Paris.

At the start of the Civil War, on 18 July 1936, he was at Montroig, but continued to paint until news reached him that the FAI (the Iberian Anarchist Federation) was out to kill him. Surprised, he left sensibly and rapidly for Paris. The anarchists did kill Miró's sister's husband, a notorious ultra-rightist ("an absolute imbecile", according to Miró). Miró was in their sights by accident because he had been a guest at his sister's wedding.

In Paris during the war he adopted his first public, political positions. He designed a stamp to raise money for the Republican side: it was an image of a Catalan peasant in a *barretina*. He was then commissioned to paint a mural for the Pavilion of the Republican Government at the Paris Exhibition, for which his friend Picasso painted his famous *Gernika*. Miró chose again a Catalan theme, a sickle brandished by a reaper in a *barretina*. It was a clear reference to the War of the Reapers, when Catalan peasants rose against Castilian oppression in 1640. The stirring and somewhat violent *Song of the Reapers* is now the National Anthem of Catalonia. It climaxes in the ferocious repeated line *Bon cop de falç*—"Good blow of the sickle". Miró's third political painting was the most famous poster of the Civil War, his "Aidez l'Espagne", a tortured face clenching a huge yellow fist.

Though he had shunned public political expression before, Miró had now clearly taken sides. Yet after the Civil War he avoided the passage to Mexican exile he was offered and that so many Catalans had to take. He returned to Catalonia as soon as he could, testing the waters first in his mother's and his wife Pilar's native Mallorca in 1941.

During the Franco dictatorship his presence, fame and stubborn Catalanism meant that he became a leading representative of what was known as the internal resistance. He went further than just surviving, talking in Catalan and waiting. He designed Raimon's first album cover in 1966 (see Chapter Eleven). Aged 77, he took part in the occupation of Montserrat monastery in protest against Franco's 1970 Burgos show-trial of Basque activists. He also designed the 1974 poster for Barcelona

Football Club's 75th anniversary. In 1976 he attended the opening of *Avui*, the first daily paper in Catalan since the 1930s.

Today, Miró is present, over twenty years after his death on Christmas Day 1983, all over Catalonia through his design of the ubiquitous logo of Catalonia's biggest bank La Caixa (bright red and yellow coins dropping into a money-box). Tourists tramp over his circle of coloured tiles at the central point of Barcelona's Ramblas. Miró also has an enormous square named after him, between the Plaça d'Espanya and Sants in Barcelona, just behind the Las Arenas bullring, converted now under Richard Rogers' direction into a shopping mall. The bus to the airport runs past the Plaça de Joan Miró, which used to be named—more excitingly—the Plaça de l'Escorxador after the municipal slaughterhouse. Now it has Miró's last work, completed when he was 89, the 72 foot-tall sculpture *Woman and Bird*, in his characteristic bright green, yellow and red, dominating one corner opposite the mock-Moorish ex-bullring. A huge palm grove has been planted between statue and shopping mall. It is such a wide, thick grove that the city traffic is muffled inside. Palms are not autochthonous to Catalonia, nor are the hoarsely croaking parrots that also thrive in the grove and throughout the city after their appearance in the mid-1970s (probably escapees from a private collection). Barcelona's parrots, flashes of Miró-like colours in the trees above the city traffic, bring both exotic pleasure and a hint of doom, for they tell us global warming is here: they have bred and spread in recent years because of milder winters. The combination of surrealist statue, Moorish bullring/shopping mall and African palms is characteristic of the eclecticism, very often as in this case successful, of modern Barcelona's styles.

The Man Who Could Not Draw

Miró was a strange young man: Josep Pla described him in 1918 on his appearance in Paris as perfectly dressed—something of a dandy, as the young Gaudí had been—and silent. This may have been shock at his first trip outside Catalonia. He was well protected in his first months; not just Pla, but the poet Salvat i Papasseit were fellow-Catalans staying in a cheap pension run by Catalans. The sculptor Pau Gargallo, most famous today for his wonderful head of Picasso, rented Miró his studio.

His fellow-Catalans in Paris found it hard to believe that just a few years later this shy, polite, well-dressed man became a notorious surrealist. It is perhaps like the man in a business suit on an anarchist demonstration; among the torn-trousered, nose-ringed squatters with piebald dogs, he is the most outrageous of all. The quiet, undemonstrative Miró in suit, waistcoat and watch-chain would shout "Death to the Mediterranean" as he wandered around Paris, somewhat to the consternation of Picasso, who was rediscovering his Mediterranean roots.

Miró had never lost them. He was born in Barcelona's Old City in 1893, in the Passatge del Crèdit, a handsome and large middle-class apartment block just off the elegant Carrer Ferran and by the Plaça Sant Jaume. In 1911 his parents bought the farm at Montroig from an *indiano*. Miró's fierce attachment to the place dates from a long period of convalescence there shortly afterwards, recovering from something like a nervous breakdown through his parents' obliging him to work in an office. This is reminiscent of Picasso's convalescence at Horta, in the mountains not so far from Montroig, as a key moment in his development. But in everything else Miró was quite unlike Picasso, the genius who could draw better than his father from the beginning and by the age of 17 had exhausted all the art education his country could offer him.

Miró found painting intensely difficult. He was in no way naturally gifted and it was stubbornness and will that carried him through. In 1912, when his parents finally let him enrol at Francesc Gali's Art School in Barcelona, he found it hard to draw from life. Inability to draw is something said of several great painters, including Cézanne, perhaps to underline their determination and to contrast this kind of painting with the fluency of a Picasso. Lluís Permanyer, Miró's friend and biographer, goes as far as to affirm: "Miró found it difficult to distinguish a straight line from a curve."

The art critic Sebastià Gasch, a supporter of Miró, Dalí and later Tàpies, said that Miró at Gali's school looked like a child, with his round face, his tongue hanging out and "sweating like a slave" as he tried to draw from life. The results looked like "sacks of potatoes". Whatever the case, Gali encouraged him in the sense of colour he did have and helped him discover forms by getting him to touch objects, eyes shut, on the frequent excursions the art school made to the country. Miró also attended the Artistic Circle of St. Luke, where among the hopeful young painters was an elderly man who said nothing, but with enormous concentration was trying to learn to draw. Miró often talked in later years of his impression when he was told that the old man was Antoni Gaudí, Catalonia's greatest living architect. For Miró, Gaudí gave a moving example of humility and determination, which served him well through the hardships of his own early years and when he embarked later on other disciplines such as tapestry, ceramics and sculpture.

His first exhibition, in 1918, at the Dalmau Gallery at Portaferrissa 18, near his parents' house, was the object of open mockery in the press. He sold nothing. Typically Miró made no recorded comments, but imbibed the positive lesson that painting really must be important if it caused such outrage in people. Despite his difficulties in drawing and communicating, Miró was as stubborn as a mule.

Like Picasso a generation earlier and Dalí a few years later, Miró went to Paris to make himself a painter. Whereas Rusiñol and Casas had gone to Paris and brought back the modern-art message to Catalonia, and Picasso had needed to settle permanently away from the confines of Spain, Miró used Paris to learn and to make his career, but remained rooted in his adopted Montroig. Despite the difference in their styles, talents, personalities and manners of painting, Picasso was perceptive and generous with Miró. Already famous, Picasso encouraged Miró by understanding his work and used his influence to force his dealers to tramp up the stairs to Miró's garret. They did not buy anything. Miró, something of the archetypical starving artist in 1920s Paris (though he returned to fatten up on his mother's Montroig cooking every summer) continued to follow his own path, which reached its first climax in *La masia* and the other masterpieces of Montroig.

Then, around 1922/1923 Miró broke with figurative painting. These were the hardest years for him. Miró was searching for a new pictorial language, based on colours and shapes, while most acquaintances urged him to return to paintings like *La masia*. Like Picasso twenty years earlier, Miró used violent words to describe what he was trying to do, affirming that he wanted to "murder painting." All the cheap imitators of Picasso and Braque were now painting Cubist guitars. Miró was out to "smash their guitars."

Despite André Breton's well-known comment that "Miró is the greatest surrealist of us all," Miró remained on the fringes of the surrealist group, not quarrelling with them but following his own stub-

born route. In later years he would say of himself with pride, both politically and artistically, *No he sigut puta*, I've not been a whore. Though his
new language appeared abstract, it was representational. Every dot or
stripe or ball of colour represented a thing: for him pictures meant something. He was no Abstract Expressionist, painting only in colours and
shapes and rejecting the question: "But what does it mean?" Miró followed on from his earlier, more realist painting in concentrating on the
detail of blades of grass, insects or stones, until they became distilled in
a dot, line or colour. While Dalí was the flamboyant surrealist who
painted, in Freudian language, the landscape of the human mind, Miró
was the quiet surrealist painter of the colours and forms of the land.

Fundació Miró

Barcelona is not a city on hills, as Rome is, but a city surrounded by hills.
One of the best vantage-points for looking over the city is the Miró
Foundation on Montjuïc. It is easy enough to get to by jumping in a taxi.
There is a more adventurous way: to walk. (A true Miró fan might run.)
Nowadays the walk is well sign-posted. From the Paral·lel, go straight up
Carrer Margarit, which runs through Poble Sec (Dry Town). On
Margarit, on the right going up, the visitor will pass one of the many
modernista houses scattered around Catalonia, but the Foundation,
designed by Josep Lluís Sert in the early 1970s, is in a completely differ-
ent style. Catalan architecture has not stayed in a rut, resting on its
Gaudian laurels, but has sought to remain in the vanguard of artistic
movements.

The career of Miró's friend, Josep Lluís Sert, tells something of the
story of architecture in Catalonia post-*modernisme*. In 1928 Le
Corbusier received a telegram in Madrid, where he was acting as a con-
sultant for the building of its rationalist University City. The telegram,
signed by Sert, an unknown student, asked Le Corbusier if, on his return
to France, he could stop off in Barcelona to give a talk. The great man
agreed, was met by Sert at Sants station at 10 pm and was whisked
straight off to his talk. The following day Sert and his fellow architecture
students, "all short but full of fire and energy," in Le Corbusier's words,
took him to Sitges and then around the sights of Barcelona, including
the Sagrada Família. The architect became an immediate fan of Gaudí,
which is surprising because Gaudí's extremely ornate style and insistence

on working in stone seem the polar opposite of Le Corbusier's emphasis on modern cement and functional straight lines. Le Corbusier responded to the daring and spirit of Gaudí, qualities he valued in himself: "Gaudí was a great artist: only those who touch the sensitive part of men's hearts last and will last... architecture is a fruit of character or, better said, a manifestation of character."

Le Corbusier, then at the height of his fame and as skilled a publicist as he was an architect, was receptive to this group of students seeking to revive Catalan culture. He was at this time designing simple concrete apartment blocks, consonant both with the need to overcome slum conditions and with new mass-produced materials. Sert and his companions rejected the bombast of the 1929 Exhibition, including the Royal Palace, on Montjuïc and founded the GATCPAC (Group of Catalan Architects and Technicians for the Progress of Contemporary Architecture) to push forward the ideas of Le Corbusier and the modern movement. In the early 1930s Sert himself went to work with Le Corbusier in Paris, where he met Joan Miró. Back in Catalonia, during the exciting early and optimistic years of the Republic (declared 14 April 1931), the GATCPAC found government and society receptive to their ideas. Le Corbusier paid other visits, saw and admired Catalonia's President Francesc Macià, and designed a total remodelling of Barcelona. This Plan Macià was not so much revolutionary, but rather designed to *esponjar* the old quarters and open up straight roads to aid commerce and social control, under the architect's maxim: "Architecture or Revolution. Revolution can be avoided."

The coming of the Civil War and actual revolution cut short Le Corbusier and the GATCPAC's dreams, but some of Sert's buildings from the 1930s remain. Most well-known is the Tuberculosis Clinic (1934-36), commissioned by the Generalitat and located just off Barcelona's Plaça de la Universitat on the edge of the Raval, an area ravaged by TB. Today it is a health centre, nestling on its irregularly shaped plot beside an atypical church with a golden Byzantine-looking dome. The Scot David Mackay, an architect in Barcelona since the 1950s, emphasized the TB clinic's careful design to take advantage of the Mediterranean climate and protect against summer heat:

The Dispensari [Clinic] is a steel-framed L shaped building that encloses a courtyard, an area forming an open-air "hall" from which

Sert's Tuberculosis Clinic, Raval, Barcelona

the patients have direct access to the different departments... a traditional entrance courtyard so typical of the medieval houses and palaces
of Barcelona... Consulting rooms on the three upper floors... are
arranged facing northwards, with the corridor on the south side protecting these rooms from the excessive summer heat... High strip
windows run along these passages which are also punctuated with
occasional viewing panels at eye-level.

For Mackay it is a totally modern and rationalist building, whose "metic-
ulous attention to all aspects of design makes [it]... a miniature repertoire
of the language of modern architecture." Looking at such a building
creates nostalgia for the public health system that might have been.

Sert co-designed the Spanish Republican Pavilion in Paris in 1937,
for which Picasso and Miró painted their *Gernika* and Catalan peasant,
respectively. This pavilion was faithfully reconstructed in 1992 in the
outlying Barcelona area of Horta, set off by the magnificent *Mistos*—
Matches—sculpture of Claes Oldenburg opposite. Unlike Miró, Sert

stayed in exile and eventually succeeded Walter Gropius in the Chair of Architecture at Harvard. Unlike many, who died in exile, Sert returned to work again in Spain. In 1956 he was responsible for Miró's huge white studio with an undulating roof overlooking the sea in Mallorca and then in the early 1970s the magnificent Miró Foundation. Among the trees and bushes of the Montjuïc hill, the foundation is a building of shining white concrete, with few windows, an octagonal tower echoing Gothic and what looks like a row of factory ventilators on the roof. They serve to give light to the gallery rooms. This form of overhead lighting is common in Le Corbusier's work and can be seen in several of the *modernista* factory buildings, such as the Casa Casaramona: an example of how one style learns from and integrates another. The rooms themselves are simple and functional, designed to focus attention on the exhibits and facilitate the flow of visitors. There are two inner courtyards, one at the heart of the building and one that looks over the city below with the moving and kinetic *Mercury Fountain* of Alexander Calder, Miró's American friend, in the foreground. The twinkling mercury slinks along its silver gutters.

As in the case of Picasso and Dalí, most of Miró's work was sold in France and the United States decades before his foundation was opened. Thus, there is over-representation of his late sculptures and giant colourful tapestries. There are three large, late canvases that are little more than one curving line. In his late paintings he is using less and less in order to achieve maximum impact—that sudden punch on the jaw. This triptych is entitled *The Hope of Someone Sentenced to Death I-III, 9-2-1974* and must refer to one of Franco's last victims, the Catalan anarchist Salvador Puig Antich, executed on 2 March 1974 in revenge for ETA's assassination of Spanish prime minister Carrero Blanco in December 1973. The line in the third picture of the triptych, still strong, has become shorter; the head traced in the first is disappearing, now just a half-line. The blood mark looming over the victim's head in the first picture becomes a yellow sun in the third. What does it mean? Is the hope of the person condemned to death to merge with the Mediterranean sun?

It is a contemplative work: the quiet man's condensed style, his feet planted firmly on Catalan soil. His other, more public style shines in the tapestries and is scattered round the city in colours that make children's faces light up in pleasure. Whatever the inner violence one senses in the boxer Miró, his colour brings pleasure, a pleasure hard fought for by the artist if we remember his distorted child's face as he tried to draw. One has to agree with Hadley: it would be wonderful to have a Miró brightening your bedroom wall.

1970: clumsy censorship of a Raimon concert

Chapter Eleven
I Come from a Silence: Catalan Music

Raimon

In 1958 a 17-year-old working-class lad from Xàtiva, an industrial town in the province of Alacant (Alicante), wrote an apparently conventional teenage song about riding pillion on a motorbike. He was called Raimon and the song was *Al vent*, In the Wind: "Face in the wind/heart in the wind/hands in the wind/eyes in the wind/the wind of the world."

With the raw, rhythmic voice of Raimon, backed by just a strumming guitar, and at the particular moment of the dictatorship, it became a song about riding free. This was the voice of the new generation, not cowed by the terrible defeat of the Civil War. For many who heard this voice coming out of the far reaches—for a *barceloní*—of where Catalan was spoken, its impact, new and authentic, was like that of hearing Verdaguer at the 1866 *Jocs Florals*: "And all/all full of night/searching for light/searching for peace/searching for God/in the wind of the world."

Raimon's early songs did not analyze the world. They expressed what masses of young people felt. They wanted to ride in the wind, free, and they were longing for a better life. It showed that music could reach beyond the censorship. Even Franco's censors, notoriously inconsistent and foolish as they were, might draw back from censoring a song about a motorbike. Yet these *crits cantats* (sung shouts) were profoundly political.

The *nova cançó* (new song) was a movement of *cantautors* (singer-songwriters) which swept Catalonia in the early 1960s. It started with a loose group of singers who called themselves the *Setze jutges* (sixteen judges). It was a name derived from a Catalan tongue-twister, containing sounds difficult for a Castilian speaker to pronounce correctly, though curiously the *tz*, *tj* and *tg* are easier for an English speaker: *Setze jutges d'un jutjat mengen fetge d'un penjat*, sixteen judges from a court eat liver of a hanged man. There were not sixteen singers in the group, though later, by 1968, they expanded to sixteen.

The *Setze jutges* and Catalan song festivals were not seen as any great threat by the Franco authorities at the start of the 1960s. It was a folkloric, minority activity: as Raimon put it, "Singing in Catalan had to be: oh! What lovely mountains, oh! What a beautiful sea, oh! What a beautiful land we have here!" The economic boom of the late 1950s, based on foreign investment in a country with a cheap labour force and on the arrival of tourism, thawed slightly the fear and repression. Very slightly, but it was enough for the *Setze jutges* to emerge and for Raimon to present a song in Catalan to the Barcelona international Festival of the Mediterranean in 1963—and win. The thaw did not last, neither culturally (the festival was closed down) nor politically: repression of working-class struggle returned with a vengeance in the late 1960s.

The *nova cançó* grew quickly. This mass cultural-political movement welded together a new generation fighting for its liberty. Under censorship it was of course not possible to sing protest songs as explicit as Víctor Jara's in Chile or Bob Dylan and Joan Baez's in the United States; but when Raimon stepped on stage and sang so powerfully and directly *Diguem no!*—Let's Say No!—goose-pimples stood out on his audience's arms and everyone knew what he was talking about. Later, for many years, he was forbidden to sing *Diguem no!* by the censors, who demanded a list of performers' songs before each concert and crossed out what must not be sung—arbitrarily, for censorship varied from province to province. But *Diguem no!* was forbidden everywhere, so clear was its message: "We have seen fear/made law for all./We have seen blood/that only makes blood/become law in the world. No, I say no/let's say no./We are not part of this world." It is worth showing the Catalan original of this translation, to show the aptness of this language of short, spat words for protest songs. How powerful the single two-consonant syllable "tots" is: *Hem vist la por/ser llei per a tots./Hem vist la sang/que sols fa sang /ser llei del món./No, jo dic no /diguem no./Nosaltres no som d'eixe món*. At the end of his concerts, when Raimon was about to leave the stage, the audience would begin to sing this song. He was not himself infringing the law, and the police could hardly arrest the whole audience. That was the collective political power of the *nova cançó*.

The immediate influences on the *nova cançó* were Juliette Greco, Jacques Brel and George Brassens, French singers of the 1950s. Brassens, in fact, was born at Sète, the "Venice of Languedoc", very close to Catalonia. The *nova cançó* also showed the breadth of the Catalan linguistic area: Raimon came from Xàtiva, Ovidi Montllor, the most worker-radical of the *cantautors*, from nearby Alcoi, while Maria del Mar Bonet was from Mallorca.

It was Raimon, still today a singer of great personality and power, who made the *nova cançó* a mass movement. Though he was not one of the *Setze jutges*, when they heard him they brought him to Barcelona, where his directness broke with their more French, intellectual airs. His first recording came out in 1963 and by 1965 he was singing to mass audiences. In 1966, with problems performing in Spain, he was acclaimed at the Olympia in Paris, where he was the first of several banned Catalan *cantautors* to find refuge. Raimon's concert, entitled *Chansons d'amour, Chansons de lutte*, demonstrated his refusal to distinguish between a love song and a political song. Any song that stood for freedom was both intimate and political.

It was Raimon who, while Franco was dying, sang to a mass audience in the Sports Palace on Montjuïc the extraordinarily moving *Jo vinc d'un silenci*, I Come from a Silence, in which he places his working-class heritage at the centre of the struggle against the dictatorship. For Raimon there was no separation between the national struggle for Catalan rights and a working-class social struggle. He is the Woody Guthrie of Catalonia, a socialist poet.

> I come from a silence,
> ancient and very long,
> of people who keep rising up
> from the depths of centuries,
> of people who they call
> subordinate classes,
>
> I come from the squares
> and from the streets full
> of kids who play
> and the old who wait,

while men and women
are working
in the small firms,
at home or in the fields.

I come from a silence
that is not resigned
...
Who loses origins
loses identity.

Music was a vital part of the rebirth of struggle in the 1960s. Raimon came out of the silence imposed by the fear that Franco's executions and dictatorship had imposed. He often says that "all songs are against fear." Song helped unite the struggle that the underground unions and residents' associations waged more immediately. They were heady days when art really could affect politics. In 1969 Raimon, part of an undefeated generation, connected quite consciously to the earlier generation that had experienced the Civil War defeat in his song *To Joan Miró*: "In lit-up red, I want songs." It was the famous double-meaning of people living under dictatorships. Of course, the fiery red balls of Miró's late paintings were suns, but red was politics, the sun rising on a new age. "In lit-up red/I want the world/and to tell things/just as they are."

The *nova cançó* was a movement whose history clashes with received wisdom. Before the death of Franco in 1975, Raimon was not permitted more than eight minutes of television time in his entire career. He was hardly played on the radio; between 1968 and 1972 he could not publish a record. All the songs he submitted were censored. Yet he was one of the biggest singers in Spain; his concerts were packed by people who knew his songs by heart. And this, of course, was before the age of downloading songs from the internet. In a time of mass struggle culture can bypass the market.

Raimon has explained how he spent six months in England when he was twenty, working on road construction and then travelling. When the English learned he was Spanish, they teased him with a Spain of bulls and El Cid. Shocked, Raimon realized that he came from a different country. Castilian "austerity", bulls and religion had nothing to do with him: he came from a Mediterranean Valencia of light and pleasure, of fire, orange groves and paella. The people of Xàtiva were known as *socarrats*, "the burned", because the city had been burnt down in 1707 by the Spanish King Philip V's troops. Today Philip V's portrait hangs in the city museum—head down.

At school Raimon was taught the Castilian poets, but nothing (not even the fact of his existence) was mentioned of Ausiàs March (1397-1459), a Valencian who was the major fifteenth-century poet in Catalan. Raimon identified strongly with March, who wrote of love and domestic affairs in a practical way, breaking from the Provençal courtly love tradition. March questioned religion and brought a rich philosophy into his down-to-earth poetry. Raimon's songs of March's poetry and of others such as Salvador Espriu helped make these poets widely available to Catalans. Espriu (1913-85) spent the dictatorship in what was known as "inner exile", somewhat like Joan Miró. An inner exile expressed beautifully in one of his poems sung by Raimon:

> We have lived to guard words for you.
> To return the name of each thing.
> You lose names, you lose precision,
> you lose your place in the world if your
> culture and language are crushed.

Raimon came from a silence where his language had been suppressed—and not just his language. He told Uruguayan socialist Eduardo Galeano in an interview:

> Any history that is not sectarian of what we now call the Spanish state recognizes that the process of affirmation of Spanish nationality as such involved the destruction of the Galician, Basque and Catalan nationalities. How have they achieved this? By stealing the collective memory of the popular classes within these nationalities.

The achievement of Raimon is not just to have made great poets newly accessible, but to address directly through music the mass of Catalan speakers. Profoundly democratic, in a way which went way beyond the confines of party politics, he was able in the 1960s and 1970s to connect his art with the people he came from. He was offered TV and radio space under the dictatorship if he sang in Castilian Spanish, but he chose not to do so. When Galeano asked him why he did not sing in Castilian to reach a Latin American audience, Raimon countered with "Why don't you write in English to reach a wider public?" There is no need: great songs or poems in minority languages can reach beyond the linguistic barrier. If you translate them, you water them down, they lose the edge of the native language. This is especially so in Raimon's case, as his vital force came from his feeling that he belonged to an oppressed people and that his songs were part of the struggle of that people.

Chimes to the Dead

In the ancient town of Verges in the Baix Empordà, the Dance of Death that takes place every Easter Thursday is the last example of a medieval tradition that was widespread throughout Europe. As Jesus' crucifixion is remembered, the dance reminds spectators of their own deaths— what really matters to each of us. Towards 10 pm, by the light of torches, five figures with white bones glowing on their skin-tight black suits parade through the town to the dirge beat of a single drum. The leading skeleton carries a huge scythe, to reap our lives; the second, an hourglass, to show how little time we have; the third, the dust and ash we will become; the fourth bears a flag with skull and crossbones; and the fifth beats the obsessive, nagging drum, slowing heart-beats and raising the tension.

The realistic Easter pageant is enacted in the great detail character-istic of Holy Week rituals in Spain. With soldiers present in full Roman dress, Pontius Pilate reads the death sentence as the five dancers enter the main square. In the choir of this simple and deeply effective annual rite sings Lluís Llach, born in Verges in 1948.

Raimon was part of an extraordinarily talented and diverse genera-tion of singer-songwriters, thrown up by the struggle against the Franco dictatorship. In 1968 the younger Lluís Llach was one of the last two judges to be incorporated to the *Setze jutjes*, along with Maria del Mar Bonet. Their songs are more ornate than Raimon's, and their range much greater, though neither of these great singers quite has the power to make you want to fight that Raimon had.

The ceremony of the Dance of Death suggests how deeply, even under Franco, the young Llach could grow up within Catalan and Mediterranean culture, just as Raimon did, though at the opposite end of the Catalan linguistic area. Franco thought he could keep Catalan culture regional and folkloric: no more than a choir or a medieval dance. Yet the reverse occurred. These folklore traditions fed into the cultural revival of the 1960s; they reminded Catalans how ancient their roots were.

Like Raimon, Lluís Llach won a Festival prize, at the age of twenty in 1968, and was offered a succulent recording contract of two million pesetas... if he sang in Castilian. He refused and went on to sell hundreds of thousands of records. One of his first, *L'estaca*, The Stake, became the anthem of Catalonia's 1968 generation:

If you all pull that way, it'll fall
And it can't last long,
So push, push, push it down
It must be rotted through by now

If I pull it hard this way
And you pull it hard that way,
So push, push, push it down
And we can all be free

Llach was, and is, blessed with a soaring, melodious voice. But it was his eyes the censors disapproved of, in their notorious 1969 four-year performance ban for "revolutionizing the public with his look." Llach has maintained a strong political commitment. He issued *Campanades a morts*, Chimes to the Dead, in memory of workers killed in a church at Vitoria by the police in 1977. In 2006 he was still there, writing the soundtrack for the film on the life of Salvador Puig Antich. He has insisted, too, on his right to sing what he wanted, to experiment with different styles. In 1985 Llach filled the Camp Nou, FC Barcelona's ground, with an audience of 100,000—few apart from Springsteen or Ronaldinho manage that.

Like most of the left, Llach was not happy with the evolution of post-Franco Catalonia. The conservative nationalists who took power in

Catalonia and the socialists who ran the Barcelona City Council modernized the country, but of course did not change the basic structures of society, as so many who had fought the dictatorship in the 1960s and 1970s had hoped. Llach said: "We thought democracy was an end in itself... a big mistake. If you don't treat it as an instrument to be perfected it becomes perverted." The politicized *nova cançó* has largely been marginalized, though Raimon, Maria del Mar Bonet or Llach retain a big audience.

Traditional Roots
Catalonia has a rich musical tradition, though its classical composers have not been in the front rank. Three of the most prominent have, coincidentally, had English connections: romantic composer Enric Granados (born Lleida, 1867) died torpedoed in the English Channel in 1916 on the way back from the first night of his opera *Goyescas* in New York. Isaac Albéniz (Camprodón, 1860), a famous pianist and composer at the end of the nineteenth century, was supported in style for many years by a music-loving member of the Coutts banking family. John Payne in his *Catalonia: History and Culture* writes interestingly of the composer Robert Gerhard (Valls, 1896), exiled in England for three decades until his death in 1970; curiously, Gerhard wrote the score for the Lindsay Anderson film, *This Sporting Life* (1963).

It is a country, though, where choral societies exist in every town. This is what led to the building of Barcelona's Palau de la Música Catalana, a sumptuous home for a local choral society. At the Palau, Domènech's most fanciful and exotic building, choir performances alternate with classical concerts and Catalan popular singers. The richest *modernista* decorations of stained glass, multi-coloured ceramics, flashing chandeliers and plaster bulging in exuberance out of the walls make a concert there a visual as well as an auditory experience. Outside, for all to see, an allegory of Catalan music hangs on the corner, giving advance flavour of the riot of *modernista* motifs inside. This "frothing mass of stone", in Michael Jacobs' words, features St. George—Sant Jordi—and a woman in a transparent dress.

Raimon started in a choir, playing the flute in Xàtiva's left-wing one (there was a right-wing counterpart, too). These choirs thrive everywhere today and help explain the high standards and varied abilities of the

The Palau de la Música Catalana, Barcelona

singers of the *nova cançó*. And not just of the *nova cançó*, for singers such as Josep Carreras, Montserrat Caballé or Victòria dels Àngels (died 2005) testify to the highest opera standards of Catalan singers.

Another Catalan festival where music plays a deep part and with roots in the Middle Ages is the Patum de Berga at Corpus Christi, which entwines pagan and profane figures and dancing with the Catholic rites. Berga is a small town in the pre-Pyrenees, whose "Patum" is the wildest festival imaginable, with the same hypnotic rhythmic drum-beat as Verges' Dance of Death, but speeded up and accompanied by dancing fire. Right along this Mediterranean coast fire festivals are common, in Catalonia especially on Midsummer Night's Eve, when bonfires and fire-works fill the night with red flames, white smoke and the thrilling tang of gunpowder.

Even the *sardanes* at the Patum are tensed by the pounding drum. The *sardana* is normally a circular group dance, not unlike English Morris dancing without the bells and uniforms; it is somewhat sedate and beloved of the Catalan middle class, who dance it in circles in the squares of small towns on Sunday mornings. It is the expression of Catalan *seny*, good sense. At Berga, among the hills at Corpus Christi, the *sardana* rhythms are driven wild and this good sense is converted to the *rauxa* of whirling motion and screaming crowds.

Yearning *Havanera* and Sexy Rumba

There are two other styles of popular music particularly associated with Catalonia that have emerged in recent decades: *havaneres* and the Catalan rumba. *Havaneres* are melancholy, sentimental sea-faring songs of nostalgia, well suited for choral singing. They originate in the Catalans who went to Cuba in the nineteenth century, many on Antonio López' ships, or who worked on the ships that plied to and forth. They can be heard all along Catalonia's coast at festivals, but are particularly associated with the town of Calella de Palafrugell on the Costa Brava. Here, on the first Saturday of July, some 35,000 people attend the *havaneres* contest at the main beach, distinguished by its fine arcades on the front. Some 300 small boats out in the bay add to the atmosphere, the songs accompanied by the flame of torches and the sucking of gentle waves.

The origins of the *havanera* are curious. If tradition is to be believed, it derives from an eighteenth-century English ballroom dance called the "country dance", taken by French colonists to Haiti. These, on fleeing the 1790s slave revolution, took it to Cuba, where its name was hispanicized to the *contradansa* and mixed with Cuban Afro-American rhythms to become today's haunting song of longing for another country. Incongruous roots: landowners yearning for Haiti and slaves yearning for Africa, mingling with traces of flamenco and Catalan choral singing. It fitted the nostalgic mood of Catalan émigrés stumbling across it in the waterfront bars of Havana.

Popular in Catalonia in the early twentieth century, it then almost disappeared. In 1966 a fishermen's and sailors' bar in the Port Bo cove at Calella de Palafrugell, one of the few places where *havaneres* were still sung, organized a contest. Its huge success stimulated a revival throughout Catalonia, centred on the bewitching beach festival that is now televised and draws huge crowds to the cove.

The existence of the *nova cançó* created the climate for the recuperation of *havaneres*. As their origin in Cuba suggests, they were originally sung in Spanish, but in the last forty years this has changed with the recovery of Catalan. Now nearly all are sung in Catalan, which leads purists to lament this distortion of a genuinely popular style of Catalan singing in Castilian.

Havaneres are traditionally accompanied by *rom cremat*—flambéed rum, consisting of Cuban rum, coffee, lemon (or cinnamon) and sugar. It is set on fire to burn off the alcohol. The taste divides opinion; many cannot comprehend a drink that sends its best part, the alcohol, wafting into the summer night's air. However, coffee and sugar keep you going and singing till dawn, which alcohol does not. Many say the mixture tastes of urine.

The other modern, hybrid musical form that has become massively popular in recent decades is the Catalan rumba. Its roots are very different from the *havanera*'s. In the old town of Gràcia, part of the city of Barcelona since 1897 but retaining its old air of craft workshops, rebellion and bohemia, there is a gypsy quarter. From this area, around the Plaça Raspall, came Antonio el Pescadilla, husband of Lola Flores (Spain's most famous post-war popular singer) and father of Rosario Flores, a very high-class singer and fond of mixing in rumbas with her flamenco-pop. On the corner of Llibertat and Fraternitat streets (names testifying to Gràcia's radical traditions), is a plaque on the house where this "father of the Catalan rumba" was born. If an outsider, a *payo*, a non-gypsy, walks into a bar here, the locals may well walk out. This is what happened the first time a young Argentine walked into the Bar Petxina in the 1970s. He ordered a bottle of whisky and nursed it at his table in the corner, saying nothing. He went back day after day. Gradually people got used to him. He started to learn the local music and in the 1980s became the greatest exponent of Catalan rumba, a mix of flamenco and Cuban rhythms. He was Gato (Cat) Pérez, who died young in October 1990 and now has a small square named after him near the Plaça Raspall. That an Argentine should revive Catalan gypsy music is as strange as an English country tune becoming a Costa Brava beach song.

The rumba is much more upbeat than the *havanera*, as befits its urban Barcelona origins. It shares with flamenco the use of guitar, voice and *palmes*, hands clapped to the rhythm, but unlike flamenco, characterized by lamentation, it is happy dance music. Cassettes of rumba music adorn racks in bars and petrol stations. The rumba is sensual, provocative and noisy, in many ways Catalan rock-and-roll. It is identifiable by a particular off-beat rhythm, which Tomás Graves describes as *a-chika-bom, a-chika bom*, the fingers flicking up and down on the guitar ("as if to brush crumbs off your shirtfront"), then the thumb darting up to the chin again. Music of urban outsiders, the gypsies, it was implicitly anti-racist, expressing "a tolerance impossible to hide," in the words of a Gato song. In his reflective story-songs Gato managed both to intellectualize and to popularize rumba.

Before Gato Pérez, the great popularizer of the rumba was a gypsy known as Peret. A spectacular performer, in Graves' words: "In the 1960s Peret created rumba-pop, complete with twitching hips and spectacular *ventilador* technique [the ventilator is the way the guitar is strummed in rumba rhythm, the *a-chika bom*], often spinning the guitar along the axis of the fretboard without losing a beat." Peret sang political songs, too, but in the 1980s became religious and only sang in his evangelical church (whose worshippers doubled and tripled). He came back to sing *Barcelona's Got the Power* at the 1992 Olympic closing ceremony.

The year 1992 was the breakthrough year for commercial Catalan rumba: Los Manolos made it famous with their upbeat version of the sugary Olympic hymn *Amics per sempre*, "Friends for Ever". Then the French group, the Gypsy Kings, made rumba internationally famous.

The latest stars are Ojos de brujo, drawing on rumba, flamenco and hip-hop, in an eclectic mix of "world music" styles. Their third record *Techarí* (Free, in *caló*, the gypsy language) has already taken them on international tours. They are conscious of how the new youth Barcelona music scene, promoted as Barcelona *mestissa*, is appropriated by Barcelona's rulers, fond of putting on music festivals and showing their progressive credentials. Guitarist in the cooperatively organized Ojos de brujo, Ramón Jiménez, told *Catalonia Today*: "In Barcelona students have to pay 1,000 euros a month for a flat... In the end we'll all be thrown out and there'll only be tourists and *mestissa* extras on the streets."

The *nova cançó*, *havaneres* and the rumba show the strength of Catalonia's music culture. It has combined influences into original forms, with genuine popular roots. Music is not just international rock or local choirs. Like the blues or jazz, it is music linked deeply to a sense of history or identity. Raimon, the singer-songwriter on whom this chapter has focused, sang, in his *Quatre rius de sang*, Four Rivers of Blood, a song inspired by the Catalan flag or *senyera* in a painting by Antoni Tàpies:

> Old and dusty land
> where new hands grow,
> where thousands and thousands of mouths,
> tired of silence,
> are getting ready to speak
> from the four rivers of blood.

Based on ancient traditions, today's Catalonia is not prepared to remain silent.

Part Three

Tourism and War

The Raval, Barcelona

Chapter Twelve
The Sweaty Groin: Barcelona's Raval

The first two parts of this book have circled round Catalonia's capital, Barcelona, a city whose name today has a romantic resonance of beautiful architecture and good living. Chapters have visited the coastal plains and the Pyrenees, Tarragona, Poblet, Figueres, Montroig and Sitges... but inevitably Barcelona dominates Catalonia. Over four million of Catalonia's eight million people live in the Barcelona conurbation, which means Barcelona itself with its million and a half inhabitants, plus the cities wrapped round it.

If you are walking near the Camp Nou, FC Barcelona's ground in the Les Corts area, you can easily step into L'Hospitalet, the second city of Catalonia with a quarter of a million inhabitants, without noticing you had crossed a municipal boundary. On its northern side, though here separated by the River Besòs, Barcelona is embraced by Santa Coloma de Gramenet and coastal Badalona, both cities bigger than Catalonia's provincial capitals, Girona, Tarragona and Lleida. In Barcelona's hinterland, less than twenty miles away, just behind the Collserola coastal range that fringes the city, lie Sabadell and Terrassa, major manufacturing cities of the Industrial Revolution.

The capital's dominance over the rest of Catalonia is for many Catalan nationalists a source of regret. In Barcelona more Castilian Spanish than Catalan is spoken, due to migration to Catalonia from other parts of Spain, and its Catalan suffers a certain influence, or "corruption", for this reason. It is common in Barcelona Catalan to hear Castilian words pronounced with a Catalan intonation rather than the standard Catalan word.

In addition, Barcelona inevitably sucks in economic resources from the rest of the country: one can find towns in the Ebro area as lost and poor as in other remote parts of Spain. It throws out its wealth, too, distorting development on the Costa Brava and Pyrenees, as its wealthy urban citizens cover promontories and mountain pastures with their second homes, swimming-pools and four-wheel drives.

Despite the size of the Barcelona conurbation, visitors who stay in one of the many new hotels in the Old City—in the last twenty years hotel space has quadrupled—will find it is a city like Florence or Oxford, whose sights are best covered on foot. What is known as the *Ciutat vella*, or Old City, is the part that was confined within the city walls until their demolition in 1859 for the city expansion of the Eixample.

The *Ciutat vella* has four districts. The first is the upside-down triangle between the Paral·lel and the Ramblas, called the Raval. The area mingles sordid, nineteenth-century slums with today's constant demolition and rebuilding and the dynamism of immigration from (mainly) Ecuador, Pakistan and Morocco. The second area, known as the *barri gòtic*, or Gothic Quarter, lies between the Ramblas and the Via Laietana. It contains the narrow soft-lit streets of the old Jewish quarter, medieval monuments such as the cathedral and the royal buildings on the Plaça del Rei, and the government buildings around the Plaça Sant Jaume. Across the Via Laietana lies the third area, the Ribera, meaning shore: today the once mercantile, seafaring Born area has been transformed into chic bars and boutiques. The fourth area of the Old City is the fishing and stevedores' quarter, Barceloneta, jutting out on a promontory along one side of the harbour. This and the next chapter look at the Old City, modern-day tourist Barcelona par excellence.

Chinatown

The Paral·lel is a straight six-lane avenue dividing the Old City from the Poble Sec quarter that begins to climb the Montjuïc hill. The Paral·lel's heyday was the first four decades of the twentieth century. Old photos show enormous cafés, tables spilling across the wide pavements, packed with customers, mostly men in hats and caps, a haze of smoke rising even in the open air. One of these was the Café Español, much smaller now, but still there beside the Paral·lel's subway station at the junction with Nou de la Rambla. The Belgian-Russian revolutionary and novelist Victor Serge described the café in his 1917 paean to revolutionary Barcelona, *Birth of our Power*: "This enormous room was extended indefinitely by mirrors framed in heavy gilt and by terraces animated with voices crackling like the wind over dry grass: it opened onto a street flood-lit by little theaters, night clubs, dance halls, and big working class bars."

The Paral·lel was Barcelona's Montmartre, the city's great centre of working-class relaxation, its open space a sudden relief from the "uniformly gray, cool and dank" (Serge again) narrow streets of the Old City and its sweatshops. A few of its numerous music halls and revue theatres remain: the Apolo, opposite the underground station, or the Molino, the Windmill, which opened in 1916 and has now been closed for a decade, though its long red sails, like arms folded, still cross the building's façade. Ordinary theatres, too, mingled with the music halls: theatre, of all kinds, was a major popular leisure occupation in Catalonia, a love that has lasted right to this day.

Today, the general cultural decay of the avenue is signalled by the Sala Bagdad, offering live sex on stage (and "audience participation"), just by the subway station. From the Sala Bagdad, walk up the Carrer Tàpies. This was once one of the most dismal streets of the Old City, home to the Criolla, a transvestite dance bar featured in both Jean Genet's embroidered memoir *The Thief's Journal* (1949) and Georges Bataille's novel *Blue of Noon* (1957). The Criolla was a destination for members of the upper class on a daring night out in the slums. Josep Maria de Sagarra, in his powerful 1932 novel, *Private Life*, describes a visit:

> The women who had never been there felt a little disappointed. Though they had been told horrifying details, they found just an ordinary café with pretensions to being a dance-hall. The place was an adapted warehouse: the old iron columns supporting the roof were painted to give the illusion they were palm trees; the leaves were painted on the ceiling.

Vice is pretty dull, the party felt, though later a play of lights "in scandalously pharmaceutical colors" highlighted the grotesque that Sagarra's characters sought:

> Certain faces took on a terrifying inexpressiveness, bringing to mind ideas of the scaffold, the madhouse... A boy in a trench coat and with a red kerchief at his neck, his face painted and hair like a woman's,

became more and more defined in the blue light and his cheeks turned
a grey green like cemetery grass...

It was all a question of lighting. Today, one side of Carrer Tàpies has
been pulled down to create a small park. This selective demolition, known
as *esponjament* or "sponging out", is the practice followed with success by
Barcelona's post-Franco councils of opening small spaces in densely populated zones. The Plaça Orwell is another example. On the other side of
Tàpies is a row of abandoned buildings, warehouses and closed shops.
Tàpies will be completely overhauled in a few years: at the far end, brand-
new buildings currently house Council offices and the Catalan-language
daily *El Punt* with its English-language associate *Catalonia Today*. The
sordid, but all-too-real *Criolla* is now just a literary memory.

Yet, just a hundred yards on, lies the Plaça de Mandiargues. Middle-
aged prostitutes hang around under the acacia trees and hiss at any
man—to attract, not to disapprove—at almost any hour of the day or
night. Along one side is a hotel with rooms by the hour, or by the
quarter-hour, affirmed the novelist Mandiargues himself. It seems you
have fallen through a time-warp back into the 1950s, when the lack of
social security, the death of so many men in the Civil War and their exile
or imprisonment after confronted many women with the choice of prostitution or their children's starvation. Mass prostitution, which the
anarchists had tried to abolish during the 1936 Revolution by closing
brothels and encouraging women to take up arms against fascism, pros-
pered under the rule of Franco and the Church. Part of the Raval became
notorious as one of the biggest red-light districts in Europe, known as
the *barrio chino*—or Chinatown. There were no Chinese, except the
occasional restaurateur, but a 1920s journalist named it after similar red-
light districts in San Francisco or New York.

The fact that the sex industry exists in the twilight zone between
night and day, between legality and prohibition, means that by definition there are no statistics, but streets like Tàpies, Robador or San
Olegario were packed with bars, brothels and small "hotels". These
narrow, pestilential, cobbled streets were full of men circulating and
staring.

In the 1950s, the area's nadir under the poverty of Francoism, Juan
Goytisolo was, like Sagarra a generation before him, a ruthlessly honest

and observant upper-class raider into the *barrio chino*. Born in 1931, Goytisolo grew up in the wealthy area of Sant Gervasi in an impoverished, upper-class family. In the first volume of his autobiography, *Forbidden Territory* (1985), he explains:

> Oscillation between literature, lust for the slums and political commitment... Trawling through the dirtiest and most wretched urban areas, rubbing shoulders with crooks and prostitutes, smoking joints, became a kind of political militancy... This attitude, common to the small bourgeois nucleus of our dawning "progressiveness", was clearly unorthodox in Marxist terms.

The Plaça de Mandiargues, full of its middle-aged women at 11 am, is not, alas, just an isolated leftover from the impoverished past. Eight hours later, the neighbouring Nou de la Rambla is lined with teenaged African girls, their short shorts and bare bellies in contrast with the almost homely look of the women in the Plaça de Mandiargues. These black women are the casualties of emigration. Each one has a story of a search for a better life, ending before it has hardly begun in the sewers of Europe. They are the new slaves, like the women filling the border brothels at La Jonquera.

Squalor and Gentrification
The fact that this area is also where tourists bring in the revenue poses a problem for the City Council. The Plaça de Mandiargues is no more than 200 yards from Gaudí's Palau Güell. In 2006 the Council passed a controversial bye-law "against anti-social behaviour" whereby everything "unpleasant" in the streets is lumped together. Urinating in the street (frequent in a densely populated city without public toilets, though not as common as in Rome), dog-shit not scooped up or noise at night are mixed in with begging and prostitution. The Council, unwilling or unable to address the root causes of homelessness or prostitution, merely moves the prostitutes on from near your hotel to somewhere else.

Chapter Seven discussed the Palau Güell, erected stubbornly by the industrialist Eusebi Güell to dominate the slums. In Chapter Ten I commented how the Parc de Joan Miró combines eclectically different styles. The Old City can be read profitably in this way. Barcelona is particularly rich and attractive to visitors because so many contrasting buildings and people were packed together over the centuries into one relatively small area: old beside new, poor beside rich, sordid beside elegant, tasteless beside exquisite.

It was here in the Raval that Jean Genet spent a few months in 1933, later glorified in *The Thief's Journal* as one of the most abject parts of his life. Other writers from neighbouring France have also contributed to the quarter's sordid legend. André Pieyre de Mandiargues—he of the square—set a whole novel here, *La marge* (The Margin), which won the Prix Goncourt in 1967. Its mix of existential anguish, anti-Francoism and revelling in the mud made it popular as well as prized. *La marge* is a powerfully imaginative evocation of the country that Franco's dictatorship created. For Mandiargues, the Columbus column at the foot of the Ramblas was a giant phallus presiding over the *barrio chino*, whose streets are coloured the yellow of excrement or the orange-red of prostitutes' sweaters, of blood and of the butane-gas cylinders stored on balconies (yellow and red are the colours of the hated Spanish flag). In Mandiargues, as in Sagarra, the colours of bars are green, with "olive-green faces" of men with green bald patches: "Three tarts are on display in front of the Ramona bar, and above their faded night-dresses, under the artificial blonde of their washed-out curls, their skin is green in the places where the make-up has rubbed off."

His character Segismond dreams his way through a nightmarish stay in Barcelona. Segismond is fleeing from his world; he carries a letter in his pocket he refuses to open, for he knows it will recall him to a terrible reality. Mandiargues' phantasmagoric record pinpoints shops, people, bars and streets, making *La marge* a valuable social history of the *barrio chino* at one of its most wretched moments. As in Dalí, surreal imagination combines with obsessive detail, the flat "styleless" detail of the French *nouveau roman* in Mandiargues' case.

Though Mandiargues' city still exists, especially in the square named after him, his "Fuhrúnculo"—a made-up amalgam of "Führer" and "furúnculo", the Spanish for "boil", i.e. Franco—died in 1975, and Barcelona has been transformed since. The infamous Robador slum has gone, to be replaced by a hotel, cooperative housing and the Rambla del Raval. Since before the 1992 Olympics, the Council has been engaged in an extremely ambitious reform programme, involving a mixture of private and public money. It has renewed streets and squares, provided grants for rehabilitation of crumbling buildings and demolished blocks to create space. On some streets the sun now shines for the first time in two centuries.

City Council policy is contradictory. It is based explicitly on two main points: a) returning the Old City to its position as "the nerve-centre" of Barcelona; and b) maintaining its residential use, i.e. not allowing it to become a desolate services-hotels-museum area abandoned by inhabitants. Yet the gentrification of the Old City has pushed property prices through the roof, leading the trend throughout the city since the 1992 Olympics. Despite Council protestations to the contrary, the new inhabitants drawn to the reformed Raval and Ribera inevitably exclude the heirs of the poorer (mainly old) residents of the *barris*.

In fact, the Council has consciously pursued a policy of gentrification to try to make the area safe for tourism, developing a museum area round Richard Meier's Contemporary Art Museum (MACBA) in the north of the Raval, which has brought in its wake arty bars, bookshops, art galleries—and higher housing prices. For several years, the rather sinister term "benevolent metastasis" was used to describe this process.

At the same time, the Raval is the part of the city where new immigration is seen most clearly. In 2005, according to the Council's own statistics, almost 44 per cent of the *Ciutat vella*'s population was made up of immigrants arrived in the previous two decades. In 1991 the figure had been six per cent. Such multiracial, multicultural quarters are normal in New York and London, but quite new in Spain whose poverty until recently made it a country with more emigrants than immigrants.

Like London's East End and New York City's borough of Brooklyn, the Raval has seen successive waves of migration. A hundred and fifty years ago, migrants were Catalans cast off the land by the Industrial Revolution and thrown into the Raval's factories. Fifty years ago, its poor were the migrants from other parts of Spain; now they are those fleeing war and the effects of IMF debt rescheduling. Thus, the Raval is simultaneously experiencing an influx of poor migrants and an attempt to prettify it for tourists and drive out the poor. How these contradictory processes will work out remains to be seen.

Rambling

The dividing-line between the Raval and the monumental *barri gòtic*, the oldest part of the city, is one of the world's most famous avenues, the Ramblas in Castilian Spanish, or Rambles in Catalan, though the two are pronounced the same. In the early 1840s, Richard Ford defined it:

> The word Rambla is Arabic Ramla, a sandy heap: it properly means a river bed, which often in Spain being dry in summer is used as a road. The channel was on the extension of the city... now it is the great aorta, and a charming walk planted with trees.

From the Plaça de Catalunya, the Ramblas follows a slightly zigzag line, the contour of the sewage-filled medieval stream it was, down to the Columbus column and the sea. On its left walking towards the sea stood the city walls, removed in the eighteenth century, to be rebuilt where the Paral·lel is today to include the Raval and so convert the Ramblas into the "aorta" of the old city, which it still is. When it rains torrentially, as is customary in spring and autumn, the water is now channelled safely underground, but in many other towns along the Catalan coast the dry *rambles* still turn into raging torrents, often carrying away cars or even sometimes an unwary person. Even more water comes down now than before, as the stripping of vegetation from the hills and the building of second homes do not allow rain to so easily soak into the hard ground.

Barcelona's Ramblas is the city's great intimate boulevard. Not a wide, noble street like the Passeig de Gràcia, which is the broad avenue of the bourgeois Eixample, the Ramblas gives the impression of always being packed with people because in fact there is little space on the central pedestrian walkway. The kiosks and performers lining it, the plane trees' broad pale-green leaves shading it and the one lane of traffic on each side create the feel of a comfortable, intimate space.

Since its development 200 years ago, it has been a place where people go to walk and be seen and where others go to stare at them. George Sand in her 1837 *Winter in Majorca*, later translated by Robert Graves, noted "...the women, beautiful, graceful and coquettish, preoccupied by the fold of their mantillas and the play of their fans; the men by their cigars, as they strolled along, laughing, chatting, ogling the ladies, discussing the Italian opera."

It is less fashionable now, with its mass of tourists. The shops are no longer the leading businesses of the city as they were in George Sand's and Richard Ford's day, but souvenir bazaars and fast-food restaurants. Hotels, on the other hand, have remained: there were always hotels on the Ramblas, opened originally by Italians in the eighteenth and nineteenth centuries. One such is the Cuatro Naciones (Four Nations). Once Barcelona's greatest hotel, it has come down in the world, but is still open and a lot cheaper now than when Stendhal (1837), Einstein (1923) or Buffalo Bill, who brought his Wild West Show to the 1889 Exhibition, lodged there in style. Hardly anyone actually lives on the Ramblas, they just lodge there.

If the Ramblas is indisputably Barcelona's central street, there is no central square. The huge Plaça de Catalunya, where the Ramblas starts, acts as the gateway between the plebeian Old City and the wealthier Eixample of spacious roads and plush apartment blocks. The square has never entered the affections of Catalans, as the multiple reforms it has undergone in recent decades show.

The Ramblas, between the Plaça de Catalunya and the sea, is divided into five parts. The first, the Rambla de Canaletes, is named after the fountain on the right: drink from it and you will fall in love with Barcelona. It is here, by the magic fountain, that FC Barcelona's football triumphs are celebrated. There used to be mass *tertúlies*, too, with hundreds of men blocking the boulevard to discuss football and politics.

The second part is the Rambla dels Estudis, named because it was the site of the Jesuit University, built outside the walls in the sixteenth century. The only remaining part is the Church of Betlem (Bethlehem), its long, sooty side-wall facing the Ramblas like a cobbled street heaved onto its side. Here Verdaguer spent his last years after his expulsion from Claudio López' Palau Moja opposite. Like most churches, it was burnt out in the Civil War, then rebuilt in the ugly style under Franco. It inspired commentator Carles Soldevila to write sardonically—and boldly for the 1950s: "This baroque factory was ferociously mistreated by revolutionaries incapable of seeing the sole consequence of their deeds: more churches and less art."

The entire Ramblas are lined with newspaper and magazine kiosks, where you can buy all the international press and a gaudy array of pornography at the eye level of the exquisitely dressed and pampered toddlers: evidence for some of Catalonia's "freedom from sexual repression". Rather, the porn magazines represent a continuing sexual repression, following on from the packed bars in the *barrio chino* of the 1950s and 1960s. Even so, after several decades of dictatorship, people are still aghast at anything, such as removing pornography from the sight of babies, that might be interpreted as censorship.

In the Rambla dels Estudis, eleven bird stalls are interspersed with the news kiosks, containing songbirds and exotic parrots, often quite big birds in small cages. The free pigeons group round, pecking up the seed that spills out. The stalls' days are numbered; the Council, reflecting tourist reaction, intends to shut down the bird stalls. Nevertheless, their existence reflects a passion for caged birds, mainly among migrants from other parts of Spain. A lot of (usually) middle-aged men in Barcelona keep and breed goldfinches, budgerigars and canaries. They carry their cages through the streets to a local park, where they whip off the covers and listen to the birds sing while they discuss, buy and sell the birds. "I don't eat my birds," responded a cage-carrier to a relative of mine who complained about keeping animals in dark captivity.

The next section down, the Rambla de les Flors, is sweeter-smelling, full of flower-, plant- and seed-stalls. A hundred years ago, before the existence of cut-flower shops, it was the city's only flower market. Still today people from outlying quarters "go down to Barcelona" to buy seeds or birds. On the right, set back, is the huge mansion known as the Palau de la Virreina (Palace of the Vice-reine), named after the young wife of Catalonia's first *indiano*, the eighteenth-century Viceroy of Peru, Manuel Amat. He built the house with what he stole from the fabulous silver mines of Potosí (in present-day Bolivia). In poetic justice, he died before he could enjoy his house and it was named after his widow. Scribes used to have their tables in front of the Virreina right up to the mid-1980s, writing letters for the illiterate. "With tears or without?" they would ask of a letter home to the distant village from which the client had emigrated. "With tears". "Ten cents extra," said the scribe.

The middle of the walk down the Ramblas is marked by the Liceu subway station and Joan Miró's *The Egg Yolk*, a mosaic in stone set in the pavement. Philistines can stamp here on abstract art. As the Ramblas is Barcelona's central street, so this mosaic and the small square it inhabits, the Pla de la Boqueria, is the centre of the Ramblas. Here is the famous

Boqueria food market (see Chapter Seventeen) and the former place of execution. John Langdon-Davies wrote: "Beneath the creaking gallows, the inevitable brothels sprang up so that love and death in their gloomiest aspects prevented the rise of property values."

Miró's carpet of tiles marks a certain frontier, or junction, between an upper Ramblas of flowers, birds and food, and a seedier Ramblas towards the sea and port. In the lower, more lawless part, the *barrio chino* crosses the Ramblas from the Raval to penetrate the run-down streets round Escudillers and the Plaça Reial.

The fourth section is the Rambla dels Caputxins, dominated by the Liceu opera house on the right. It burned down in 1994 and has been restored and extended to fill a whole block. The Liceu was the great social and business meeting-place of the nineteenth-century and early twentieth-century textiles magnates and their families. Its construction had been paid for by their subscriptions. Here the great nights of the bourgeoisie, a class otherwise little seen in the Old City, still take place. This section is named for the Capuchin monastery that was destroyed to open up the Plaça Reial, built in the 1840s. This French-style enclosed *plaça* has tall arcades, slender palms reaching up for the light and two lamp-standards topped by Mercury's flying helmet, which was the first public commission Gaudí ever did. There are cafés and clubs all around the square, including the Taxidermista, now a restaurant, but until the mid-1990s a famous shop. Ava Gardner had the head of a bull killed by her Catalan boyfriend Mario Cabré stuffed there.

The beautiful Plaça Reial is a good example of the semi-permanent struggle or balance between the *barrio chino* and the tourist industry. It is heavily policed, because for decades this is where hippies have lain around with backpacks (the Kabul hostel on the square still offers cheap dormitory beds), vagrants have sat with wine bottles and bag-snatchers and drug-dealers have snatched and dealt. The tourists soak up the winter sun on the café terraces or shelter in summer under the arcades, watching the marginal and criminal behaviour, and are, in turn, watched.

The fifth and last section of the Ramblas is the Rambla de Santa Mònica, named after the Santa Mònica convent, now a contemporary art centre. This building is the last surviving example of what was once a street of monasteries and convents. Here at the bottom, the Ramblas

The tower of Santa Maria del Pi, seen through the Palau Nou, Ramblas, Barcelona

widens, losing intensity. Skilful pavement artists will draw you, where only a couple of decades ago ageing prostitutes lined up from the monument to the playwright Pitarra in the Plaça del Teatre down to the Columbus column. Manuel Vázquez Montalbán, in *The Pianist* (1985), described his middle-class characters venturing into the dangerous territory with a characteristic heightened realism:

> A stretch of solitudes and fleeting lights, on both sides entries into the
> forbidden city of cheap whores and rotting drugs... the sweaty groin of
> the city awaiting another police raid hunting for the system's parasites.
> And in the bodies of all the explorers, the tension of a patrol under
> threat in a hostile zone of a river-street, flowing from the purity of the
> fountain of Canaletas to death in the oily water of the port pond.

The faded Cuatro Naciones Hotel is on this strip, alongside the Cosmos, the Jazz Colón, respectively a former by-the-hour hotel and a club full of black American sailors—exotic in the 1950s. Now, as part of the City Council's determined and successful drive to smarten up Barcelona for tourists, buildings for the new University Pompeu Fabra have been located here. To use a mixed metaphor, the sweaty groin of the city has had a face-lift.

The Ramblas is city bustle, its street performers, beggars, kiosks, workers, tourists, unemployed: the "throbbing aorta" or "river of people" every guidebook raves about. After the Ramblas, step into the quiet of neighbouring streets. This is one of the Old City's greatest pleasures. It is why Gabriel García Márquez called Barcelona "the most secret of cities" or the designer Mariscal commented: "This most beautiful city is like a wonderful woman hiding in a cupboard." You can walk out of the roaring noise, sunlight, colour and bustle and, fifty yards away, stroll alone in a dark, narrow medieval street.

The city's careful, determined and successful drive to smarten up

Chapter Thirteen
The Gothic Quarter, Barcelona

Gòtic describes well the relatively small, monumental area which holds not just the cathedral, but where all the buildings of Catalonia's religious and political power are packed together. They were mainly built six and seven centuries ago at the time of Barcelona's glory as capital of a great maritime power—and the heyday of the Gothic style.

The Museum-City

In the *barri gòtic*, the Gothic Quarter, the tourist city draws closest to the "museum-city" into which the City Council and its hoteliers are converting the centre of Barcelona. The museum-city is also conversely what the hoteliers, restaurateurs and City Council fear, for without the great monuments being mixed in with daily life, i.e. the survival of local shops and ordinary residents, the Old City runs the risk of losing its vibrancy and becoming just another town full of old stones, a stage-set for weekend shopping or clubbing trips.

Still today, despite the slide towards the "museum-city", the visitor's encounters are breathtaking. In a narrow street like Roca, parallel to and only a hundred feet from the Ramblas, you walk alone among the buildings of brown crumbling stone. Or strolling on a summer's night down Avinyó, for example, from the more gentrified top end to the rougher part where it crosses Escudillers, suddenly the great dome of the Mercè Church with the Virgin balanced on top like a ballerina comes into view. Most buildings in the *barri gòtic* are not actually medieval (though those unbrushed by the reform programme look old enough to be so), but the street layout is. Carrer Marlet has Hebraic inscriptions still visible on its wall, and the very ancient synagogue nearby. Or, in contrast, stand the three happy, Parisian-style interlinking squares of the Plaça del Pí, with its painters' market on Saturdays; or, darker, the Plaça de Sant Felip Neri, long a lost, secret square only stumbled on by chance, as if one was in a film in Venice. Now it is popular on the *Shadow of the Wind* tourist trail.

Even so, there is often no-one there at all, except for a few down-and-outs drinking beer and insulting their lean dogs.

The wall of the church in the Plaça de Sant Felip Neri is spectacularly pitted: some say by the machine-gun bullets of anarchists taking the building from pro-*coup* police at the start of the Civil War; others say the marks were caused by the volleys of executions. In fact, the wall was damaged in March 1938, when a bomb fell on an air-raid shelter and twenty children were killed. The knowledge of the dead children adds to the square's dank gloom. It is one of the few places in Barcelona that make an apt setting for the best-selling *Shadow of the Wind*, which strangely confuses this light-filled Mediterranean city with the chill fog of the nightmarish London/Edinburgh of Stevenson's *Jekyll and Hyde*.

At night in the *barri gòtic* the street-lighting is soft in the damp air (Barcelona is humid, which is why August is exhausting, even though maximum temperatures are only 32ºC). Langdon-Davies put it beautifully: "There is great peace in the narrow streets; and the naked electric light bulbs create a golden nimbus through which the ancient honey-coloured stonework towers to unmeasured heights." The diffused, soft light makes the sudden encounters—contrasts, secret corners, architecture glimpsed from an unusual angle—particularly dramatic.

The *barri gòtic* is not only Gothic. On the Via Laietana side of the area, by the statue of Ramon Berenguer IV, one of the first counts of Barcelona, the Roman walls are seen at their best. They are extensively restored—at times, rather touchingly, in red brick: no deceit intended here, unlike Tarragona—but nevertheless recognizably Roman. Roman remains are scattered through the area; there is a gift shop on the Carrer Boqueria with a piece of Roman wall behind the trinkets. The excellent Museu de l'Història de la Ciutat excavated downwards and found the line of the original Roman street in the basement. Now, visitors can walk through the foundations of the Roman houses, baths and alleys in their original positions. There is, in summer, an outdoor café in a small square, Sant Iu. From a rickety table under the orange trees, the visitor is shaded by the back of the monarchs' palace and can look out over the Roman walls. At this peaceful corner, Roman, Gothic and the Arab trees join.

What is known today as the Plaça Sant Jaume has been the seat of city government for two thousand years and of Catalan government for a thousand. The Barcelona City Hall faces the Palau de la Generalitat across the square. Up the small zigzagging Carrer Paradís running off one of the corners of the Plaça Sant Jaume is the Centre Excursionista (Ramblers' Centre) de Catalunya, in whose building the three Roman columns of the temple of Augustus on the highest point, "Mount Taber", of the old city are conserved. Verdaguer, in his *Oda a Barcelona*, wanted to make these "three columns of Hercules" the centre of a huge, new square that would unite the Plaça de Sant Jaume with the Plaça del Rei on the other side of the columns. It would have meant demolishing at least three city blocks, a madly grandiose scheme perhaps, but no more so than carving the Via Laietana through the Old City in 1909, a straight lance through the festering streets, or today demolishing brothel-filled streets and tenements to build the Rambla del Raval.

Verdaguer's idea shows the desire of the Catalan nationalist *renaixença* for a big open space to reflect the revival of Catalonia's medieval greatness and place it on a par with other nations. Verdaguer mixes in every evocative symbol of antiquity to create his "immense square", not just calling the three columns the columns of Hercules (mythical founder of the city), but comparing them to the Three Graces and to the temple on the Acropolis. They were to form the:

... great door letting through light and air.
The Cross has nothing to fear from a pagan tripod.

Cathedral and Cloister

Barcelona's Gothic cathedral should be entered through the side-door into the cloister. This is no sober inner patio like those at Poblet or Santes Creus, or even the Convent of Pedralbes on the outskirts of Barcelona. No place for silent contemplation, the cloister is an extension of the noisy city. Its railed-off middle is filled with magnolias, orange trees, palms so slim they are held up with wire, a pool of goldfish and two fountains (one with Catalonia's patron St. George and the dragon on top). The thick vegetation picks up the leaves and flowers carved in the Gothic iron and stone. The cloister is also home to thirteen pure-white geese. If you hear mass in the august, high cathedral, the priest is happily punctuated by the panting shrieks of the geese.

The open side-chapels of the cloister include one to the youthful-looking illuminated Virgin of Light, patron of electricity and plumbing. There are monthly masses for members of the trade. In the cloister floor tombs to members of guilds are marked with the signs of their trade. One was a *candeler de sera*, a wax candle-maker. A beautiful sun indicates that Ignasi, master-tailor, "and his family" were buried there in 1754. This is notably unlike the grand cathedrals of Castile, where only nobles' heraldry adorns the tombs and chapels. These features are often cited as evidence of Catalonia's greater democracy and practicality. In Barcelona, making money was respected, and "trade was never held to be a degradation, as among the Castilians" (Richard Ford). This is part of Catalans' self-image as practical, business people, unlike the less industrious rest of Spain. Catalans flee the cliché of lazy Spaniards always putting off business till *mañana*.

This cloister used to be the most relaxing, open, public cathedral cloister in Europe. Friends would arrange to meet there. Office-workers ate packed lunches. Students chatted in the shade. Tourism and the avarice of the Church have stopped this; in 2002 the Church hired private security guards, installed a box office and now charges four euros to enter cloister and cathedral. Curiously, one is asked for a donation, but on trying not to give a "donation", I was informed that the donation is compulsory. The people of Barcelona have lost the easy, day-to-day use of the cloister.

The Catholic Church, as elsewhere in Western Europe, is at a curious point of both popular decline and increased militancy. Young Catholics have learnt from John-Paul II the power of mass demonstrations. In anomalous scenes in front of Barcelona's cathedral in 2005 silver-haired priests mingled nervously with groups of young people demonstrating against the socialist government's legalization of homosexual marriage. With guitars, songs, laughter and chants, the "pro-family" militants seemed more like an evangelical sect than the Church of Rome.

Popular decline is relative. At Sunday mass, churches in Catalonia are often full (the four-euro donation at the cathedral is waived on Sunday mornings) and church weddings are surprisingly on the up. Private, Church-run schools are popular: Catalonia has the highest rate of private education in Europe at about 42 per cent and most private schools are Church-run. Catalonia also has Europe's highest school failure rate in the state system, a product of chronic under-financing as most private schools are subsidised by the state. Yet the convents, monasteries and seminaries are empty, and priests in Catalan parishes often come from Africa or Latin America. And papal edicts on contraception and abortion are routinely ignored in a country where ninety per cent of people fill out "Catholic" on their census forms.

Catalonia, like the rest of Spain, has always been a profoundly devout country and, by the rule of dialectical opposites, a profoundly anti-clerical country. The chapters on Verdaguer and Gaudí showed the religious character of much of the nineteenth-century *renaixença*. Chapter Sixteen on revolutionary anarchism will explore the opposite pole.

Barcelona's cathedral, the Seu, can be traced back to a Christian basilica on the site in the fourth century. This was sacked in the 985 Moorish raid and the present building was started in 1298. Building was slow, though, and came to a complete halt in the centuries of Catalonia's decline. Ford in 1840 found: "The principal façade is unfinished, is only painted in stucco, which is a disgrace to the chapter, who for three centuries received a fee on every marriage, for this very purpose of completing it."

The cathedral was finally paid for, not by 300 years of fees, but by a rich man worried in his final years that his worldly sins needed expiation. In this case, the banker Manuel Girona paid for the "disgrace" of the façade to be finished in the 1880s. The 600 years taken to complete a cathedral can only reassure the fans of Gaudí worrying about the unfinished Sagrada Família, some 125 years old today.

Like other Catalan cathedrals—at Manresa, Lleida, Tarragona or Girona—Barcelona cathedral has a flight of steps leading up to the entrance, where beggars can sit and importune the ascending tourists and faithful. But unlike other cathedrals enclosed in the old quarters of their cities, Barcelona's can be photographed from a distance. This is thanks to Mussolini's airforce pilots, flying from their bases on Mallorca in 1938, who bombed the houses in front of the cathedral, allowing the present wide square, by far the biggest in the *barri gòtic*, to be opened.

Not everyone thinks it a good thing to be able to see the cathedral from a distance. John Langdon-Davies wrote that Barcelona cathedral had "the ugliest facade in Catalonia... this crippled sham." He urged tourists to visit the *barri gòtic* by night so as not to see it or at Christmas when the Santa Llúcia market is on: "The steps... are so covered with booths selling figurines that one has no temptation to lift up one's eyes to the dishonest structure above." Langdon-Davies' point is that the nineteenth-century neo-Gothic façade was inevitably kitsch; nothing could be constructed "in the same spirit of ruthless abnegation as the rest of the structure... Things had been going too well in the business world."

The pre-Christmas Santa Llúcia market is nowadays as kitsch as Langdon-Davies alleges the façade to be. Full of plastic figures for cribs, it includes the best souvenir of Catalonia that can be bought. Forget the Mexican sombreros, Ronaldinho shirts or drying-cloths with Sagrada Família designs that fill the shops along the Ramblas: at Santa Llúcia you can buy a *caganer*. This is a figure of a man, usually in a *barretina* and smoking a pipe, with his trousers down and an enormous pile of shit curved onto the ground beneath him. The *caganer*—shitter—is an integral part of the Christmas crib. There are many interpretations of Catalan fascination with *caca*. It may be that Catalans eat so much pork sausage that they are often constipated. Or it may be a certain anal retentiveness: this is not a people as spontaneous as Italians or *Madrileños*. Or again it may just be greater naturalness about bodily function than in the Protestant North. Whatever the explanation, the *caganer* is an integral part of Christmas, and the Catalan family firm Roca has turned shit into gold. It is the world's biggest toilet manufacturer.

Inside the main door of the cathedral, look straight up and you see the high hollow inside the spires. The lofty roof of the nave, with its slim columns bound together in sheaves of stone, is a characteristic feature of Catalan Gothic, and the few windows make the cathedral a particularly dark and cool place. The Protestants alleged that Spaniards kept their churches dark so that the dominion of priests was maintained: the faithful had no light to read bibles by. Whatever the truth of this, the dimness of a cathedral such as Barcelona facilitates repose. Each person can be alone with his/her thoughts, even in the age of the Virgin of Electric Light.

The many columns and the choir placed right in the middle clutter the cathedral. Unlike any other church in Barcelona, the side-chapels add to the clutter, for they are rich with gold leaf, painting and statuary.

Most Catalan churches were burnt in the 1936 Revolution at the start of the Civil War and many were dismantled brick by brick, but the Generalitat, its building nearby, made a particular effort to protect the cathedral.

There are four great specific features of Barcelona's cathedral. The first is the gold-plated first chapel on the right, dedicated to the Christ of Lepanto. This is the smoke-blackened figurehead from the prow of the ship of Don John of Austria at that decisive victory over the Moors on 7 October 1571. The battle settled Islamic-Christian rivalry in the Mediterranean. There is a little plaque outside the chapel that explains that the real victor of Lepanto was not the Castilian member of the royal family, Don Juan, but Admiral Lluís de Requesens, a Catalan, who then arranged for the flagship's figurehead to be offered to the cathedral. Apart from the truth or falsehood of the comment, it is interesting as an example of the need for Catalan nationalists to combat the official Spanish version of history and make sure credit is given where due.

The second special feature is the choir, right in the centre of the nave. Behind seat number six is painted the English coat of arms, for Henry VIII sat here in 1519 for the one and only meeting of the Order of the Golden Fleece. This conference of monarchs, despite its pagan name, was convened by Emperor Charles V to unite Christian Europe against a possible Turkish invasion. Unity did not last, for Henry split off the Church of England little more than ten years later.

Under another of the choir seats can be seen a Moor's Head, two naked women pulling his beard. There is an even bigger one below the organ. These were trophy heads, not uncommon in Spanish churches and carved/hung as signs of victory. They are a sanguinary reminder of centuries of military struggle against the Muslim Moors. If fundamentalist Protestant militancy is alive today, in medieval times, after the failure of the Crusades and expulsion of the Moors from Spain, the Church was even more explicitly bloodthirsty in its imagery.

The third feature is the crypt, which contains the tomb of Santa Eulàlia, the co-patron saint of Barcelona. Her statue stands in the Plaça del Padró, where she was martyred by the Romans in the fourth century for refusing to abjure Christ. She was rolled down a hill in a barrel full of broken glass in the street now called Baixada de Santa Eulàlia, St. Eulalia Slope. Then her breasts were cut off and she was crucified. She was only thirteen, the reason why there are thirteen geese in the cathedral cloister. A sweet smell revealed her uncorrupted body to a passing bishop in 878. After further vicissitudes, Eulàlia was re-buried in the crypt in 1339, once the main body of the cathedral was completed. The crypt is still kept perfumed, with a huge wreath of scented flowers—gardenias, white lilies, freesias—permanently before her marble tomb. Carved round the sarcophagus are the terrible scenes of her martyrdom at the hands of the Romans, a sobering story of sadistic fantasy at the heart of a system of belief.

The fourth and final feature of the cathedral is not a religious one, but the trip in a lift to the roof. It gives you a great view over the city of Barcelona: the dome of the Generalitat Palace with its several flags and beyond it the City Hall; down into the cloister, and beyond the cloister, the *call*, and past that, the hill of Montjuïc; and finally the numerous flat roofs with washing drying. From this vantage-point one can look across the Old City as if it were a scale model and reflect how cities do not just grow arbitrarily, even when they look random. Barcelona was urbanized in a certain way by the need to control its revolutions. On the hill of Montjuïc the military fortress pointed its guns over the city. The Ciutadella fortress, built after the destruction of Catalan sovereignty by the Spanish government in 1714, dominated the other side of the Old City. The streets of Nou de la Rambla, Unió, Ferran and Princesa were built as straight lines through the twisting medieval streets that followed contours and streams, so that cavalry could charge along them. It was not just theoretical: they often did in revolutionary Barcelona.

Now the Ciutadella fortress, the ugly scar on the pretty face of the city, has been knocked down and the park of the same name, "Citadel Park", located there. The Catalan parliament occupies the citadel's former arsenal: a democratic improvement on the former military occupation.

Plaça del Rei
Stand at twilight for several minutes at the entrance (there is only one) to the Plaça del Rei (Square of the King). This dream-like square lies between the cathedral and the Via Laietana. Dream-like because, while its buildings are in reality palatial and substantial—at the back is the Palace of the Counts of Barcelona, on the left the late-Gothic Castilian Viceroy's palace—they seem intimate, as if part of a toy-town.

King Martí's Tower, Plaça del Rei

At the far side of the square, curving steps like a fan open from the palace, where in 1493 the new monarchs of a united Spain, Ferdinand and Isabel, received Columbus on his return from his first visit to the Americas. Ferdinand was suffering from a stiff neck, where he had been stabbed four months earlier by a Catalan peasant, Joan Canyamars. The King and Queen were unpopular. It was common knowledge that Isabel wanted to centralize Spain and do away with Catalan rights. Ferdinand, of the Crown of Aragon, was seen as a traitor for marrying her.

The noble stories told in school history lessons were usually dirty deeds, just as the beautiful buildings we revere today hid foul crimes. In 1493 the Portuguese claimed that Columbus' discovery of America took place in the area allocated to them in the 1480 Treaty of Alcacovas-Toledo, by which everything South of the Canaries was ceded to Portugal. Thus, Portugal protected its African colonies. In the new situation of Columbus' discovery, the Spanish monarchs petitioned Pope Alexander VI, who just happened to be a Borgia, a Valencian family (Borja, still a common name in Catalonia), whose native tongue was Valencian, i.e. Catalan. Ferdinand and Isabel's presence in Barcelona, their use of links of language and country and the payment of a certain sum to Alexander VI made sure that the Americas were assigned to newly united Spain. It was the last time that a Papal bull was used to settle a question of universal sovereignty. In 1494, the Treaty of Tordesillas was to renegotiate Alejandro's edict, giving Brasil to Portugal.

Ownership established, Isabel sent Columbus back on his second voyage, financed by goods confiscated from the expelled Jews, rounded off by "loans" extracted from Barcelona's leading citizens. The ruthless Isabel's final attack on the Catalans she had exploited was posthumous: in the 1518 codicil to her will she excluded Catalonia from trade with the Americas, which was to have dire consequences on Catalonia's economy until the measure was revoked in 1780.

This palace was earlier the residence of the counts of Barcelona. Its King Martí tower has five storeys of galleries opened by seven symmetrical arches on each floor, overlooking the square. It is not exactly a tower, but rather a wide and slim building. The repetition of the tower's architectural motifs and its height combine with the small scale of the square to contribute to the place's dream-like effect, resembling a surrealist painting of a medieval city. The tower has no obvious function, except that of looking out over the city. It was, one assumes, for internal defence rather than just pleasure and dreams. The king needed to know if a riot was developing: for the same reason, the bishop's palace is backed up against the Roman wall.

The second great feature of this closed square is up the steps and inside the palace, the Saló del Tinell (Banqueting Hall). In Catalonia's medieval heyday meetings of the parliament took place here and the bodies of the Counts of Barcelona lay in state. The knights would ride up the steps and gallop round the coffin, sometimes throwing themselves off their horses to demonstrate their grief. There is no record of this causing any further deaths. Later, the hall was used by the Inquisition, introduced by the united Spanish monarchy, and more recently was where the solemn pact leading to the three-party government led by the socialists was signed in 2003. The Saló del Tinell was thought lost until its rediscovery behind a Baroque chapel in 1934. Now its six huge rounded arches that start not from head height but from ground level are left bare.

Beside it, on the right of the square from the entrance, is the Royal Chapel of St. Agatha, whose roof is completely different, narrow and high with pointed arches. While outside in the square proportions seem intimate, it is here inside the palace that the bareness of hall and chapel create an effect of space and majesty. As at Santes Creus monastery, it is not adornment that shows the grandeur of brick and stone, but the absence of clutter that reveals the presence of space.

Visitors can spend several days exploring the *barri gòtic*'s medieval palaces and religious and political buildings (a combined ticket is available). The City Hall has a magnificent Council Chamber, the Saló del Cent, the Hall of the Hundred, where in those days of glory the hundred burghers who ruled the city met. Its rounded arches are reminiscent of the other great hall, the Saló del Tinell. On the façade of the Generalitat palace facing the City Hall across the square, Sant Jordi, St. George, once again kills the dragon. The outstanding feature of the Generalitat is the Orange-tree Courtyard on the first floor. The only way to see it is by joining the queues on the few bank holidays it is open or by getting yourself invited to a Generalitat reception on a spring evening, when the rich, heady orange blossom mixes with the sharp taste of the best Catalan *cava*.

The more lived-in part of the Gothic Quarter lies downhill towards the sea. Look for the odd-shaped Plaça dels Traginers (carters), narrow on one side, more open on the other (few squares are square in the *barri gòtic*), a space like Sant Felip Neri more often stumbled on by chance in the labyrinth of streets than found deliberately. Unlike the austere Sant Felip Neri, Traginers is poor and homely. The residents bring down chairs on summer nights and sit out in the street, as if they were in a village and not a few hundred yards from the country's government buildings. Carrying on towards the sea, one meets the Carrer Ample. Ample means wide, but the street is narrow, only "wide" because it is wider than all the others nearby. Here is where at night you can feast on fish and shellfish *tapas*.

Barcelona's authorities boast that the *barri gòtic* is one of the best-preserved medieval cities in Europe. There is a host of places (think of Florence, Prague, Heidelberg or Avignon) that can legitimately claim monuments of greater beauty and/or artistic interest. Yet there is some truth in the boast, if one looks at the shape of the Gothic Quarter, not just its monuments. The street lay-out of the area is unchanged since medieval times, with rare exceptions caused by bombs or *esponjament*. In this respect it is like the City of London, with its original narrow streets among the skyscrapers.

In the case of Barcelona, the street plan of its Gothic Quarter was maintained because of poverty. Its wealthy citizens fled overcrowding and cholera *en masse* when the walls came down in 1859. The poor were left in stone and brick houses that were built (usually with stone from Montjuïc, riddled now with quarries) in that century with the advent of the Industrial Revolution. In Florence, for centuries a tourist attraction and not a modern industrial city, the old wooden houses of the poor were cleared for its great palaces and squares. In Barcelona, the street layout was retained because its centuries of decline and poverty meant that there was no construction industry interested in the Old City nor any tourists to speak of until the 1980s.

Through this journey down through the Old City there is no hint of the sea, no smells, mariners, chandlers' shops or customs agencies, until suddenly the narrow streets give way to the open seafront and harbour. This feel of an inland city only a few blocks from the dock contributed to the legend that Barcelona "turned its back on the sea."

Santa Maria del Mar

For the non-religious, Santa Maria del Mar, the "fisherman's church" across the Via Laietana in the Ribera area, is more attractive than the cathedral. It is uncluttered, high and empty. This is both thanks to the anarchists who burned its contents in 1936 and to its origins in the medieval city's seafaring parish. It never had the sumptuous side-chapels of the cathedral. Its majesty resides in its brick.

Though Santa Maria del Mar (St. Mary of the Sea) is sentimentally said to be a people's or fisherman's church, in reality it was raised as the church of imperial trade by the Catalan conquerors of the western Mediterranean. Whereas the cathedral was at the heart of the Old City of the counts of Barcelona, Santa Maria was on the beach and in the quarter of artisans, traders, ship-owners, sailors and fishermen. All the local guilds were taxed for its construction, including porters and apprentices, many of whom are represented on its pillars and walls: this has given it its reputation as a people's church.

Started in 1329, it was finished by the end of the century. This demonstrates the extent of the wealth flowing into Barcelona at that time from its overseas possessions and makes it the only pure-Gothic church in all Catalonia. It was built in one period, in one style. It is famous for its bareness and its huge interior space, with the supports reduced to a minimum. Unlike French Gothic, but like the Barcelona cathedral, it has little light.

In the last generation, the Born, as this area is called after the cast-iron market still standing, has changed from the slum it had been for centuries to the Old City's most up-market area of trendy bars and newly reformed, expensive apartments, replacing the local shops and cold-water flats. The price of an apartment has risen five-fold in just the last decade.

From the thirteenth to the seventeenth century the Plaça del Born, between the market and Santa Maria, was the focus of all festivals and markets: tournaments, carnivals, ceramic or silversmiths' markets. No. 17 is the only surviving house from that epoch, though the arches giving onto the side-streets conserve a medieval air, as do some of the windows and porches of neighbouring streets, the Carrer Rec in particular. Now all this is the perfect setting for the fashionable bars, where tourists and the incoming wealthy can lounge and cause noise for other residents.

The City Council exalts the Born as showing how a run-down area can be regenerated. This process happens all the time in all the cities of the world: areas come up, others go down. The old residents, the poor, are displaced to new slums. The Council sees the Born, on one side of the Old City, as the way the Raval, on the other side, can go. As urban renewal seen narrowly, the Born works. Tourists wander narrow, well-preserved streets with houses reformed rather than knocked down and rebuilt from scratch. The predominance, however, of high-priced bars, galleries, clothes boutiques and antique shops supports the views of Barcelona's critics that the city has become a shop-window, at the service of the tourist industry, not of its residents. The city's main attraction was its mix of local and cosmopolitan, of sumptuous squares like Sant Jaume beside malodorous alleys like Roca. In an operation favouring the building speculators, the Born's inhabitants are being driven out for the sake of tourists—a process that makes it less attractive to tourists.

Unplanned suburbia

Chapter Fourteen
Mass Migration and Mass Tourism: Lloret

Contested Spaces

Visitors stay in city centres and see the sites. This is why guidebooks are full of churches. People who never step into a church in their home town spend a holiday gazing at saints' statues and high roofs. Most visitors to Barcelona stay in or near the Old City and only emerge from it on one of the two tourist buses or for quick raids on the Park Güell or the Sagrada Família.

The majority of Catalonia's eight million inhabitants live in the out-lying suburbs of Barcelona and its satellite towns. Barcelona is one of the most densely populated cities in Europe. Its surrounding cities, such as L'Hospitalet, are even more crowded. In Spanish cities people live in apartments on top of each other, which gives the streets the feel of bustle, noise and "life" that those who dwell in the straggling and often empty cities of England or the United States find so attractive.

The first impression on leaving the subway at Vilapicina on the blue no. 5 line (subway lines are coloured and numbered) is bleak. Ten-storey blocks of flats line a four-lane road with traffic hurtling along both ways. Vilapicina is in Barcelona's District of Nou barris (Nine Quarters), an area of over 200,000 inhabitants. It was developed in the 1950s and 1960s to house some of the million and a half immigrants who poured into Catalonia from other parts of Spain, mainly the South, in the years of hunger after the Civil War.

A walk along this street, the Passeig de Fabra i Puig, comes to a sudden village-like interruption in the blocks of flats: an old church, a low-rise row of shops and a mansion converted into a community centre. Next to this area stands the Virrei Amat market, one of the food markets found all over the city. Beside the market lies the Virrei Amat Square, a big traffic intersection. Behind the square an entire block has been demolished and a park with fountains and shade created, opening up views and giving space to sit and stroll. This sort of development, attractively increasing public space, is one of the reasons the Socialist Party, in coalition with other forces, has maintained power in Barcelona since the first democratic elections after Franco in 1979.

Yet such improvements as the urban park at Virrei Amat should not be attributed to the kind hearts of the socialists. Space in cities is contested. Barcelona had an extremely strong network of residents' associations that arose in the late 1960s as part of the general struggle against the dictatorship. They fought tenaciously over space: was it to be publicly or privately owned? The network of community centres and many of the city's parks are the result of the residents' associations mobilizing. To conserve its votes the Council has had to construct such public, open space.

City of Noise

The Passeig de Fabra i Puig continues on the further side of Virrei Amat as a five-lane one-way street filtering traffic in from the Meridiana, the main avenue in and out to France. The traffic reminds us that Spain is the noisiest country in Europe, and said to be after Japan the second noisiest country in the world. A major culprit is the Council, whose trucks empty the rubbish containers in the street during the night, in some areas passing as late as 4 am. Some years ago this was worse, as the containers were made of metal. But even now, the lorry lifting the plastic containers, turning them upside down and shaking out every bit of sticky rubbish, makes a racket that awakes any newcomer to the city in a cold sweat.

Other Council employees, the municipal police, are part of this pro-noise culture and do nothing as souped-up motorbikes roar along at all hours of day or night. Bus-drivers do not turn off their engines at the end of a run. Drivers press their horns as an expression of frustration. Everyone shouts: what else can you do to make yourself heard? And deafness is common, so you have to shout more, though I have been unable to find figures comparing deafness indices in different countries.

Fabra i Puig is at its best in the evening, with its broad pavements packed. People come down from their flats into the streets in almost any month of the year and stroll: a consequence of migration to the city bringing village habits, the dinginess and smallness of many flats, and a certain working-class solidarity. People move comfortably in groups and crowds, a phenomenon which has its negative counterpart in conformism and fear of standing out. The bars, cafés and public benches are full, and gaggles of chatting people block the street. There is no automatic awareness of others, no instinct to move out of the way when someone approaches. You have to ask (shout, if they're deaf or really engrossed in the expression of self that often passes for conversation). If you do, people are almost invariably courteous and move.

On Friday or Saturday evenings these broad pavements are filled with people at leisure. Working-hours are long in Spain, wages low. A postal worker, for example, takes home in 2007 about 1,100 euros (US$1,400) net a month. So leisure hours are lived intensely: cafés and tables on café terraces are full. Family groups are common: elderly parents often live with their children as there are few welfare state provisions in Spain. Children with bikes or playing football hurtle through the crowds, as do the waiters with trays heading for the terraces. The scene is rowdy, riotous and friendly.

In Fabra i Puig there is a wide range of shops serving the whole of Nou barris, so that it is possible to buy anything in the area without having to "go down to Barcelona," as people often say. Shops usually shut from 2 pm to 5 pm, but then stay open till 8 or 9 pm. These are terrible hours to work, but it means that the streets are alive late: none of the deathly quiet of British provincial shopping streets after 5.30 pm.

If noise is one great social problem in Catalonia, car-driving is another. Car ownership has soared in the last thirty years and has reached unfeasible levels. This leads to double-parking, parking on zebra-crossings, on pavements. Two-lane roads are inevitably reduced to one, as people park illegally for errands or just to take a drink. Contamination is high and crouches poisonously over the city for days until the wind bears it away. Noise and cars come together in the frequent traffic jams, when grown adults press the heel of a hand on their horns with no thought for the pedestrian passing and, obviously, no effect on the traffic jam.

The fact that most people live on top of each other in flats also means that it is impossible to park your car in front of your house, which leads to every new block having an underground car-park. This is not always practicable close to the coast and in some areas their flooding is regular. In Tarragona car ownership has led to a curious situation in which underground parking lots measuring some fifty square feet sold for as much as 24,000 euros in 2006. The high price of parking here is in part because extensive Roman remains in the city's sub-soil have impeded subterranean construction. In cities with little surface area bicycles could be the answer. Here, though, you have to be daring to cycle in dense, aggressive traffic, even if cycle lanes are on the increase. Cycling is not part of the driving culture, although motorbikes (*motos*) are.

Twenty years ago, Alastair Boyd went driving round Catalonia to research his thorough *The Essence of Catalonia*. It would not be advisable today, as Catalonia is the region of Europe with most fatal accidents on its roads. Perfectly sensible people in other walks of life become demons behind the wheel. There are various theories as to why this should be so: love of motor-sports is one. Car and bike racing are enormously popular; the Montmeló track near Barcelona draws huge crowds to its Formula One Grand Prix. Catalans like Alex Crivillé and Dani Pedrosa are world motorbike champions who come from a long tradition of bike-riding. When Barcelona Football Club returned from El Prat airport after winning the 2006 league title, it was thought quite normal that 300 motorcyclists should accompany the team coach. With a quarter of a million, Barcelona has more motorbikes registered than any European city except Rome. At red traffic lights they weave through traffic to position themselves on the grid (also known as the pedestrian crossing-place) in front of the cars.

Catalonia also has the highest cocaine consumption in Europe. Attitudes to drink/drug-driving are relaxed. Or maybe the real reason for high accident rates is the one favoured by James G. Ballard in his novel *Crash*: driving riskily at high speeds is sexually thrilling. If you add in the number of *moto* riders who think it cool to ride around with their helmet strap undone (the majority) and one foot trailing the ground, it is surprising there are so few broken heads and legs.

This is an increasingly stressed society at many levels: from schoolchildren facing a future without stable jobs or the prospect of buying a flat to executives working long hours. Alcoholism is high (EU figures: second in Europe), disguised by the infrequency of drunkenness and nourished by the habit of drinking through the day. Catalonia's education system is in deep crisis, trailing the rest of Europe in its 34 per cent school failure rate. The two languages in use is also a pressure. The greatest pressure, though, may lie buried; compared with Britain or the United States, Spain is a traumatized society, with no-one who does not know of somebody in their family killed in the Civil War, imprisoned under Franco or who spent years in exile. Add to this the pressure of widespread anti-Catalanism in Spain, exacerbated in recent years by the row over Catalonia's new Autonomy Statute, and the *seny*, the calm that Catalans pride themselves on, flares up in rage on the roads.

Near Vilapicina subway station lies the area of Turó de la Peira. On streets curving round the *turó* (hill) are some of the poorest apartment blocks in Barcelona. Many flats measure no more than ninety square feet. They have no balconies and some have no outside windows, but give onto inner wells where kitchen and bathroom smells mingle, linger and rise gently to the roofs.

Lack of housing drove many 1950s migrants into shantytowns on the Montjuïc hill, the Carmel hill and on the beach of Somorrostro, now the Forum site. The city authorities' solution to the housing problem was to give free rein to speculation. Fortunes were made by builders who bought agricultural land on the city outskirts and threw up blocks without sewage, electricity, services or communications. The best interpreter of modern Barcelona, Manuel Vázquez Montalbán, summarized this process soberly in his anti-Olympic *Barcelonas* (1991): "The architecture which emerged was lacklustre and profoundly conservative, and construction firms used materials of the poorest quality." The same author, his anger released by fiction, put it more sarcastically in his novel *Southern Seas* (1979): "ugly poverty prefabricated by prefabricated speculators prefabricating quarters of prefabs."

The tenements on Turó de la Peira date from this period. Here a block collapsed in 1991 due to weakness in the concrete beams from mixing the concrete too cheaply. One person was killed. In 2006 the overhaul of all the tenements was still not complete—an example of how shop-window projects like the Olympic redevelopment of the entire waterfront can be finished incredibly quickly, while the poor decay on the city's outlying hills. Now, it is the new poor, immigrants from South America, who are taking over these flats.

Only 500 yards from Turó de la Peira, but inhabiting another world, is Horta. In the nineteenth century there were a number of villages scattered across the plain, which were incorporated into Barcelona as the city spread from the Old City after the walls came down. The most prominent of these is Gràcia, a town of 60,000 people when it was joined to Barcelona in 1897. A place with a long radical tradition, Gràcia is still today a bohemian, alternative area, the Greenwich Village of Barcelona, with a network of interlacing squares. Horta, as its name indicates, was the market garden of Barcelona. The old village that it was is still present in the low-rise housing in its centre and the narrow streets, many of them pedestrianized.

The old centre of Horta, along with the other former village centres within Barcelona, Clot (meaning "Dell"), Sarrià, Sant Andreu, Gràcia and Sants, has been partially conserved by the City Council. Council policy is to develop high-rise blocks while conserving and prettifying selected older areas. The relatively low-rise housing, the inner gardens, the neighbourhood shops just about clinging on against the new supermarkets, make such areas attractive islands among the non-stop construction of high-rise housing. Horta, too, has *modernista*-influenced houses, often summer chalets for a new middle class a century ago, and lies close to the Collserola hills, once the outer ring-road has been negotiated. As noted in the chapter on Verdaguer, Collserola is a marvel for Barcelona, a wilder Central Park or Hampstead Heath.

In Horta one can clearly see the disorganized, unplanned way in which Barcelona has developed. A roof-top view shows blocks of all different heights, facing different ways, in different styles and interspersed with low houses. It is common to see the sides of an apartment block left in temporarily finished bare brick or corrugated iron, hanging like a threat over the tiny house and garden beside it. Such unfinished bare walls may last for thirty years. Commonly, too, home-made constructions are tacked on top of blocks or alongside houses. Such chaos has created many nooks and crannies. Gardens flower on flat roofs, in the interstices of apartment blocks facing different ways, or on tiny balconies. Roofs are often covered with palms, flowers, or even vegetable gardens.

Though influential politicians like London's Mayor Ken Livingstone and architects like Lord Richard Rogers praise Barcelona's development, this is not sustainable development. "Sustainable" is a word appropriated for many uses. Rogers talks of Barcelona as a "city for the twenty-first century", but it cannot go on in the same way. Barcelona's consumption of resources and production of pollution means that its development is as unsustainable as any other major city's. Its traffic is dense and aggressive, noise is intolerable, air pollution is high, there is no decent housing or jobs for the young. Barcelona shares these problems with most cities, but few dare to claim that their city is sustainable, as Barcelona's rulers do.

Package Holidays and the Changing Costa Brava

While most people in Catalonia live in the outer suburbs of Barcelona, most tourists come to the Costa Brava. This is not the landscape that visitors would have seen a hundred, or even fifty, years ago. The mountains that fed the imagination of Verdaguer and the rugged coast that Dalí loved have been largely destroyed. In *Voices of the Old Sea*, Norman Lewis wrote of fishing on the Costa Brava, where he lived in the 1940s:

> Past every headland the view opened on a new adventure of riven cliffs and pinnacles, of caves sucking at the water, of rock strate twisted and kneaded like old-fashioned toffee... the shallows were of such transparency that the weeds under us showed through, like the fronds, the fanned-out petals and the plumes of a William Morris design.

His overwritten book portrayed an ancient fishing community, still largely outside the market economy but just on the point of changing radically. Chapter Two touched on this fall from the innocence of virgin sand that James G. Ballard experienced. When Ballard's wife Miriam died suddenly on the Costa Brava in the early 1960s, he already saw the coast "through a dream more lurid than any of Dalí's paintings, a vision of the world's end seen in terms of polluted sand, the stench of sun-oil and terraces of over-exposed flesh."

The fishermen of Norman Lewis have long stopped "listening to the voices of the old sea." The lucky ones sold their whitewashed sea-front shacks to developers. Now the Costa Brava is a string of concrete-covered package holiday resorts: Blanes, Lloret, Tossa, Sant Feliu, Platja d'Aro, Calella... There is, of course, no such thing as an unspoiled fishing village nowadays. How could there be? The very notion is a nostalgic dream evoking a past that never was (except for the rich and foreigners like Lewis or Ballard), for these coastal villages were poverty-stricken.

Since the tourist boom began in the late 1950s, Catalonia's coast, with a few exceptions such as remote, un-pretty Portbou or wealthy Sitges and Cadaqués, where many of the people who made their money from plundering the rest of the coastline have their homes, has been systematically ruined. The construction industry, intimately linked to tourism, has been the motor of Catalonia's development.

The symbol of Catalonia should be the crane. In a 2006 newspaper photograph of developments round Barcelona's Plaça Cerdà, I counted twenty-four cranes. From the roof of the apartment block in Horta where I live, eight cranes rise above the low-rise housing. They are curiously like the huge bird of the same name, standing on one leg, with their long beaks dipping over the landscape. The ecologist-novelist Toni Sala calls them giant crosses in cemeteries, marking where the earth has been buried under concrete.

Spain's ubiquitous construction industry has the highest proportion of fatal accidents of any industry in Western Europe. This is a consequence of years of dictatorship and the absence of a reforming social-democratic party. There has been no inspectorate, obliged by strong unions, to insist that safety measures are taken on building sites. Despite the magnificent multi-coloured notice boards listing all the excellent legislation that one sees on each site, workers habitually work at height without railings, helmets or safety nets. If a pavement is cut, very often there is no alternative route for pedestrians: they have to walk in the road.

This situation is exacerbated by the employment of new immigrants from Africa, Eastern Europe or America, often without papers and therefore without rights. Horta provides a cameo of life in Catalonia today. Many lead peaceful lives in pretty houses with gardens and on quiet café terraces in squares shaded by plane trees, while male immigrants work in the heat under dangerous conditions on a construction site nearby, and women immigrants scrub the hallways of apartment blocks or look after the old.

The first package holidays in the sun were marketed in the 1960s. Lloret de Mar and Benidorm rapidly became household names in the United Kingdom. The post-war boom meant that there was a layer of middle- and working-class people who could for the first time contemplate the possibility of a continental holiday, previously the preserve of

Monument to the Woman of the Sea, Lloret de Mar

the rich. Flights were not cheap, but the package was, for food, drink and hotel prices in Spain were rock-bottom. Despite restrictions—for much of the 1960s, £50—on the amount of money a British person could take out of the country, the money could stretch to a fortnight of bars and restaurants on the Costa Brava or Málaga's Costa del Sol. Nowadays the flights are so cheap that some people fly Ryanair from London to Girona airport on a two-hour turnaround just to buy tobacco and alcohol at the airport shops.

In the mid-1960s women wearing bikinis began to appear on the covers of tourist brochures, thus setting into place the image of the Spanish package holiday in its vulgar splendour: cheap, beach, sun, alcohol and sex. This was "Blackpool in the sun", and it was a massive step forward for millions of people to have (almost) guaranteed sun on their holidays.

Lloret

Lloret de Mar became synonymous in following decades with a holiday of discos till dawn, sleeping it off on the beach and starting again. The image of the British "lobster" in shorts, straw hat and sunburned torso entered the Spanish popular imagination. Dehydration and serious burns were common problems in local casualty departments. One wonders where the sex fitted in if the holiday-makers were drunk, asleep or in hospital.

Stories of loutish behaviour became common in the Spanish press: urinating from balconies, all-night noise, early-morning brawls, smashing up bars and urban furniture. Catalans, whose 1950s view of the British was of courteous, quiet people looking at monuments or walking in the country, now revised their mental images to include loud-mouthed drunks. The British media regularly featured horror stories of the bad behaviour of working-class youths, who were encouraged by tour companies' advertising to behave in a certain way. The Spanish could not understand the apparent alcohol fixation of the British working class. They did not know about its extraordinarily high price in the UK, the restrictive opening hours of pubs, nor that holiday-makers were escaping from routine or from the reproving eyes of their own communities and families. All surveys and figures show, in fact, that alcoholism is more prevalent in Spain than in the UK. Mass drunkenness, though, was something new on Spanish streets.

Another piece of mutual incomprehension concerned *suecas*, or Swedish girls. The foreign women who wore bikinis on the Costa Brava beaches in the 1960s were considered little different from prostitutes by older generations of men who had suffered decades of sexual repression, and as easy pickings by young Spaniards. All of them, of whatever nationality, became known as *suecas*—the first package-holidaymakers, as Sweden was the wealthiest country in Europe as well as the coldest. In his brilliant book about Mallorca, *Tuning up at Dawn*, Tomás Graves believes that in the 1960s:

> The Northern Female was drawn by the Legend of the Latin Lover. All the girls' comics and magazines lying around the common room at my English boarding school—*Jackie, Bunty, Mandy, Petticoat*—seemed to be in the pay of the Spanish Tourist Office because the holiday romances that filled their pages always involved a dishy, dark, square-jawed heart-throb called Manuel or Antonio.

Whereas in Britain mothers warned against the dangers of the love-em-and-leave-em Latin Lover, Graves came to see the local Mallorcan youngsters as "unwitting victims of the flocks of Valkyries that flew South every summer to prey on them." Maybe it was not so much mutual incomprehension as mutual satisfaction.

In one basic respect the Spanish were not, and are not, satisfied by the tourist boom. Someone wanting a job in Lloret can certainly find one, but hours are long, work is seasonal, pay is rock-bottom and Spanish employment law means that you can be sacked at the drop of a hat. The tourism industry on the Costa Brava has always been based on low wages and massive exploitation: how else could holidays be so cheap? Its corollary was the enrichment of a few builders and hotel owners.

The idea of Lloret, Torremolinos and Benidorm was a good one: put all the holidaymakers in one place to enjoy a disco-beach holiday. Today, in places such as the Piccadilly pub on the front at Lloret, men in shorts can while away the afternoon drinking and watching English football on TV, before strolling down to the beach or along the front. Yet it would be wrong to assume that tourists want nothing more than the Piccadilly Pub and are uninterested in Spanish, or Catalan, culture. Resorts like Lloret have contributed greatly to making British society less insular and more sophisticated. The coaches organized for day-trips to Figueres for the Dalí Museum or to Barcelona to see Gaudí are frequent and full. The view of Spanish culture presented is a curious one, though: the shops of Lloret are stacked with wide-brimmed Mexican hats, Che Guevara T-shirts, extremely cheap bottles of sangria and whisky, children's flamenco dresses or beach towels in the gaudy red and yellow of the Spanish flag with a black bull charging out of the middle.

If the above is an accumulation of distortions of Spanish culture, Catalan culture itself hardly gets a look in. One can have a hilarious (or painful) time trying to speak Catalan in Lloret: none of the shops expects you to, and many of the workers are as foreign as the visitors. Nor can you find Catalan food among the Italian, Asian and English cuisine. None of this is the fault of the tourists, many of whom earnestly attempt to find out about local culture. There is a mutual non-meeting, whereby the clichéd vision of Spanish culture that the tour companies, shopkeepers and local authorities believe that tourists want is served up to them.

At its peak, around 1990, Lloret (a town of 10,000 inhabitants) had 120,000 visitors a week throughout the summer in its 200 hotels. Four hundred coaches from northern Europe arrived every Saturday. Its holidays were the cheapest on the market and this led to many of the abuses that damaged its reputation. Hotels had paper-thin walls and were often a long walk across the main road to the beach; over-booking was common, noise was constant, the junk-food was... junk.

But there is change at Lloret. Club 18-30, one of the most notorious sex-profiteering travel companies, started in 1965 and is still going strong. But it has now withdrawn from Lloret in favour of Mallorca, alleging that Lloret is not "sophisticated" enough. The question, though, was not sophistication, but the Town Council's awareness that the boom was ending. Hotels thrown up in the 1960s were looking too rough even for the cheap package by the 1990s. In August 2003, after drunken brawling had smashed up much of the front, the Councillor for Tourism Anna Gallart told the press: "Some tour operators sell Lloret de Mar as a paradise for alcohol, drugs and sex. We want to put an end to that." The Council, of course, had encouraged just this image for decades. Now Gallart was expressing the realization of hoteliers and the commerce-aware Council that Lloret had to change its image or die. And in Lloret there are no other jobs but in tourism.

Drinking beer in Lloret

I visited Lloret in 2006, prepared to write a chapter about the exploitation of tourists and locals and satirical paragraphs about drunken British youth, only to find a town full of pensioners on holiday. Lloret has cleaned up its act. In the summer season many of the above problems may still apply, but in May or the winter months especially, this is no bad place for a holiday.

The front at Lloret and the old town are pretty. The Town Hall, in a square at the south of the front, is a particularly beautiful building, with a Catalan cast-iron open bell tower, where one bell hangs above the other. From the cliff by the Town Hall, the *Monument to the Woman of the Sea* stares out across the Mediterranean in honour of the women who put out to sea or waited for men out fishing or gone to the Americas. Her feet and calves are big and muscular: this is a working woman.

There is only one extremely high-rise building on the front, to the north of the long, slightly curving, shale beach. The rest are seven-storey blocks in varied styles, fronted by wide pavements and palms. This main beach is enclosed by rocky headlands and paths along the cliffs. The

Costa Brava has a wild, spectacularly beautiful shoreline that stretches from Blanes, just south of Lloret, to the French border, with the exception of the marshy fluvial plain round the Bay of Roses, which divides the Costa Brava in two. Little coves with sheer paths winding down the cliffs, and the round-crowned Mediterranean pine seemingly growing out of the rocks right by the edge of transparent water, can still be found along the coast. Many coves are only accessible by boat or by cliff paths more suited to goats than holiday trippers. As much of the coast is too steep to build on, it has not suffered the ribbon skyscraper development of the other Spanish Mediterranean *costas*. Lloret and its neighbours Tossa and Blanes are the sea-towns of the county known as *La Selva*, the jungle. The name comes from the thick forest covering the coastal hills: still today, despite development and forest fires, nearly forty per cent of *La Selva* is forested with oak, cork, beech and chestnut trees. It is similar to the thick vegetation around the house where Verdaguer died in Collserola and can be found in ranges all along the coast, where mountain rains meet coastal heat.

On the walk out of Lloret along the cliff path north, the trees, mostly pines, cling to the rocks and, clinging, force their roots into crevices and crack the rocks. Jasmine and bougainvillea rampage through cliff-top gardens, filling the ground and air with foliage, flowers and perfume. With waves splashing on the jagged rocks, gulls watching from the streaked black cliffs and the cormorants diving, it is hard to believe you are sandwiched between two of the biggest, most down-market resorts on the Mediterranean.

If walking up and down cliffs is too strenuous, from Lloret beach there are boats—including a glass-bottomed one—that motor along the coast to Tossa or Blanes and show the kind of unspoiled, inaccessible sandy coves and jagged cliffs that Norman Lewis discovered in his fishing-boat.

As the *Monument to the Woman of the Sea* has intimated, Lloret's history was bound up with the emigration from poverty to America. There are many museums to the sea in Catalonia's coastal towns, such as the Maritime Museum in the Drassanes at Barcelona or the Fishing Museum at Palamós. Lloret has Catalonia's main museum to the *indianos*, those who sought their fortune in Latin America and the Caribbean, in a *modernista* house with its original furniture (Centre

Cultural Verdaguer). We know about those who returned rich. They founded capitalist dynasties like the Güell family or built ostentatious houses in their home villages with a tall palm in the garden to demonstrate the source of their new wealth. There are several of these in Lloret itself and in *La Selva's* inland towns such as Santa Coloma or Caldes de Malavella. Lloret has a unique plaque, a poignant tribute on the north of the front to the people of Lloret who "emigrated to America to make their fortune and were not lucky."

At Torremolinos and Benidorm it is hard to see under the concrete the old *costa* that existed before the tourist boom. The charm of Lloret is that this old Costa Brava can still be perceived. It is present in the cliff walks or the fantasy 1930s castle on Lloret's north headland, with its path across the rocks to a tiny jetty. When the makers of the film *Capote* were looking for a site for the villa where Truman Capote wrote part of *In Cold Blood* in the early 1960s, they used Dr. Faust's Mar i murtra (Sea and Myrtle) garden at Blanes. Faust's 1920s forty-acre cliff-top botanical garden is only half-a-dozen miles south of Lloret. The wealthy Costa Brava of before the boom can still be inhaled there.

In Catalonia three-quarters of the population live within fifteen miles of the coast. In the last 25 years there has been more building here than in the previous 2,000 years. Whatever one's views on mass tourism at resorts like Lloret, it is clear that the profit-driven (not need-driven: if it was need-driven, cheap apartments for immigrants and young people would be built) construction boom cannot be sustained, especially in a country with a deficit of water. The problem is not one or five Llorets, but of the whole buildable coast becoming covered by concrete. In 2005, it was reported by Spain's Sustainability Observatory, there was more construction in Spain than in France, Germany and the UK combined. One-third of the entire Spanish Mediterranean coastline is now under concrete. In response to this report, the melancholy and portly Joaquim Nadal, the same no. 2 in the Generalitat who went to Greece to apologize for Roger de Flor, affirmed depressingly that there were plans for 100,000 more houses and that "we have not reached saturation."

There will not be any more water. And the water that there is will pour dangerously off the slopes as the forests behind Lloret are cleared, taking the topsoil with it.

The hill-top Cloister of the Seu at Lleida

Chapter Fifteen

Plain and River: Lleida and the Ebro

City of the Plain

Catalonia is not just *mar i muntanya*, the humid coast and the hills that rise rapidly from the shoreline. It also has an inland coastal plain where temperatures dip to -10° in winter and regularly reach a dry 40° in summer.

Thirty miles up the River Segre from where it joins the Ebro stands the city of Lleida, the capital of Catalonia's inland province. Lleida's rows of twelve-storey apartment blocks bordering the Segre are not encouraging as a first view. These outskirts are little different from those of most Spanish cities. In Lleida, though, high-rise development makes sense, as it means that less of the plain's valuable agricultural land is gobbled up by housing. Pear, peach and apple orchards spread across the Plain of Urgell all around Lleida. The apples are densely farmed in espalier style, their branches stretched out along the wire, so that each tree is slim and flattened. They look like rows of frightened ghosts, arms raised and outstretched so that every leaf and fruit catches the sun. Space is maximized and picking the apples from the alleys between the wires is easy. The dusty plain is turned to orchards by the freezing waters of the Canal d'Urgell, channelling Pyrenean melt-water off the Segre. In spring the mixed blossom is as fragrant as in the Garden of Eden before the fall.

On this plain, the greatest extension of flat land in Catalonia, the rock on which the old cathedral of Lleida is built can be seen from miles around. Once inside the ring of high-rise buildings, Lleida has its charm. The central area of this small city (c. 110,000 population) mixes old and new, rich and poor, in a more intense and intimate way than anywhere else in the country. At the top of the Carrer Cavallers the houses (the typical older four- or five-storey apartment blocks of Spain) have been falling apart for decades. Some are being done up, several have actually fallen down, most are now inhabited by old people and by new immigrants. Africans hang out on the streets: they were drawn to Lleida by the intensive seasonal fruit-picking. Most come and go, but some find work or hope to and stay.

Toward the bottom of this street dropping attractively down the hill the shops change: a block from the river, Carrer Cavallers crosses the Carrer Major ('Main Street'). This part of Main Street is full of clothes boutiques, banks, fashion shops and tourist agencies. Within two blocks, a 90 per cent black population has given way to 90 per cent white; the crumbling houses are replaced by restorations with pretty roof-gardens and varnished bare beams. Like Reus, Lleida is wealthy because of the number of farmers with money who shop in town.

To the right of this junction of Cavallers and Major is the new cathedral. With his customary aggressive Anglicism, Richard Ford wrote that the priests were too fat and lazy to climb to the old cathedral on the hill, so had a new one built down by the river. To the left, along the Carrer Major, is the Plaça de la Paeria, with the Town Hall restored to its medieval glory and arcades round the very thin, elongated square.

The stone-floored and -roofed arcades of the Plaça de la Paeria are cool in summer. If you go round the block, you emerge onto the riverfront. The water is dull and distant, running in a concrete channel between mown grass. High-rise buildings again dominate the riverfront on both sides, but in front of this bit of the old city there are several ornate *modernista* houses. Every town in Catalonia has them.

The Plaça de la Paeria connects with the Plaça de Sant Joan, as huge and modern as the Plaça de la Paeria is tiny and medieval. Though the remodelling of this square in 1982 to the design of the Basque urbanist Peña Ganchegui was controversial, to an outsider visiting the city twenty years later, the Plaça de Sant Joan is Catalonia's finest modern square. It is constructed on two main levels, with a long bridge along one side enclosing the remains of an ancient church. On walking up the steps onto the bridge, the tower of the old cathedral, or Seu vella, rises into view on the hill above the square. In front of this causeway stands a lighthouse, like the ones that adorn the Plaça de l'Espanya Industrial in Sants, Barcelona. A great circular ring of steps, with on top a stage and another bridge running out of the square, protrudes from the hill side of the square. Unmistakably modern and bold, the multi-level square also has the feel of a medieval theatre or forum, with the neo-Gothic nineteenth-century Church of St. Joan (John) as backdrop. The houses round the square continue this mix of ancient, nineteenth-century and very modern.

The Seu, Lleida's glory on top of the hill, is a deconsecrated building, which served as stables from the time of the military occupation of the city by the Bourbons in 1707 until as recently as 1947. The Spanish monarchs destroyed much of the city on the hill round the Seu when building their castle beside it. This hated castle of occupation was severely damaged in both 1812, when Napoleon's Marshal Suchet massacred his way through Catalonia, and 1936. It is gone now, like its equivalent, the Ciutadella in Barcelona.

Lleida's civic authorities have been on the losing side in too many wars. In the Punic Wars they supported the Carthaginians against the Romans, who named it Ilerda. They supported Pompey against Caesar; Catalonia against Spain in the War of the Spanish Succession; the popular movement against Napoleon in 1810-14; the Republic against Franco. They were mostly good causes, but defeats have left this huge, empty building surrounded by waste ground on top of a sun-baked rock.

The experts explain that, like Tarragona's cathedral, Lleida's Seu vella is an outstanding example of the transition between Romanesque and Gothic. In the thirteenth century, Gothic appeared with its new ideas and shapes, but did not replace the old traditions all at once. Lleida's thick Romanesque pillars and Gothic vaults show clearly this combination of styles. For a non-expert visitor, its more direct fascination lies in its stark desolation, with no trappings of religion left.

The cloister with a giant laurel tree in the middle is built on the edge of the cliff. Its five great open windows on the south side make the cloister a place not like the closed garden of Poblet, or the cluttered bustle of Barcelona, but a bare, windswept eerie. It is possible to step higher, up the 238 steps of the bell-tower's banister-less, corkscrew stair. The view from the roof, with pigeons cooing and the bells booming every quarter hour beneath, shows miles of irrigated orchards and the mottled red roofs of the old city below.

Mequinensa: Drowned Town

The Urgell plain, surveyed in its majesty from the bell-tower of the Seu de Lleida, does not have the rolling hills of the Empordà. Flatness and intensive agriculture make it an unattractive landscape, but the frequent villages—wealth leads to towns closer together—are often pretty, though dusty in summer. Ringing the plain are bigger towns with medieval squares, churches, walls and arcades. Bellpuig is one and Agramunt has a famous sculpted Romanesque door to its church. Les Borges Blanques is an olive oil town and the village of Arbeca gives its name to the small, dark olive characteristic of the area, the *arbequina*. Tàrrega is site of Catalonia's great September theatre festival. And Cervera was where the Bourbons relocated the university from Barcelona's Ramblas after 1714, as a sort of students' exile. The first Rector of Cervera made clear the Spanish monarchs' aspirations for Catalan culture by opening his lectures with the famous dictum: "Far from us is the baleful obsession with thinking."

South of Lleida stretch arid steppes of cereal crops and olives, with a rich plant and bird-life. These steppes give way to the Ebro river (or Ebre, in Catalan). The Ebro is born in the Picos de Europa in Asturias, not far from Spain's northern coast giving onto the Bay of Biscay. From there it runs across much of northern Spain through a number of major cities, the biggest of which is Zaragoza, the capital of Aragon.

Catalonia starts a hundred miles downstream from Zaragoza, more or less where the Ebro is joined by the Segre and where the huge Riba-roja dam has drowned the town of Mequinensa. The construction of hydro-electric dams was part of the mid-twentieth-century industrial development of Spain. They are held in less high repute today, as much water evaporates and the natural habitat of the river downstream suffers from the lack of water.

Over the centuries trees were stripped from the hills round Mequinensa for ships and for firewood. Now these eroded hills are undergoing another change, as the micro-climate created by the dam has fertilized intensive cultivation. New trees have arrived: miles of peach groves among pine woods. Above the peaches the bare rock is as twisted and tortured as the stones of Cap de Creus or Portbou. These are the hills that begin the rise to Spain's central plateau. Though Catalonia is greener than most of Spain, the hills on the Catalonia-Aragon border round Mequinensa force on the traveller or resident the sense that the earth is not comfortable, but harsh and rough.

The novelist Jesús Moncada (1941-2005) made of his native Mequinensa and its dam a metaphor for the destiny of Catalonia and the passing of an old way of life, drowned. He wrote three novels and several short-story collections based around Mequinensa. In *The Towpath*, published in English in 1994, one of the maids says: "There are some things in life you can never blot out... They're like the Ebro and the Segre. The water never stops running." But of course, the water did stop running, as the dam waters covered the town, and Nelson, the old barge captain, experienced the bleakness of losing his town and livelihood, and then realized he could no longer remember the drowned town, either.

Moncada's masterpiece tells the general history of Catalonia's twentieth century from the edge, from the *franja* (fringe) rather than from the centre. Right around Catalonia's frontiers, in Aragon, there is a *franja* where people's first language is often Catalan, as is the case in Mequinensa. The peculiar and particular rise and fall of this industrial river town is told in *The Towpath* by no central character, but a mosaic of voices, whose various, sometimes conflicting memories compose its history.

The Towpath contains a socialist consciousness of class and historical change. The impact of events such as the First World War, the coming of the 1931 Republic or the start of the Civil War are explained through anecdotes connected with river commerce through the lignite barges (pulled by mules along the towpath) coming and going to and from Mequinensa. It is a town divided in two, with the coal- and barge-owners on one side and the miners and bargees on the other. Was the death of the town, drowned like unwanted kittens beneath the dam waters, Franco's final vengeance on the "reds" of the 1920s and 1930s? Moncada speculates. If so, it also destroyed the old bourgeoisie, represented by Senyora Carlota, sold out by her children, locked in her mansion and awaiting the deluge. Carlota represents that Catalan bourgeoisie that was delighted to have won the war, but then realized all their murders were in vain: she had lost the peace to a progress she did not like.

The Towpath is a fine novel whose pace speeds up, stagnates and swirls around backwaters like the winding river itself, in an impressive fusion of theme and style. It is both filled with nostalgia for time lost and unsentimental about the total destruction awaiting Mequinensa and its inhabitants. Moreover, Moncada offers us a historical insight into modern Catalonia, told from the periphery and not the more usual tale through the prism of Barcelona. And he expresses magnificently the classic warning of Walter Benjamin: if we lose our history, our memory, we become like Senyora Carlota's callow, money-grabbing children or like the inhabitants in the new town built on the hill, who live in square, brick houses in symmetrical blocks on streets scourged by the wind. Moncada's elegy ends bitterly, with an undercurrent of hope that life flows on:

> The north winds were broader than before and came direct from the Monegros plateau; the straight streets with their rows of identical houses got more of a battering as there were no cul-de-sacs where the winds could swirl around, no maze of alleys where they could blow themselves out... only the youngest inhabitants, the babies, would forget completely; a part of the memories of the rest would hang on like a root beneath the waters of the Segre and the Ebro. They would often hear old words in the new rooms where the furniture still smelt of varnish and in the mists of winter they would catch the raised voices of old crews and the screams of other seagulls.

The dams on the river stopped the river barge traffic: and hydro-electric and nuclear electricity ended the demand for lignite from Mequinensa's mines. Now that the water has stopped flowing, Mequinensa has surprisingly become a rather odd tourist resort. Not just peaches, but beaches surround the dam. Holiday apartments have been built. There are fishing stores in the new town. Introduced black bass and giant carp have colonized the dam waters, gobbling up autochthonous fish. Carp are a good trophy catch, but almost as tasteless as battery chicken. There are camels, their humps and necks poking above the peaches, to ride through the fruit groves; and power-boats roar along the huge lake with its swampy shoreline filled with migrating birds. The Oxford University rowing squad comes each year to train on the calm water. The hill-tops are lined with new long-sailed windmills whirling in silent beauty, as they bring clean energy and make visible the moving air we normally do not see.

Yellow Fog along the Ebro Valley

The lower Ebro, around Mora, was the site of the last and biggest battle of the Spanish Civil War. On one night, 24 July 1938, some

60,000 Republican troops crossed the river in rowing-boats and on pontoon bridges in a last-ditch attempt to defend Catalonia by a counter-attack against Franco's army. They established a considerable bridgehead to the south of the river, but were forced back over the following months. Some 100,000 Republican soldiers were killed (mostly by Franco's vastly superior aviation), wounded or captured. The retreat back across the Ebro in November 1938 represented the end of the Republic's effective military resistance. Barcelona fell two months later and the Civil War ended on Franco's entry into Madrid on 1 April 1939.

The victory of fascism in Spain led to a forty-year dictatorship whose scars, submerged and visible, still affect everyday life. In Catalonia, as in all of Spain, there is not a family unaffected by the war and dictatorship. Until the past few years it has hardly been talked about publicly. The "pact of forgetfulness" of the 1970s transition from dictatorship to democracy meant that many people who had suffered the dictatorship in silence continued to do so.

All around the Terra Alta, or highlands, on the south side of the Ebro valley the scars of the Civil War are still visible. As part of the recovery of historical memory a number of monuments are rising to commemorate the dead. Some 2,000 of these were International Brigaders, including the Lincoln Battalion—the first non-segregated military unit in American history. The Brigades were recruited by communist parties from idealists all over the world to fight fascism in Spain. Some 35,000 came and nearly a third of these died.

The Republican advance in July 1938 reached Corbera. Today this is a prosperous town on the main road from Reus and Falset into Lower Aragon. The tree-lined main street is full of shops selling local wine and olive oil. The drama of Corbera is seen on the hill above this new town, where the ruins of pre-war Corbera have not been knocked down, but left as they were after the battle. The Church of St. Pere still stands, but with great chunks of masonry gouged out by bombs. From old Corbera's hill-top square there is a remarkable view over the rolling valleys of the Serra de Pàndols, a landscape of grapes, forest and small villages: one of them with the beautiful name of Bot, so characteristic a Catalan word spat out with one vowel between two hard consonants. Among the hills, too, lies Horta de Sant Joan, the town where Picasso completed his education. Jorge Reverte, author of a recent popular history, *La Batalla del Ebro*, wrote:

[The Terra Alta] is full of powerful, imposing ranges, with bare stone peaks that make perfect natural look-out points, and hair-raising slopes which the pines cling to with difficulty... Where each range finishes, barely seen valleys open, crossed by numerous escarpments and rivers that sometimes turn into torrents, collecting the waters that the hillsides cannot retain... In summer, the heat dismays the birds and in winter the fog accentuates the devastating cold.

Ruined Corbera and the view of the hills remind us that the Ebro offensive by the Republic was futile. Contravening the most basic military tactics, the Republic conducted a frontal attack on a superior army. This was for political reasons: the Republic was gambling on a spectacular action that would appeal to the Western democracies. But it was a forlorn hope, as the principal Western governments, mainly Britain, had no intention of intervening in Spain or even allowing arms to reach the Republic. Their policy was to appease fascism, as the Munich Pact that same autumn showed. The Republic, at the time of the Ebro offensive in southern Catalonia, had just spent a year suppressing the revolution in Barcelona and dissolving by force the anarchist collectives in Aragon. It had smashed its own militant popular base to try and convince Britain that it was a reliable democracy. War is often lost by politics. The very word *guerrilla* was invented in Spain, due to the country's rugged landscape, but that sort of warfare was never seriously considered.

As the main street of Corbera suggests, this is a land of olives, red wine and olive oil, and has been for two millennia. Just up the road from Corbera is Gandesa, near where the Franco armies situated their headquarters for much of the Battle of the Ebro. Gandesa today hosts the official Museum of the Battle and a huge *modernista* wine vault, designed by Gaudí's associate Cèsar Martinell in 1919.

Outside Gandesa lies a hill, named Cim (Hill) 705 in the argot of war, where a plaque was unveiled in May 2005 to commemorate the ninety British volunteers from the 15th Division of the International Brigade who died in the Battle of the Ebro seventy years earlier. In a moving ceremony four of the last survivors of the International Brigades attended and spoke. The youngest was 89; the oldest, at 92, was Jack Jones, General Secretary in the 1970s of the Transport and General Workers' Union, Britain's largest trade union. Journalist Michael Bunn wrote:

> ... there was an impromptu rendering of the *Internationale*, followed by a minute's silence during which we, the representatives of the present, gazed at these selfless heroes of the past, the surviving representatives of the millions who died in the bloody 20th century to ensure that we in Europe would enjoy lasting peace. Jack Jones' words hung in the air: "Remember the past, but look to the future."

Another of the four volunteers at Hill 705 that day was the Welsh paramedic, Alun Menai Williams (1913-July 2006). In the Battle of the Ebro he had crawled around the battlefields attending to the wounded: "I witnessed most of the carnage from a height of six to 12 inches from ground level—a kind of worm's eye view of the bloody proceedings. I became an expert in the taste and texture of the Spanish earth."

This quote from Williams' autobiography is included in an article (*Catalonia Today*, 12 May 2005) by the British historian, Angela Jackson. She highlights how few of the tens of thousands of books about the Spanish Civil War deal with the experience of the medical units. Researching British volunteer women in the Civil War, she found that several had nursed at the Santa Llúcia cave at La Bisbal de Falset, which was used as an improvised hospital during the battle. She rediscovered the enormous cave, protected by a slab of rock against the constant bombing. She also found out that the people who died in the cave-hospital were buried in a communal grave in the cemetery and that the Town Hall had carefully kept a register of all their names.

In this article Jackson pinpoints a change in Spain and Catalonia in recent years and identifies two key reasons why the truth about the past should be "disinterred". First, she tells the story of two men who discovered where their mother's brother had died only when the list of the dead from the Santa Llúcia cave was published in 2001. They brought their mother to the cemetery to place a plaque: thus an open wound from the Civil War was staunched. Second, she argues: "... by recovering memories of what happened at a local level, we can better understand the terrible tragedy of war—a tragedy for individuals that is often ignored in political and military history books."

Angela Jackson's work in the Terra Alta is very much part of the movement to recover historical memory and tell the truth about the Civil War and what Paul Preston called the "long holocaust of the defeated", the forty post-war years of Franco's dictatorship. This movement has erupted in Spain in the last few years, and means that in Catalonia the monuments to Benjamin and Companys are not now the only antifascist memorials.

The best-known journalist of the Civil War was Ernest Hemingway. From lower down the Ebro, at Tortosa, Hemingway sent dispatches to the North American News Agency when the fascists first reached the river in April 1938. Hemingway has often been criticized for saving his best material for *For Whom the Bell Tolls*, but the dispatches from Tortosa are brilliant. His reports pinpoint how the Republic was bombed to defeat in what Robert Capa called "a war of no non-combatants".

> Above us in the high cloudless sky, fleet after fleet of bombers roared over Tortosa. When they dropped the sudden thunder of their loads, the little city on the Ebro disappeared in a yellow mounting cloud of dust. The dust never settled, as more bombers came, and, finally, it hung like a yellow fog all down the Ebro valley.

In several other Ebro dispatches Hemingway describes the effects of war on the civilian population, as he does in one of the greatest short stories of the twentieth century, first published as a news dispatch, his *Old Man at the Bridge*:

> An old man with steel rimmed spectacles and very dusty clothes sat by the side of the road. There was a pontoon bridge across the river and carts, trucks, and men, women and children were crossing it. The mule-drawn carts staggered up the steep bank from the bridge with soldiers helping push against the spokes of the wheels. The trucks ground up and away heading out of it all and the peasants plodded along in the ankle deep dust. But the old man sat there without moving. He was too tired to go any further.

A Dying Delta

At the mouth of the Ebro, below Tortosa, lies a great triangle whose point pushes out into the sea. In Catalonia the mountains nearly always press down on the Mediterranean, except in the wide wild beaches, lagoons and rice fields of the Ebro Delta. Out on the delta, sea, sky and land seem to merge. The bare rocks of the Serra de Montsià behind shimmer purple in a heat haze and, seemingly far away, underline the flatness of the delta.

Though the Ebro Delta appears an ancient landscape, it is recent. The deposits of soil carried down to the sea are much greater now than in Roman times. The delta was fed by the terrible erosion round Mequinensa after the forested hills were denuded. But if you were to visit in a hundred years, it is very likely to have disappeared. Franco's several dams on the Ebro have meant less soil and water coming down the river, and increasing water demand has since reduced the flow further.

The complex effects of global warming make this delta one of the most vulnerable landscapes in Europe. Reduced rainfall in the last decade is already leading to salinization of some of the rice-fields, with the crop yield dropping. It is calculated that an 18-inch rise in sea level will obliterate the delta. One ecological disaster has already occurred: in the summer of 2003 sea temperature rose to an unprecedented 30°C in the shallow waters of the Alfacs Bay protected by an arm of the delta. The mussels farmed there died. Normally over a million kilos a year are produced, with some 400 people employed. The mussels are taped to ropes and lowered into the water, where they breed, and then the dripping ropes are hauled out on pulleys. The low salinity and high temperature, if not too high, are ideal for them.

Despite its temporary nature, the delta seems ancient because you can still escape into little-spoiled nature and long beaches, making it the last wild expanse of land on the Italian, French or Spanish shores of the Mediterranean. There is a reason for the delta's isolation: until the middle of the twentieth century malaria was endemic. Its landscape is only comparable to the Rhône Delta, the Camargue, but the Ebro Delta is much less commercialized. It is subtly different, too. More to the south than the Camargue, the Ebro Delta has a South American air (Hemingway said "African"), which comes from the width of the river, its banks of matted canes, reeds and rickety, low jetties, and its one-

The white lighthouse of the Punta del Fangar

storey, flat-roofed, mosquito-netted houses. At dusk if you sit out with a lamp lit, the volume of mayfly and mosquitoes hurling themselves against the wall behind the light is tropical. At the long straggling town of Deltebre, right in the middle of the delta, there are three car-ferries, low home-made platforms of planks with railings that loop across the river in a figure of eight. As you chug across on one of these ferries, you are only a couple of feet above the water, and it is easy to imagine you are crossing a branch of the Amazon.

The delta's hardy, sunburned and wind-beaten people speak a rough dialect of Catalan. Rice is a tough business. Though farmers use huge-wheeled special tractors, they are still often up to their knees in water, churning through mud in long waders that protect their legs against leeches. Tough though they are to work, rice fields are impressive to look at, with bare earth in winter, flooded in spring and green with rice in the summer. There is an uneasy balance in the delta between agriculture, the ancient hunting and fishing rights of its inhabitants and growing environmental consciousness. Some people like to eat and shoot the thousands of indigenous and migrating wildfowl on the marshes; others, often outsiders, like to encourage tourists to come and look at live birds.

On the question of maintaining water in the river to stop the progressive entry of salt water into the delta, all parties—locals and incomers, farmers, hunters and birders—agree. The second government of José María Aznar's Partido Popular (2000-2004) made a political blunder when it proposed building a pipeline to transfer Ebro water to the dry south-eastern provinces of Spain. Whereas Murcia and Almeria had tourism with new resorts and golf courses, together with agro-business and intensive agriculture bringing off-season fruit to Northern Europe; the Ebro Delta had much-desired water. The government did not imagine that a poor, rural area like the lower Ebro valley would cause problems, but in 2002 and 2003 a mass movement developed against this transfer of water. The Ebro awoke. There were demonstrations of 400,000 people in Zaragoza, Barcelona and Madrid. The Socialist Party was pushed into opposition to the National Water Plan.

The pipeline would have meant the rapid death of the delta. First, its agriculture would be stopped by the entry of salt water; then the land itself would disappear as still less sediment came down the river. The National Water Plan was halted by the victory of the Socialist Party in the 14 March 2004, elections. The delta will continue to die, but more slowly.

The wide Ebro is deceptively shallow, but enough soil and chemical nutrients are still washed down to make the sea off the mouth of the river alive with fish. Go to the fish auction on the dock at Sant Carles de la Ràpita at 4 or 5 pm, when its fishing fleet—the biggest in Catalonia— comes back from scooping up the shoals in nets.

The auction is still traditional, the fish in open boxes sprinkled with crushed ice on the floor of the long, open sheds. The buyers' vans and trucks are lined up along the quay behind the sheds for the overnight trip to the markets and restaurants of Madrid. The fish are sorted on the boats and dripping wooden boxes of them, some still twitching, are wheeled shining on trolleys into the sheds. Here the auctioneers start high, not low (a "Dutch auction") and drop the price with the speed and joy of a schoolchild who has learned to count backwards. The system is quicker than the bidding upward system, but tougher, for buyers have only one chance to bid. When you signal, the box is yours and that is that. Hesitate a moment and you have lost the boxes you had your eye on. The buyers keep themselves awake on the long night drive back up to Spain's central plain by wondering whether, had they waited a moment longer, they could have bought cheaper.

As you leave the auction sheds, the fishermen and women are repair- ing nets, with the singular stench of diesel oil, rotting fish remains and salt-encrusted nets and ropes drying in the sun. The restaurants at Sant Carles are famous. The well-to-do make the two-hour drive down from Barcelona for weekend lunch. A paella, using delta rice, or a *parrillada* (assorted grilled fish) with a dry chilled Penedès white wine at one of the dockside restaurants, where flashing-tongued lizards ("we have them for the mosquitoes," explains the waiter) dart in and out of the vines cover- ing the whitewashed walls, is not cheap, but is worth the experience.

Or drive out to the horns of the delta to savour the sensation that the land is ending. These tips are long slim promontories of sand that hang back towards the land, like the drooping flowers of a plant whose stem is the river. On the southern promontory, in front of Sant Carles, the salt plant occupies the land bulge at the end of a 100 yard-wide four- mile tongue of land. A blindingly white hill of salt stands beside the pools where shallow sea-water is dried out by the sun and the salt left behind swept up into the hill. They are sea-fields where the sun turns sea-water solid. All along the spit waves crash onto the outside beach while the shallow, fish-filled Alfacs Bay on the land side is still. Fishermen in galoshes make a living scooping out fish from the bay with nets. Even in this Eden, alongside the claw-marks of gulls, oil streaks the sand like black veins, reminding us there is no escape from the modern world.

On the northern spit, dunes have formed, with hardy sand birds hopping among the coarse marram grass. Beyond the dunes stands the white lighthouse of the Punta del Fangar, at the end of such an expanse of sand that mirages of lakes appear. It is hard to be sure whether they are mirages or not, as the whole delta is dotted with lagoons.

The delta has changed enormously in the past twenty years. One of the main changes has been its development as a protected natural park and a place to watch birds. On the main lagoons, raised wooden hides have been built. All year round there are numerous birds, but in October the lagoons and fields are filled with migrants. Some 300 species are counted here, sixty per cent of Europe's total species. Herons, egrets, ducks, coots, gulls, grebes and cormorants (monopolizing any wooden posts) are as common as sparrows in a suburban garden. So are pink flamingos, whose long legs step daintily through the mud. For bird-watchers there are rarer sightings, too: an array of birds of prey or ibis, but for the lay viewer the sheer quantity of diverse sizes and shapes of waterfowl covering the lagoons is impressive. Everywhere herons lurk.

Here on the southern edge of Catalonia the wind batters you again, as in the north. Despite the delta's slow death, both rice-farmers and ecologists can derive some pleasure from the doomed beach development by the river mouth at Riumar. The greatest efforts of speculators and, now, the unfortunate proprietors have failed to stop the sand, which is swept by the wind month after month over the garden walls and up against the walls of the villas.

The Plaça Orwell, Barcelona

Chapter Sixteen

The Anarchist Dream: George Orwell and Revolution

On 10 February 1939 the army of General Franco reached the French border at La Jonquera and completed the occupation of Catalonia. The military rebels against the Republican government had risen in Morocco on 18 July 1936, but were defeated in nearly all Spain's major cities by a massive popular response. In Barcelona a full-scale social revolution led by the anarchists erupted, though this revolution was crushed within the Spanish Republic long before an exhausted, war-torn Catalonia finally fell to Franco's armies.

After his military victory, Franco set about uprooting the "sins" of Catalonia: separatism, communism and atheism. There were several facets of this onslaught on a culture and society. The most serious, of course, was that thousands of people were summarily executed. The executions were mainly in small towns and rural areas, as anyone who believed they were in danger, such as active trade unionists, anarchists or communists, fled to France. Most of those killed had thought they were safe. In contradiction with all proper juridical systems or any sense of natural justice, the Law on Political Responsibilities was retrospective. Many people were jailed or killed for "military rebellion"—because they had opposed Franco's military rebellion.

Even more sinister were the accusations by neighbours or personal enemies. Informers were encouraged, and often benefited by the property of the person they denounced. Thus both crippling, generalized fear and a layer of people with a stake in the regime were created. Extraordinary corruption entered the educational system and civil service. Tens of thousands of workers in these fields had fled; most of the rest were sacked. Their replacements were people loyal to the regime, most of whom had no qualifications at all for their jobs.

Rose of Fire

The depth of Franco's assault on Catalan rights was a response to the radicalism of Catalonia's workers' movement in the decades before the Civil War. Catalonia boasted the most famous mass anarchist movement in history. Earlier chapters have touched on Santiago Salvador's 1893 bombing of the Liceu opera house and other bomb attacks. The idea of people like Salvador was that of exemplary action, "propaganda by deed", whereby a terrorist attack on the ruling class would inspire the poor to rise up and sweep away their bosses and oppressors.

In general, such actions killed individuals, but made the ruling class those individuals belonged to more ferocious, giving it an excuse for repression. This, in turn, produced more terrorists but did little to change the status quo. Yet the view that anarchists are just bomb-throwers, though commonly held, is wrong. In 1910 the anarchist trade union the CNT (National Labour Federation) was founded in Sants. From then until 1937, the CNT was the main organization of the Catalan working class. The CNT was not a terrorist organization; it rather believed in the mass strike as a revolutionary weapon. This is not to say that the CNT's history is not violent, for the bosses regularly murdered workers' leaders and the CNT responded in kind. In addition, as no respecters of capitalist order or property, some members of the CNT such as the famous Buenaventura Durruti engaged in bank robberies to finance their activities. The CNT struck fear into the hearts of Spanish industrialists and respectable society.

Catalan anarchism can be given a very definite starting date. Mikhail Bakunin's agent, Giuseppe Fanelli, arrived in Barcelona by train in October 1868, just at the start of the First Republic that General Prim from Reus had ushered in with his expulsion of the Bourbons. It is a romantic story: the black-bearded Fanelli had no money, knew no Spanish or Catalan and had no contacts in Barcelona. Somehow he met up with revolutionary-minded workers and communicated Bakunin's message. In fact, it was in Madrid that Fanelli made his most important contacts, though Madrid was never an anarchist stronghold, as Catalonia and Andalusia were to become. Anselmo Lorenzo, later known as the "grandfather of Spanish anarchism", explained the effect of Fanelli's speeches:

... passing rapidly from accents of anger and menace against tyrants and exploiters to take on those of suffering, regret, and consolation, when he spoke of the pains of the exploited... He spoke in French or Italian, but we could understand his expressive mimicry and follow his speech.

Fanelli was not casting seed on stony ground. Even before its industrial revolution, Barcelona was famous for ferocious urban riots, so much so that Richard Ford wrote in the 1840s that "Barcelona has taken the lead in all insurrections." Factory owners' profit margins were generally low, which allowed little room for wage rises to placate hungry workers. Barricades frequently went up and the army went in; Gràcia, for example, the radical free-thinking town incorporated into Barcelona in 1897, saw barricades built in 1870, 1874, 1902, 1909, 1917 and 1936. In 1909 protests against conscription escalated into the *Setmana tràgica*, the Tragic Week, with churches burned across the city and hundreds of workers shot down. Barcelona became known as the *Rosa de Foc*, the Rose of Fire. After the Canadiense electricity company strike in winter 1919 had brought the city to near collapse, the bosses organized the Sindicats lliures (Free Unions), squads of armed thugs who murdered hundreds of anarchist leaders. Their most famous victim was the CNT's General Secretary, Salvador Seguí, the *Noi del Sucre*, Sugar Boy, gunned down in 1923 in the Raval. A square with his name has now been opened there.

Victor Serge wrote of a Raval workshop in 1917:

We suffocated, about thirty of us, from seven in the morning to six-thirty at night, in the Gaubert y Pia print shop. Skinny kids, naked under their loose smocks, went back and forth across the shop carrying heavy frames, their thin brown arms standing out like cables of flesh. At the back of the shop, the women were folding away... repeating the same motions seven thousand times a day to the rumbling of the machines.

These were the conditions that fostered anarchist ideas. Anarcho-syndicalism, aiming to use the mass strike to destroy bourgeois society and the capitalist order, preached solidarity as an alternative morality to the appalling conditions of life at the bottom of capitalist society. In the *barris* the anarchists organized food kitchens for the unemployed, and educational activities of all sorts—not just history and politics, but reading and writing, the arts and sciences. If a family had housing or employment problems, as was frequent, personal and group solidarity was the norm.

Ruling-class violence culminated with Franco's military uprising in 1936. The anarchists' organization at the base of society meant they could respond rapidly to the generals' coup. They led the popular defeat of the army in the days after 18 July. They then implemented their dream of the organization of society. "We carry a new world in our hearts," as Durruti put it. Factories, transport, businesses, all aspects of daily life were rapidly taken over by the workers and peasants. Barcelona's Hotel Ritz dining-room became a free restaurant.

Meanwhile, the CNT organized militia columns to march on Zaragoza and Huesca, the Aragonese cities that had fallen to the military rebellion. Though they failed to take these two cities, they spread their revolutionary ideas throughout inland Catalonia and Upper Aragon. Peasants were encouraged to collectivize the land; churches were burned throughout Catalonia. The source of anarchist hostility towards the Church is well represented in Ken Loach's film *Land and Freedom* (1995), set in rural Aragon at this period. The Catalan anarchists and POUMists taking the village are fired on from the church bell-tower by the priest, who is then shot in reprisal. This cameo suggests quite simply how priests were often collaborators of the landowners, who were hated because of their centuries-old exploitation.

The historian Chris Ealham, brushing against the grain of history (in Benjamin's phrase), explains how this revolutionary process worked. One example was the case of the women's prison in the Raval's Carrer Amàlia. Its prisoners had been peacefully freed by the crowds on the 14 April 1931 proclamation of the Republic. On 19 July 1936 a crowd attacked the prison and again freed the prisoners. The nuns who ran it had a reputation for brutality and several of them were killed. A large notice was raised above the open front gate: "This torture house was closed by the people, July 1936." Then an assembly of Mujeres Libres, Free Women, the main anarchist women's association, took the decision to demolish the hated building. This was then done by the Building

Workers' Union on 21 August. I cite this process to show how direct, mass action was then followed by open assemblies to decide what to do next, which led rapidly to action to carry out the decision of the assembly. The anarchists were highly disciplined and democratic in their organization of the new society.

Hatred of employers, state and Church led to frequent murders in the first months of this revolution. Landowners, priests, sometimes personal enemies were killed. This became a major propaganda point for the Franco side. It also allows many commentators today to argue that both sides in the Civil War were as bad as each other. Yet as all historians affirm (except the most Franco-partisan ones), the Republic throughout Spain and the Generalitat in Catalonia brought these killings under control as rapidly as possible, whereas the Franco forces made murder a question of policy in order to intimidate the opposition. It is for this reason that they slaughtered prisoners and the wounded in the hospital beds of captured cities.

The anarchist leaders were profoundly moral in their approach: Ronald Fraser cites a story of how, when raiding a gun-shop in Barcelona's Ramblas for arms, a CNT militiaman broke open the safe. He pulled out a bundle of banknotes and set them alight, explaining that the Revolution had no need for the old order's money.

It is common today to view such revolutionary zeal as a scandalous waste of life and effort, inevitably leading to disaster. Anarchist utopias are regarded as impossible. It is a view showing a certain lack of historical imagination; many of the people murdered in Catalonia in 1936 were the village bosses who had raped any young peasant girl they fancied; or priests and police who had accepted that state of affairs; or bosses who lived in luxury whilst their employees slaved away in sweatshops like the one Serge describes above. It is common, too, to feel that debates about revolution and fascism are old hat, part of history. But the Civil War defeat has cast a long shadow over most areas of Catalan life, which stretches right down to today. Just think of the inability of many people to write their own language, Catalan; the weakness of labour unions in present-day Spain, which makes it the country with the highest percentages of short-term contracts and of deaths from accidents at work in Western Europe; the ferocious anti-Catalan centralism of many in Spain; or the suffering caused, even two or three generations later, by having family members who were exiled or murdered.

The right also takes this history seriously. We are back here on Walter Benjamin's terrain, touched on in Chapter One, in which he/she who controls the interpretation of the past may more easily control the present. There is a recent movement of historical revisionism, with big-selling books by authors such as Pío Moa, promoted by Spain's main opposition party, the Partido Popular. These historians recover the climate of 1940s Spain by denying or minimizing fascist atrocities and exaggerating anarchist and communist murders. Moa justifies Franco's 1936 military uprising against the legally elected government by moving the start of the Civil War back to the Asturias workers' revolt of 1934.

Writers like Moa are responding to a significant movement in Spain in recent years to recover the truth about historical memory. Schools under the dictatorship had purveyed a totally false view of the military uprising. The hundreds of thousands who had been imprisoned or had family members imprisoned or killed under Franco or had lost friends or family in war had to keep their mouths shut for forty years. In the 1970s transition an implicit "pact of forgetfulness" was agreed. It was argued that Franco's army would not accept democracy if torturers and murderers were tried or if victims of the dictatorship were rehabilitated. Thus all those who had suffered had to remain silent for a further thirty years.

Only recently has the dam cracked and an extraordinary and diverse movement to re-examine the legacy of the Civil War has swept through Spanish society. At the time of writing, Spain's Socialist Party government is debating legislation on historical memory, which is likely to be very much watered down but would include annulment of some of the summary sentences of death, imprisonment and confiscation of property.

Revolutionary Days: Orwell in Catalonia

George Orwell, the most famous foreign writer on Catalonia, arrived in Barcelona on 26 December 1936. This was already five months after the start of the Revolution, but he found a city still in ferment. At the start of *Homage to Catalonia*, he described in a famous page what he saw:

Practically every building of any size had been seized by the workers and was draped with red flags or with the red and black flag of the Anarchists; every wall was scrawled with the hammer and sickle and with the initials of the revolutionary parties; almost every church had been gutted and its images burnt. Churches here and there were being systematically demolished by gangs of workmen. Every shop and café had an inscription saying that it had been collectivized; even the boot-blacks had been collectivized and their boxes painted red and black. Waiters and shop-walkers looked you in the face and treated you as an equal. Servile and even ceremonial forms of speech had temporarily disappeared. Nobody said 'Señor' or 'Don' or even 'Usted'; everyone called everyone else 'Comrade' and 'Thou', and said 'Salud!' instead of 'Buenos días'. Tipping was forbidden by law... There were no private motor-cars, they had all been commandeered... Down the Ramblas ...the loudspeakers were bellowing revolutionary songs all day and far into the night...

Orwell came to Barcelona with the idea of writing newspaper arti-cles, but the atmosphere was so enthralling that he at once joined the militia. He had a letter of introduction to John McNair, the British Independent Labour Party (ILP) representative in Barcelona, which is why he ended up training with the ILP's allies, the Partido Obrero de Unificación Marxista (POUM), a small revolutionary party close to the anarchists, at their Lenin barracks near Sants railway station. It was there that he met the Italian militiaman mentioned in Chapter One.

Homage to Catalonia is now thought by most critics and general readers to be Orwell's best book. At the time, though, he could not at first find a publisher and, when it was published in London in April 1938 by Secker and Warburg, it sold under a thousand copies. Later, *Animal Farm* and *Nineteen Eighty-Four* buried *Homage to Catalonia* under their fame. Orwell became "a symbolic figure of disillusion" (Raymond Williams), with *Animal Farm* and *Nineteen Eighty-Four* used as weapons against communism in the Cold War. Orwell's actual posi-tion of being, at the same time, against both capitalism and Stalinism was obscured. It was not until the political generation of 1968, also both anti-capitalist and anti-Stalinist, that *Homage to Catalonia* was recovered.

¡UNION!
¡DISCIPLINA! POR EL
SOCIALISMO

General readers were put off by *Homage to Catalonia*'s revolutionary politics; and much of the substantial left-wing constituency interested in the Civil War did not like its criticism of the Communist Party. It is a tribute to the book's quality that it has survived. This is in part due to its freshness; it is written out of the joy of his experience in Spain and in real anger at what he saw. The loner Orwell found happiness in collective struggle despite his hatred of death, dirt and disorganization. His pleasure in off-beat details pervades the book. This is from Chapter Eight on peasants hunting quails:

> They... spread the net over the tops of the grasses and then lay down and made a noise like a female quail. Any male quail that was within hearing then came running towards you, and when he was underneath the net you threw a stone to scare him, whereupon he sprang into the air and was entangled in the net. Apparently only male quails were caught, which struck me as unfair.

The last line is classic Orwell: he was a stickler for fair play, which stood him in good stead when he had to interpret political lies.

The book's greatest quality is this honesty: Orwell wrote what he saw, with clarity and passion. Christopher Hitchens, in the introduction to the Penguin *Orwell in Spain*, comments: "The intellectuals and writers of enlightened Europe generated shelf upon shelf of prose and poetry during the Spanish Civil War, but it is absolutely safe to say that most of this stuff would not bear reprinting except as a textbook in credulity and/or bad faith." Orwell's approach to the Civil War was that of an independent mind, not following any party line. He was like Stephen Spender in his individualist honesty, but whereas Spender expressed his liberalism, his "divided mind", Orwell's book explained his evolution to full revolutionary commitment.

It was chance that Orwell did not join the International Brigades: in London he visited Harry Pollitt, the General Secretary of the British Communist Party, to seek contacts in Spain, but Pollitt put him off, finding him too politically independent. His association with the ILP and the POUM meant that he became not just a witness to war, as Hemingway was in his dispatches from the Ebro, but a witness to the revolution within the war. He felt at times marginal, from January to

April 1937 on a relatively quiet front near Huesca, but his experience on leave in Barcelona during the events of May 1937 made him a central witness to the defeat of the revolution that had enthused him. He had been thinking again of joining the International Brigades to see more action, but after the May days he refused the offer of a transfer. This time it was not chance but choice to stay with the POUM and anarchists.

The May events changed Orwell. They matured him into his definitive political stance. More importantly for us, his readers, they gave him the grasp of politics and history that turned him from a second-rate novelist into a world-famous writer.

When Orwell and other ILP members got back to Barcelona from three months on the Aragon front on 26 April 1937, their intention was to rest. But on 3 May the Generalitat police moved to take control of the telephone exchange in the Plaça de Catalunya. The anarchist-led telephone workers refused to cede the control they had seized the previous July. Fighting between the Generalitat police, backed by the Communist Party, and the anarchists, backed by the POUM, left several hundred dead in four days.

From the government point of view it was intolerable that the anarchists could interrupt phone calls of people such as the Spanish President Manuel Azaña, which had actually occurred on at least one occasion. The anarchists found it intolerable that bourgeois order should be restored: they saw that this signalled the defeat of their revolution. Raymond Carr summarized succinctly: "As a consequence of the May events both the revolutionary forces in Barcelona and Catalan independence of the central government were destroyed."

After the victory of the government side Orwell returned to the front, where he survived a near-fatal neck wound on 20 May. Evacuated back to Barcelona, he had to go underground (while still convalescing) after the round-up of members of the now-illegal POUM started, then flee the country. He left Catalonia, on the train through Portbou, on 23 June. He and his comrades got out by wearing their best clothes and posing as English tourists. Catalonia was no longer a country in the grip of revolution.

Crushing the Revolution
The Communist Party (the PSUC in Catalonia) used the May 1937

events to help break anarchist power. They believed that the anarchist revolution reduced the Spanish Republic's chances of attracting Britain and France to an international common front against Hitler, Mussolini and Franco. After May the communists would be the main movers in changing the Spanish government, removing Prime Minister Largo Caballero, installing in his place their ally, Juan Negrín, and strengthening their own presence. They persuaded the new government to declare the POUM illegal and were responsible for the imprisonment and murder of many of its members, including its main leader, Andreu Nin.

In this complex situation Orwell had to take sides. Along with the other ILP activists who had been on the Aragon front, he had no hesitation when fighting broke out in offering his services to the POUM. He was sent to the roof of the Poliorama cinema (now theatre) to help guard the POUM offices in what is now the luxury Rivoli Rambla. Assault guards were entrenched in the Café Moka beside the POUM offices.

These experiences decisively changed Orwell. He who had been a colonial policeman in Burma until 1927 crowned his evolution by writing the famous phrase:
"When I see an actual flesh-and-blood worker in conflict with his natural enemy, the policeman, I do not have to ask myself which side I am on." He had supported the common-sense line, argued by the Spanish Popular Front government and the Communist Party, that first everyone had to unite to defeat Franco, and only afterwards make the revolution. Now he saw to his shock that, in practice, the Communist Party had no intention of making the revolution at any time. It was, in fact, intent on crushing the anarchist revolution that had already occurred, to try and win the support of the British government. It was a forlorn policy, as the British government had no intention of selling arms to the Republic however "respectable" it became. Communist policy led later, as the previous chapter observed, to the disaster of the Battle of the Ebro.

In its propaganda the Communist Party had to use what Orwell would in *Nineteen Eighty-Four* call "doublethink", i.e. attacking revolutionaries while saying they were themselves revolutionaries; and "newspeak", such as calling the POUM fascists, when they were the opposite, i.e. revolutionary socialists. In this "terribly distressing and disillusioning" experience (Orwell in a letter) lie the main sources of *Animal*

Farm and *Nineteen Eighty-Four*. Orwell knew from his own experience that neither Nin nor the POUM rank-and-file were fascists. Here, too, he witnessed what his later novel termed "thoughtcrime": the crime of deviating from the party line, watched over by Stalin, Big Brother. These and other phrases that have entered the English language originate in Orwell's experience in Catalonia.

There are also telling details of Orwell's six months in Aragon and Catalonia that found their way into those two famous books: Georges Kopp, Orwell's Belgian friend and POUM comrade, was put into a bin "without light, air, or food where enormous rats ran in and out of his legs" because he refused to sign a document saying the POUM was "a nest of spies and traitors"—a clear precursor of Winston's torture in *Nineteen Eighty-Four*. Goldstein, the opposition figure in that novel, is generally taken to be Trotsky, but Orwell's papers suggest the portrayal is based as much on Nin. Orwell noted the terrible irony that Antonov-Ovseenko, the Soviet consul sent to Barcelona by Stalin to oversee the smashing of the POUM ("Trotskyists" for the Communist Parties), was himself liquidated by Stalin in 1939 after his recall to Russia in 1937—for "Trotskyism".

The unique Catalan anarchist movement of the first decades of the twentieth century has left no lasting jewels of architecture, except the ugliness of many churches, pulled down in 1936 and rebuilt in utilitarian style by the dictatorship. It has left, like most defeated movements of the poor, only an idea in people's memories of what might have been. In a residual sense, though, anarchism has lasted. There is a large squatting movement in Catalonia against the high housing prices that make it impossible for most young people to rent or buy a flat. The Catalan anti-globalization movement of the past few years is heavily influenced by anarchist ideas in its direct action and rejection of political parties. There are also small, militant trade unions (the CGT is the largest) that define themselves as anarchist.

The "Picasso approach" is an attitude that has lasted, too, in a general sympathy towards anarchism, but without any practical implications. A few years ago I met a literary editor of a conservative Catalan newspaper. He told me he was an anarchist. Somewhat surprised, I asked him which group he belonged to. He was as puzzled at my question as I was at his comment. I had wrongly assumed that anarchism was a positive commitment. What he had meant, I surmised later, was that he was anti-authoritarian, not that he acted as an anarchist.

Catalonia's revolutionary political tradition was defeated decisively in 1937 and 1939. Orwell recorded it in his *Homage to Catalonia*. Later, when he was agonizing over whether the resistance to Franco was worth all the death and suffering, he wrote again of the Italian militiaman:

> When I remember—oh, how vividly!—his shabby uniform and fierce, pathetic, innocent face, the complex side-issues of the war seem to fade away and I see clearly that there was at any rate no doubt as to who was in the right. In spite of power politics and journalistic lying, the central issue of the war was the attempt of people like this to win the decent life which they knew to be their birthright.

Chapter Seventeen
The Landscape in the Pot: Food, Drink and Identity

Cava

Sant Sadurní d'Anoia is the world's cava capital, with some eighty cellars in a town of 11,000 people. *Cava* is the Catalan word for a wine cellar, but in the Alt Penedès, the area round Sant Sadurní, it has come to mean what is usually stored in them: Catalan sparkling wine made with the traditional method. They used to call it Catalan champagne, but in the 1980s were prevented from doing so by the French Champagne district. International law ruled that Champagne was an area, not a method, and so Catalan champagne was a contradiction in terms. This verdict, which seemed then a fatal blow to the cava industry, turned out to be a blessing, because it allowed cava to create its own identity.

Many of the grapes from the Penedès vineyards end up at Freixenet's huge cellar, right beside the Sant Sadurní train station and the motorway south from Barcelona. Freixenet is the biggest sparkling wine company in the world, producing ninety million bottles of cava in 2005, up from 73 million in 1998. Freixenet's delivery vans, shaped like cava corks, line up in the forecourt of its long, low main building, which looks like a Mexican ranch-house, fronted with white tiles adorned with luscious bundles of juice-dripping grapes. The lobby shows off Freixenet's famous advertisements. Yellow-capped girls in shimmering yellow suits, like swimmers or early aviators, hold glasses whose constantly rising bubbles twinkle in the light. Severe beside them in the posters stand the black, frosted bottles of Cordón Negro, launched in the 1970s and today the United States' top-selling imported sparkling wine. Over the years Freixenet has spent prodigiously on publicity, its Christmas commercials a roll-call of Hollywood glamour: Nicole Kidman, Demi Moore, Penélope Cruz, Meg Ryan, Anthony Quinn, Kim Basinger, Sharon Stone and Paul Newman have all featured in Freixenet ads.

Freixenet has created a glittering image of itself, but its profits come from its low prices, making it the "working man's bubbly", the cheap alternative to posh champagne on supermarket shelves. Both Freixenet and its main rival Codorniu have become huge drinks multinationals, selling not just the sickly, semi-sweet cheap bubbly, but an enormous range of quality cava that has severely dented French champagne sales. Freixenet's and Codorniu's grapes come not only from the Penedès, but from all over Spain; and both own plants in Chile and California.

Despite these two companies' international renown, the basis of the cava business is the Spanish market. Its glamour—the fantasy of ice beading to water-drops on the bottle and the bubble rising through the glass, promising love and friendship—and relative cheapness have made it the drink of choice at Christmas, New Year and Reis (Kings) on 6 January, the main present-giving day in Spain, when the three kings bring gifts from the Orient.

Two boycotts have affected cava exports in recent years. First, the boycott of French products due to France not supporting the US invasion of Iraq in 2003 benefited Catalan cava in the US. Secondly, the boycott in the rest of the Spanish state of Catalan products due to the new Catalan Statute of Self-government dented cava sales in Spain, with a 10% sales drop in 2005-6. This was particularly irritating for Freixenet, which has always presented itself as a Spanish company overseas and does not share the Catalan nationalism of much of Catalonia's big business. It persuaded Mariano Rajoy, the leader of Spain's main opposition party, the Partido Popular, to come to Sant Sadurní and publicly oppose the boycott, which many militants in his own party were promoting.

Beneath Freixenet's main building lie 25 miles of wine cellars on various floors. Forty million gallons of wine are stored in stainless steel tanks. From the start of the grape harvest in September, one million kilos of grapes per day for six weeks enter the plant. It is possible to visit the Freixenet cava plant every day and all day, culminating in a toy-train ride round the lowest cellars. These cellars at various levels, the walls rough as they were hacked out of the rock, are kept cold—at 15°C when it can be 35° outside—and at high humidity (up to 98°): the low cellar ceilings drip. The train runs along the corridors between huge stacks of fermenting bottles; the dry *caves* (the plural of *cava*) ferment longer (Cordón Negro for two years), which is why they are dearer.

The guides explain the "traditional method" (no longer permitted to call it the "champagne method"). The bottles, pointing downwards though not completely upside down, are turned slightly each day until the yeast sediment has drained down to the mouth. Then the neck of the bottle is frozen, the bottle set upright, the temporary cap whipped off and the pressure of the gas caused by fermentation pops the frozen plug of sediment out of the bottle. Then, the bottle is filled up with cava of the same vintage and the cork, held down by wire, inserted. All this, of course, is now done mechanically, even in the smallest cellars. Before, the sediment was removed with a rapid finger in a skilled operation as the upside-down bottle was opened.

On the other side of Sant Sadurní, running out into the vineyards, lie the cellars of Freixenet's great rival, Codorniu. If Freixenet's sales are greater today, Codorniu wins hands down on architecture. Its cellars were designed in brick by the *modernista* architect Puig i Cadafalch with columns and Catalan vaults in the neo-Gothic style he liked. They are reminiscent of his Casa Casaramona factory, now museum, on the flanks of Montjuïc; or the medieval shipyard in Barcelona, the Drassanes. At Sant Sadurní the buildings are topped by green *trencadís* (mosaics of broken tile shards), to pick up the colour of the bottles. Such industrial buildings are particularly imposing out in the country, among rows of vines crossing the valley, with the holy mountain of Montserrat visible behind the forested hills. High roofs, curving arches, windows arched like the roofs, stained glass (keeping direct sunlight off the wine) and huge internal space make Codorniu's main building seem like a church, empty, large and aseptic. The smell of must hangs like incense on the still air. On the wall at Freixenet hangs a drunken Bacchus. Cava gods are real enough, but pagan. At Codorniu closer attention reveals the *modernista* detail of clusters of grapes sculpted on the brickwork and light filtered through transparent bricks shaped like bottles.

Codorniu is the oldest cava firm in Catalonia, founded in 1872 by Manuel Raventós, who learned the champagne method while working in the Champagne area as a labourer. When the phylloxera fly ravaged Catalonia, he introduced white grapes from California. Family firms are common in Catalan industry, and Codorniu is no exception; it is still run by the Raventós family. Their early posters were designed by Ramon

Casas and the tour of the cellars costs two euros: they try to be a classier outfit than Freixenet.

The cellars of the Penedès do not just produce cava. Though less known than the Rioja and Ribera de Duero brands, some Penedès red wines rival the best from these areas. The Torres family, who nearly gave up the business in the Civil War when their Vilafranca winery was destroyed by Mussolini's bombers, has renowned middling table wines, such as Sangre de Toro (Bull's Blood).

The most successful Penedès red of all is still Jean Leon's Cabernet Sauvignon Gran Reserva 1983, named by *Wine Magazine* in 1993 one of the world's eight greatest wines. Jean Leon was the name adopted by the adventurer and *bon vivant* Ceferino Carrión, born in Santander in northern Spain in 1929. His family migrated to Barcelona in 1941 after a huge fire devastated Santander; a few months later his father and brother died when their ship was sunk by a torpedo. Fleeing the misery of post-war Barcelona, Ceferino arrived in New York as a stowaway in 1947 and started washing dishes. Later, as a waiter at Los Angeles' Villa Capri, he became a friend of Frank Sinatra by giving evidence that Sinatra had been at the restaurant, when Sinatra and Joe diMaggio were accused of beating up a man suspected of having an affair with diMaggio's wife, Marilyn Monroe. Apparently they burst into the wrong motel room and attacked the wrong man. Marilyn was upstairs.

Ceferino, now Jean Leon, became friendly with James Dean and planned to open a restaurant with him. Despite Dean's death in 1956, Leon opened La Scala that year at 9455 Santa Monica Boulevard, Beverly Hills. Serving Italian pastas and Valencian paella, it became fashionable among Hollywood actors. Gary Cooper, Paul Newman, Lana Turner: as big a roll-call of 1960s stars ate there as of 1990s stars in a Freixenet commercial.

On a Costa Brava holiday in 1962, Jean Leon bought a small vineyard of 150 hectares of chalky-clay land at Torrelavit in the Penedès. To local shock, he had the vines pulled up and brought in French vines purchased from the best houses; he was a pioneer in introducing noble strains into the Penedès. Leon is credited with the first Chardonnay matured in oak in Spain, while Miguel Torres was doing much the same at that time with Merlot. Leon had a very specific aim: he had created a gourmet restaurant, but he could not find the wine to accompany the food.

He found his wine and became famous with it, when one of the 1950s habitués of La Scala, Ronald Reagan, chose it for his presidency's inaugural gala in 1981. Leon sold out to Torres in 1994 and went to sea when he found he had cancer, dying on board his yacht *La Scala a Mare* off Thailand in October 1996. He scripted his death as romantically as he created his life.

Another Penedès story, as romantic and certainly more ethical, is that of the Albet i Noya brothers, Spain's leading producers of organic wine and cava. They use no herbicides, pesticides or fertilizers. One of the ways they feed their vines is by growing grass between the rows and ploughing this back into the soil in the spring. Given the steady corruption of agricultural land and water supplies due to use of chemicals, Albet i Noya's sustainable wine marks the future. They are based at Lavern, a hamlet on the railway half-way between cava capital Sant Sadurní and wine capital Vilafranca. On his way to Lavern, journalist Jonathan Bennett caught the romance of the rural Penedès for the *Guardian*:

> The 45-minute journey [from Barcelona] takes you through the industrial area of the Llobregat valley, past the bulbous peaks of Montserrat and into the vine-fringed slopes of the Penedès. As you get off the train, there is nothing but vineyards as far as the eye can see, interrupted only by the impossibly bucolic romanesque church, with beautiful stained-glass windows and a separate walled cemetery, filled with cypress trees straight out of Van Gogh's Provence.

Catalan Cuisine

The fame of Catalan cava has been matched in the last decade by the reputation of *cuina catalana*, Catalan cuisine, a particularly successful blend of traditional Catalan cooking and French *nouvelle cuisine* that has taken Ferran Adrià onto the front pages of the *New York Times* and Carme Ruscalleda to becoming the first Spanish woman to win three Michelin stars. Adrià's restaurant, El Bulli, is up a narrow, winding road at the back of beyond, near Roses in the Alt Empordà. Ruscalleda started off at Sant Pol, a pretty beach town on the Maresme, in the 1980s and is still there.

Other famous chefs with Michelin stars are scattered around

Catalonia: Santi Santamaria has his restaurant, El Racó de Can Fabes, at Sant Celoni, in the Montseny mountains. Montse Estruch's El Cingle is at Vacarisses, under the shadow of the Montserrat massif. Carles Gaig, though he now cooks in the centre of Barcelona, started off in outlying Horta with a restaurant-inn founded by the Gaig family in 1869 and providing *cuina del mercat*, market cooking. These restaurateurs, household names in Catalonia and some like Adrià and Ruscalleda internationally known, consciously maintain their roots in local cooking and make customers come to them.

Like the country itself, jammed between Spain and France, Catalonia's cuisine is a mix of several influences: French, Castilian and Italian. Combined with these external influences, Catalonia's extremely varied geography defines its food. "Cooking," said Josep Pla, "is merely the landscape in the pot."

A clear example of geography affecting food is seen with the fish dishes of Catalonia's long coast. In the south, around the Ebro Delta and its hinterland, the Valencian paella heavily influences the *cassola* of clams, mussels and fish with red peppers. Paella is the word for the flat pan the dish is cooked in; similarly, *cassola* is a deeper pan, a casserole, and, as in English, gives its name to the casserole cooked in it. On the northern coast, however, around abrupt, rocky Cap de Creus and the Empordà, where the coves are mountain valleys that open into the sea, *suquet* is the main fish dish, a long-simmering stew with inland onion, potato and garlic joining the local fish. Sauces, too, vary, reflecting geography and history: *romesco*, based on almonds, is a sauce of Arab origins from the south of Catalonia, whereas *allioli* (garlic and oil: garlic mayonnaise) of Greco-Roman roots is found in the north.

There is a care given to food in Catalonia that is not so often found in Anglo-Saxon countries: an underlying reason for Jean Leon's success in Beverly Hills. Dishes can take a long time to cook, as slow casseroles release flavour, or sauces are reduced to leave taste lingering in the meat or fish. They take a long time to eat, too, with hours of post-meal conversation common. Food is pampered, in both preparation and consumption. It is appreciated as an art, not just gulped down as a necessity.

In most of northern Catalonia, which is neither coastal strip nor the highest mountains, but rather the coastal ranges and Pyrenean foothills, wild mushrooms are collected and eaten. In this expanse of hilly country, mushrooms (*bolets*) thrive in the long wet springs and autumns. Mushroom-collecting fits perfectly with the Catalan tradition of rambling. With baskets and knives (you cut a mushroom carefully at the base of its stalk, not tear it from the ground), groups of all kinds spend their leisure time walking the hills and collecting mushrooms, bringing back home the musty smell and taste of forest. Knowledge of the country is also needed: to find where they grow and to avoid picking poisonous fungi, tantalizingly similar at times to the delicious delicacies.

One can divine the love of Catalans for their *bolets* by the beauty of their names. Unlike so many Catalan words, most of these are long, soft and squashy, indicating richness and sensuousness, or otherwise traditional and colloquial names, suggesting their centuries-old use: the prized orange *ou de reig* (Caesar's mushroom), *camagrocs* (yellow legs), *llengua de bou* (ox-tongue), *fetge de vaca* (cow's liver), *moixernons*, *siurenys*, *llenegues*, *rossinyols* (nightingales), *trompetes de la mort* (literally "trumpets of death", known, in contradiction, as "horns of plenty" in English), *rovellons*... Bolets are ephemeral: they appear one day and are gone the next. From the damp, mossy forest floor, they dart out with playful colours in strange shapes: buttons or balls, umbrellas, sticks or funnels. There is usually a fascinating exhibition of them in the autumn in Barcelona's Virreina Palace. Of scant nutritional value, they adorn with their flavours all other dishes, whether pork, fish, omelettes or rabbit.

The other great food of this huge hilly area is *embotits*, various kinds of processed pork sausages. Pigs are very intensively farmed in Catalonia, leading to a serious problem of slurry poisoning water supplies. In mountain climes it was essential to get through long, cold winters. This was done by killing the pig (or wild boar) in November, a communal ceremony in the villages, and making *embotits*. Their names, too, are a litany of Catalan words: *butifarra*, *bull*, *bisbe*, *sobrassada*, *peltruc*, *llonganissa*, *fuet*, *xoriç*, etc., red, white and black, depending on the amounts of blood and preservative, spicy or plain-tasting, cooked or eaten raw with toast rubbed with tomato and garlic, or bread smeared with tomato, oil and salt.

A word of warning, though. In Catalonia there is a rich haute cuisine and a healthy popular cuisine, but good food is not normally found in ordinary restaurants, unlike France or Italy. Cheap reheated oil, salads swimming in water... In general, barely edible food and poor service are common in cities and tourist areas.

The Boqueria: the Religion of Food

Local produce for the basic dishes is found in the food markets. Though these have lost ground before the onslaught of pre-packaged supermarket food, they are still where most fresh food is bought. In Barcelona the markets are supplied by Mercabarna, the central wholesale food market in the Zona Franca, but in smaller towns peasants still supply markets direct. In Vic or Mataró, the main city of the Maresme coast, there are Saturday morning markets where country vendors lay out their fruit and vegetables.

The Boqueria, Barcelona's newly overhauled central market at the mid-point of the Ramblas, dates from 1836, when founded on the site of a burned convent. A market stood in roughly the same place from earlier times: its name comes from the *boc*, Catalan for goat. As in London's Covent Garden, it was the point just outside the medieval city walls where the townspeople met the peasants bringing produce from the fields of the surrounding plain.

Today's Boqueria is laid out on a grid system, with at its heart curving stalls in concentric circles. These are mainly stalls of fish and shell-fish heaped on ice, the particular target of gourmet shoppers. Its bounty, reflecting the variety and plenty of Catalonia's food, was described in memorable vocabulary by art critic Robert Hughes in his *Barcelona*, as if he were describing paintings:

> ... stalls under the iron vaults crammed with local fruits and vegetables in their season: ranks of fat fresh lettuce and lacy escarole, tight bundles of radishes, floppy bouquets of white-ribbed chard, bins of jade-colored peas and neat fagots of tiny green beans, soft cannonball peaches and russet pears, mountains of tomatoes, zucchini, melons, beets—and everywhere, in the fall, an orange glow and thick telluric perfume rising from the trays of bolets.

The Boqueria is big enough to cater to a varied clientele: the Raval poor living in the streets behind, top chefs, and visitors enraptured at the colour and variety of products.

Packed at all hours, the Boqueria is loud and riotous, its noise as strident as its colours. The fish-vendors, experts in market banter, shout at the potential customers, who shout back to make their orders heard. It is a living museum, where you can not only look at the exhibits, but smell and buy them. Some stalls are given over to very particular products, such as herbs, bananas, cook-books (!) or offal. Others have their piles of fruit and vegetables constantly assembled and undone. You can lose yourself for hours, wandering through the vision of raw food heaped high, then taste the exhibits at the restaurant stalls. Several people manoeuvring in a tiny space prepare the food before your eyes, while you perch on a high stool.

There is a close association between food and religion. Not only because the Boqueria was built on a burned convent; nor because monks more or less invented fancy cooking and cook-books; not even because Lenten fasting led to the salting of food to conserve it; but because the end of Lent saw an explosion of eating to make up for lost time. The custom of giving chocolate Easter eggs, *mones* in Catalan, on Easter

Monday is founded in this sin of gluttony encouraged by religious fasting. On a corner just down the Ramblas (no. 83) from the Boqueria is the *modernista* Escribà pastry shop. Every Easter Escribà, like dozens of other cake and chocolate shops throughout the city, makes and sells the most exotic *mones*. These are not eggs as such at all, but street scenes, well-known people (Ronaldinho, Zapatero) or characteristic Catalan activities, sculpted in chocolate.

The shop's founder, Antoni Escribà, hand-painted at least 1,500 *mones* every year. He was an all-round pastry-cook and chocolate sculptor, who delighted in avant-garde themes. He tackled three-dimensional recreations of Dalí or Picasso paintings: "I am the Che Guevara of chocolate," he pronounced. He made an extravagant chocolate Diego Maradona, when the footballer played for Barcelona, and a model of the Vatican, which he sent to the pope. They were instant works of art, to be admired and savoured all the more intensely, like *bolets*, because their life was so short. The idea was that they should taste even better than they looked. Escribà saw himself as an artist. Picasso agreed. From his exile in Provence, he ordered from Escribà a *mona* of the Columbus monument at the bottom of the Ramblas. Payment came back in the form of a painting, from one artist to another.

The Dalí of Cuisine

Catalonia's contemporary cuisine has medieval origins. The *Llibre de Coch* by Robert de Nola was the most influential cook-book of sixteenth-century Spain. It integrated into European dishes the products newly arrived from the Americas, such as tomatoes, peppers and aubergines, which would become an essential part of the Mediterranean diet. Michael Jacobs remarks: "Certain of its recipes might not be entirely to present-day tastes, such as the one for roast cat, which involves roasting the animal in oil, garlic and herbs and serving it in slices with more garlic."

Such a dish would confirm the prejudices of those Anglo-Saxon traditionalists who believe that Mediterranean sauces are only there to blot out the taste of bad meat. They would not have been comforted by the *Llibre de Coch*'s advice to remove the cat's brains before cooking, as these were "considered prejudicial to human sanity" (Jacobs). Despite these early signs that Catalans took food seriously, regional cuisine could not begin to develop until the nationalist *renaixença*. Ferran Agulló, a Girona journalist, asserted boldly in his 1908 *Book of Catalan Cuisine*: "Catalonia, just as it has its own language, constitution, customs, history and political ideals, has its own cuisine."

The identity of this cuisine was clear: it was based on the produce of Catalonia's three main geographical areas: coast, hills and Lleida plain, and especially on the vertiginous fall and rise from Pyrenean mountains to Mediterranean sea. It was also based on international influences, reflecting Catalonia's position as a *terra de pas*. Cannelloni, for example, became the Christmas luxury meal for the new nineteenth-century bourgeoisie and still is today. French and Italian sophistication was grafted onto Catalan products and traditions.

Catalan cooking is, of course, part of Mediterranean cuisine, the elixir of immortality sought after by today's rich, who see how obesity and heart disease are decimating North Americans and Europeans and note that fresh vegetables, fresh fish, olive oil and red wine in moderation are not just good, once you have washed the burger additives out of your system, but lead to longer life. The statistics tell us that Catalan women live to an average of 82 and men lag not so far behind: this makes them, despite twentieth-century war and famine, the longest-lived people in Europe apart from Icelanders, who are conserved in chill air.

During the Franco years of hunger the great pre-war French-style restaurants closed or diminished, for only the rich ate very much at all, let alone thought of cuisine. The 1970s transition brought new wealth and an expanding middle class, eager to assert their Catalan identity in a non-political way: politics was fine for getting rid of the dictator, but sport and food took its place in the 1980s. Or, as Vázquez Montalbán put it:

> Whereas the first few years of the transition were characterized by an unrealistic quest for sexual liberation, inviting friends round for a meal became the cultural paradigm when the transition slid towards moderation... post-Franco Spain had to settle for the palate and stomach rather than sex and its attributes.

This new middle class could pay the prices of the new *cuina catalana* and so laid the basis for the explosion of high-class restaurants.

When Colman Andrews wrote his *Catalan Cuisine* in 1989, he could still claim that it was "Europe's last great culinary secret". For the last decade at least the food movement in Catalonia has been widely trumpeted. It has become part of Catalans' new post-transition confidence and self-image: that we know how to work well and also to live well. The sub-text is that we are not like those Puritans from northern Europe who do not know how to relax. Nor are we like those southern Spaniards who only know how to play. In Catalonia there is a balance: we eat and drink well, we enjoy yourselves, we live well, but not to excess; and we work hard and seriously, though not to excess.

Like most self-images, it tends to be true in the sense that people make it true. When Louis van Gaal, the Dutch football coach, left FC Barcelona in the year 2000, he proffered a grave insult to Catalans, saying that Barcelona was a place where you could live well, but not work well. As van Gaal was a disciplinarian, the insult became something of a compliment: one would not want the balance of leisure and work to be defined by an ill-mannered martinet.

Ferran Adrià, already head chef at El Bulli in 1986 at the age of 24, is twenty years later Spain's most famous chef, renowned for his exotic combinations of flavours. This is nothing new for Catalans, one of whose defining dishes is *Mar i Cel* (Sea and Sky), a dish typical of the port of L'Estartit and containing pork and rabbit from the inland and monkfish and prawns from the depths. Fruits are widely used with meat, mixing sweet and savoury: duck with pears or pheasant and apple. Adrià has taken combination to extremes, making him for the *New York Times* in 2003 "the best chef in the world" and "the Salvador Dalí of cuisine". Adrià shares with Dalí not just his restaurant's location on Cap de Creus, but mastery of publicity.

It is almost impossible to get a table at El Bulli: it has just 45 places and is only open from April to September. For the remaining six months Adrià is lecturing around the world or experimenting in his food laboratory just behind Barcelona's Boqueria market, where he can often be seen eating at one of the restaurant stalls. His cooking shows an infectious *joie de vivre*. Nearly everyone who has written on one of the long meals at El Bulli with a succession of tiny dishes says, like the French food writer Cécile Thibaud: "One comes not to eat, but to test sensations." Carrot-flavoured foam, vanilla-scented mashed potato, Rice Krispies with shrimps' heads and green truffles are just some of Adrià's taste experiences. If his exclusivity, prices and combinations have become too Dalinian, remember he is not the only New Wave Catalan chef.

Carme Ruscalleda has developed her deceptively simple "home cooking" from her mother's recipes. She emphasizes the traditional basis of her kitchen, in implicit rejection of Adrià's ornate laboratory experiments:

> My recipe-book is practical and agile, natural, transparent without make-up or false hair-pieces, without hidden tricks; the magic is the nature of each ingredient and the personal touch that you will discover in each recipe.

The Camp Nou, Barcelona

Chapter Eighteen
Cradle and Refuge: FC Barcelona

Just as the *cantautors* were the main cultural expression of the struggle against the dictatorship in the 1960s, so the boom in Catalan chefs can be said to represent the new wealth and confidence of modern Catalonia. It is football, though, that has been the greatest cohesive cultural force in Catalan society, expressed through one of the world's most famous football clubs, FC Barcelona, *Barça*. Its star player of recent years, Ronaldinho, FIFA World Player of the Year in both 2004 and 2005, though not compared with Dalí as Ferran Adrià was, found inspiration, unlikely as it seems, in Dalí. He told journalist Justin Webster about the impact of one of Dalí's paintings at Figueres: *Gala Contemplating the Sea*, a picture of Gala naked doing what the title says. This is one of Dalí's renowned double images, turning at a distance into a portrait of Abraham Lincoln.

> "If you look at it normally you don't see anything. But if you do this"—he [Ronaldinho] pulls his eyes back to blur his vision—"you can see into it. To make something like that, such a fascinating picture, you have to have imagination, you have to be able to think before others. I thought to myself, yes, that is what I have to do. My imagination comes from being with a ball and wanting to do something new, like Dalí as if for the first time. This is my motivation."

One's sceptical mind says that Ronaldinho is merely doing what all football stars, cracks, as they say in Spain, have to do. As a six million euros-a-year mercenary from Brazil, he needs a Dalinian sleight of hand to make fans believe he feels in his heart the blue and scarlet colours, that he belongs to Barça and to Catalonia. In Ronaldinho's case, however, one would be ingenuous to think he was anything but genuine, although the club's publicists may well have shrewdly pointed him towards a look at Catalonia's most popular painter.

Football, like *cuina*, reflects the times. Whereas in the 1950s and 1960s, following Barça was about stubborn opposition to oppression and in the 1980s about defensive resistance to centralist power represented in people's minds by Real Madrid, we are now in supposedly prosperous and hedonistic times when we can exclaim with chef Montse Estruch "I want to laugh, eat, drink and love." Ronaldinho, with his huge smile and spontaneous grin, represents this new confidence.

When FC Barcelona won Spain's league championship for the second year running in May 2006 there were the normal, rowdy celebrations throughout the night by some 25,000 supporters on the Rambla de Canaletes. This was nothing in relation to the million or so who lined the team's victory cavalcade on an open-topped double-decker through the streets. And this, in turn, was peanuts compared to the furore after the 17 May 2006 triumph over London's Arsenal to win the European Cup, a match in Paris attended by the king, queen and prime minister of Spain, the president of the Generalitat, the mayor of Barcelona and any other dignitary who could beg a ticket.

Football is not just collective joy or woe, parodying the real feelings of personal or political triumph and disaster. In Catalonia it still has a powerful political edge. When France beat Spain in the 2006 World Cup finals, every time France scored rockets were fired into the Barcelona sky by fans. Catalan nationalists love to celebrate Spain losing. There is a profound antagonism to any success of Real (Royal) Madrid and hostility to the Spanish national team. When the fifty-year bubble of the tourism- and construction-led Spanish economy finally bursts, this hints at the political conflict that might erupt.

Triumph and Tragedy

Football triumph is cyclical. At the time of writing, Barça is nearing (or at) the top of its cycle, whereas just four years ago Real Madrid was winning its third European Cup in five years and Barça had won nothing at all for three years, had had seven managers in seven seasons and was staggering from one institutional crisis to another. Lack of titles and cups brings upheaval within big clubs. From 1996, when Johan Cruyff was summarily sacked as manager, even though his team had won four league titles on the trot in the early 1990s and the 1992 European Cup (while in addition playing attractive attacking football), until 2003, Barcelona was in crisis.

After these years of turmoil the key event in Barça's modern history was its June 2003 presidential election. The club is formally owned by its members, and thus presidential elections are held every four years. The fans of Manchester United, seeing "their" club sold over their heads, would like to have the option to vote out the club's board. The front-runner in 2003 was a wealthy head of an advertising agency Lluís Bassat (see p.44); he had on board Pep Guardiola, the recently retired midfield player who had been Barça's main icon throughout the 1990s. Among its numerous foreign players, hired "honorary Catalans" like Ronaldinho, Barça needs a local lad with whom the fans can identify. What Guardiola, the *noi* from Santpedor, was in the 1990s, Carles Puyol, from the Pyrenean Pont de Suert, is today.

However, the 2003 elections were won by the 41-year-old Joan Laporta, with a fresh, dynamic, new-broom image. Laporta's message was one of renewal, sound business management after the spendthrift previous years, manners rather than the loutish behaviour of the hotelier and previous Barça president Joan Gaspart, and reaffirmation of the club's Catalanism. Key to Laporta's campaign, though, was his promise to bring David Beckham to Barcelona. Laporta affirmed that he had a verbal agreement with Beckham that, if he won the presidency, Beckham would leave Manchester United for Barça.

Here Laporta had outrageous good luck disguised as a disaster. Beckham signed, a few days after Laporta's election victory, for Barça's historic rival, Real Madrid. Laporta was a new emperor left stark naked. Desperate for a big signing to make up for Beckham's "betrayal", he found a star who was under a cloud at Paris St. Germain. Ronaldinho's name began with "R", following in the steps of Romario, Ronaldo and Rivaldo, Barça's other Brazilian stars of the previous decade. More importantly, the cloud of melancholy that had hung over him in Paris lifted as he stepped off the plane at El Prat. Ronaldinho never stopped grinning and laughing. From the start he loved playing football and loved Barcelona. His happiness infected other players and he was a genius with the ball. Proud, sometimes arrogant, like any great media star, he was also self-effacing and self-aware. When Barça consolidated their ascendancy over Madrid—and the pin-up star Beckham—by winning 3-0 at Madrid's ground in November 2005 to the unheard-of applause of Madrid fans, Ronaldinho grinned at the press corps afterwards and said: "I may be ugly, but I think I have charm."

In December of Laporta's first season Barça's new team was languishing mid-table, but then suddenly began to function and started a winning run in the second half of the season that took them to second place in the league, above Real Madrid. Barça could not believe their luck. Ronaldinho was not just a solitary genius like Romario; he was also a team man, encouraging younger players, drawing off defenders, running the whole ninety minutes. FC Barcelona's myriad fans (most people in Catalonia) heaved a sigh of relief that the confused and confusing Beckham, an excellent player but no inspiring genius, had gone to Madrid. Beckham's presence brought in cash and sponsorship to Madrid, but he lacked the spark on the field that creates the mass following that leads to lasting cash and sponsorship. Just three seasons later, Ronaldinho was not only considered the world's greatest player, but had surpassed Beckham in the merchandising income his name generated.

Laporta also hired the ex-Dutch international Frank Rijkaard to train the team. One shuddered for him, an inexperienced trainer and a black man to boot. Spanish football crowds, Barcelona included, are almost as bad as Italian crowds in their relentless racist jeering. Laporta, though, not only hired Rijkaard—on Johan Cruyff's advice—but supported him. Laporta also confronted the *boixos nois*, the "wild kids", fans encouraged by previous presidents, especially Núñez (1979-2000) and Gaspart (2000-2003), because their fervour animated the crowd. Barça's 125,000 members suffer from manic depression. They make a lot of noise if the team is winning, but wave white handkerchiefs, boo and walk out like spoiled schoolchildren if things go badly. Often players themselves have to encourage the crowd to support the team. Nor do fans in Spain travel much to away matches. The *boixos nois*, a group formed by Núñez in the early 1980s and given offices in the ground and free tickets, were prepared to travel and make a noise, home and away. Núñez and Gaspart had always looked sympathetically on their excesses, such as racist chanting and beating up fans of visiting teams (especially Barcelona's other First Division club, Espanyol). If FC Barcelona was, in Vázquez Montalbán's words, "the symbolic unarmed army of Catalonia", the *boixos nois* were the armed thugs of FC Barcelona.

Laporta stopped their privileges and has stuck to his position, despite receiving death threats. As well as challenging violence, this is part of the "gentrification" of football, with seat prices rising and the game becoming established as a middle-class spectator event, with the working class watching on TV in bars. In these mainly male bars men scream like demons and jump from their chairs when their team scores or loudly lament, eyes wide open and clutching their heads in their hands, in a melodramatic dramatization of suffering, when chances are missed or games lost. It is permitted collective externalization of emotion.

Celebrations of great Barça victories are both manipulated and genuine. When in Paris Carles Puyol lifted the 2006 European Cup above his head, the organizers choreographed the televised moment with red-and-white smoke and multicoloured confetti pouring over the pitch, with the music rising to a crescendo. Throughout Catalonia rockets soared into the air as if it were Sant Joan (Midsummer's Eve, fireworks night), cava corks hit ceilings, people screamed "champions, champions" with orgasmic insistence, cars hooted and dogs howled. If one did not know a football match had been won, one might have hoped or feared that a dictatorship had been overthrown.

After this triumph Laporta produced a master-stroke: he gave money away. It was a long way from overthrowing the regime, but it showed his ambitions for the club. Barça had been one of the few major clubs proud not to wear sponsorship on its shirts. Laporta's directors had been negotiating with the Beijing Olympics and a bookmakers' chain. They turned them both down and instead signed an agreement with UNICEF, whereby Barça would pay the UN development agency 1.5 million euros a year instead of receiving 22 million from Bet&Win (BWin) over five years. Marketing ploy though this reverse sponsorship is, it brings pride to Catalans. Barça is not just a sports champion, they can rightly say, but invests in a good cause. In the constant wrangling between Spanish centralists and Catalan nationalists the good cause is also a good joke: Catalans are often attacked for being tight with money.

Ronaldinho, at first second-best, was the luckiest signing, but Rijkaard was an inspired choice. "Rijkaard is the perfect counter-point to the Catalan mentality, which shows no middle ground," said Johan Cruyff. Calm, polite, rarely losing his cool, not obviously playing the games of criticism of players or directors, he has known how to survive in the intense pressure of press conferences, hunger for instant success and the hothouse manoeuvring of politicians and businessmen, all of which tend to make the club chronically unstable. Such manoeuvring and instability are the downside of the club's democratic structure. Nearly all Barça's greatest players and managers have ended up victims of the directors' and members' ungracious and ill-tempered failure to digest failure. Both Kubala and Cruyff were thrown out through the back door. At present, though, success smoothes over most difficulties. The same people who scream like demons at the ground or in bars, showing the *rauxa* or raging passion that Catalans like in themselves, also admire the *seny*, the intense calm of Rijkaard's gaze. He has been dubbed a "Zen" trainer.

The failure of Ronaldinho in the Germany 2006 World Cup underlined the importance of Rijkaard. Brazil was just a group of stars, like a night with Eric Clapton and friends, not a team like Barça blended by a coach on the basis of players' differing strengths.

Football and Nationalism
The history of Barça as a major institution in Catalonia explains a lot about the nature of Catalan nationalism. Founded in 1899, like many big clubs in Spain, by expatriate British, it was from quite early days a focus for anti-centralist feeling. It was after the Civil War, however, that the club became a major channel for expression of discontent. Historian Josep Solé i Sabaté wrote of the 1940s:

> A society shivering under a white terror that extended to the language and culture of the country... Sport was a place where the population could feel freer... FC Barcelona was the refuge and the cradle, diluted and vague, of the essence of Catalonia—this feature maintained it and made it grow right down to today. In addition, it welcomed all the new-comers, the other Catalans, who were then arriving in growing numbers to search for work and a better future.

Though the Franco regime clearly favoured Barça's great rival, Real Madrid, it was far-sighted enough to understand that what was required was rivalry. If Real Madrid always won, football would lose all interest. Constant rivalry was a safety-valve for feelings of oppression. Nevertheless, the extent and political character of Catalan celebration at

Barça's first great team in the 1950s took the regime aback. Franco's aim had been to crush Catalan culture after the Civil War with executions, concentration camps and steady repression. Vázquez Montalbán explained some of the contradictions in his *Barcelonas*:

> An epic nationalist sentiment, irrational but emotionally therapeutic, gradually crystallized in support for Barça... Such anti-centralist rebelliousness did not entail an outright rejection of Franquism, but rather a feeling of collective subjection to central power... This mood... accentuated the impression that for forty years Barcelona was an occupied city, wracked by schizophrenia.

The great 1950s team was known as the team of the Five Cups and was built round the legendary figure of Ladislao Kubala (1927-2002). He was the Hungarian exile who signed for Barça after being enticed away from Madrid, just as the other great name of the 1950s Alfredo di Stefano had been "stolen" by Madrid from Barça. Franco himself was a football fan, beyond any appreciation he might have of the use of football in keeping people's minds off politics. When Hungary prevented Kubala from playing in Spain, as he had fled from behind the Iron Curtain, Franco intervened personally with the international football authorities. Sport was important in Spain's return to the United Nations after its isolation as a pariah state in the decade after the Civil War. With the Cold War just getting under way at the time of Kubala's arrival, Spain's former alliance with Hitler became less important than its anti-communist credentials. The Kubala case was a godsend for Franco: no-one wanted this genius of sport not to play.

With Kubala Barça won four league titles, five cups (known then as the Cup of the Generalísimo Franco) and two European Fairs Cups between 1951 and 1960. The mass celebrations on the Ramblas became political protests precisely because no direct political protest was permitted. In 1961 Barça knocked reigning champions Real Madrid out of the European Cup, though lost narrowly to Portugal's Benfica (2-3) in the final.

Kubala became a legend. He was tough: he could not be kicked off the pitch, though all opponents tried, and he was an artist. In 1953 he overcame tuberculosis. Joan Manel Serrat, the most internationally known of the Catalan *cantautors* who emerged in the 1960s (though by no means the least radical), sang in *Kubala*:

> Long live the knowledge and joy of his game
> Adorned with a touch of fantasy.
> Football in colours, gourmet taste,
> Fancy lace, smooth cinnamon.

Kubala did things that fans had not expected or even thought of before. He was part of a generation of great Hungarian players who brought bending free kicks, protection of the ball with their bodies and rapid passing into the game. They were showing that this subtler style of play was superior to the kick-and-run of English football. Like Cruyff and Ronaldinho after him, Kubala drew the crowds back into the stadium. The Les Corts ground proved too small by the mid-1950s, though it had a capacity of 60,000. Kubala became known as "the man who built the Camp Nou", as today's huge concrete 100,000-seater stadium was constructed and opened in 1957.

Serrat, a working-class lad from Barcelona's Poble Sec, on the flanks of the Montjuïc hill, also sang of Kubala in his list of 1950s memories in *Temps era Temps* (Time was Time), the famous forward-line acting as a collective counter-point to the centralist Franco slogan in the first line and complementing the comfort offered by cinema in the 1950s:

> Time of "One, Great and Free"
> Metro Goldwyn Mayer
> ...
> Basora César Kubala Moreno and Manchón

Football, if it is an art, is an immediate and perishable one, like dance or Escribà's chocolate sculptures. Songs like Serrat's, making poetry out of the Barça forward line, convert a fading memory into text. It was no surprise that at Barça's centenary in 1999 Kubala was voted player of the century by the club's members, ahead of Cruyff.

The 1961 European Cup defeat weighed heavily for thirty years on Barça. The club with the biggest membership in Europe failed to fulfil its potential. Many Catalans blamed Barça's failures on biased refereeing and anti-Catalanism, but such "victimism" did not help solve the problem. The weight of expectation bore down on club and players. Barça was *més que un club*, more than a club. If Barça carried the hopes of an oppressed nation, it was terrible to continually lose.

1973 saw the start of the club's association with Dutch players and coaches, which has lasted to this day. Rinus Michels and Johan Cruyff, coach and player, arrived to make Barça as great as the Ajax team they came from. They sparkled briefly, defeating Real Madrid 5-0 in Madrid and winning the 1974 league title, but failed to build the great team the club yearned for. That had to wait for Cruyff's second coming in 1988. By then the club's gloom had been deepened by defeat in the 1986 European Cup final under Terry Venables and a subsequent player rebellion.

Cruyff's 1988 arrival as trainer finally lifted Barça's inferiority complex. Ronald Koeman's goal in the 1992 European Cup final at Wembley gave them victory just three months before the Olympics came to Barcelona. More than that, Cruyff's team reflected an ideal of attacking football that the fans identified with and a *joie de vivre* that took some of the terrible pressure off the players.

Catalonia is not Spain

In 2005 the governing bodies of European football drew Barça's attention to the banners displayed in the crowd during European Cup matches, which read "Catalonia is not Spain." Since the opening of the Olympic Stadium on the Montjuïc hill in 1989, these banners in English are often unfurled on big televised sporting occasions. It is an odd slogan, for clearly Catalonia is in actual fact part of Spain, like it or not. But the slogan is not part of a campaign with any practical consequences. The assertion is part of conservative Catalan nationalism, which is not in favour of independence. In opinion polls there is surprisingly little support for independence in Catalonia (between 12 and 18 per cent, depending on the political situation of the moment), much less than in the Basque Country. The slogans "Catalonia is not Spain" and the accompanying "Freedom for Catalonia" are just bargaining chips in negotiations with the Spanish government and flags to keep party memberships happy.

Catalonia emerged in the late 1970s from the long Franco night with mass workers' and residents' movements, led by the PSUC, the Catalan Communist Party, which had organized the underground opposition to Franco. The PSUC polled twenty per cent of the popular vote in the first democratic elections of 1977. Fearful of its power, the transition government of Adolfo Suárez in Madrid and conservative Catalan nationalism worked together to restore Josep Tarradellas as president of the Catalan Generalitat. Tarradellas, a minister in the 1930s Generalitat, was the president in exile who skilfully presented himself as the living link with the past, offering the continuity of Catalan institutions.

Tarradellas' non-elected 1977-80 transition government, accepted by all the main opposition parties, PSUC included, paved the way for the conservative Catalan nationalists, in the coalition Convergència i Unió, to win the first autonomous elections in 1980. Their leader was Jordi Pujol, a Christian banker who had been tortured and imprisoned by the Franco regime in 1960 for organizing a Catalan nationalist protest in Barcelona's Palau de la Música. This background gave Pujol the authority to govern Catalonia for 23 years. The political manoeuvres to install Tarradellas in the transition have set the pattern for Catalonia's development ever since: a formal democracy strongly supportive of big business (especially construction). No-one was a more suitable minister in various Pujol governments than Joaquim Molins, the country's main cement manufacturer at the enormous plant by the motorway at Montcada i Reixach. The alliance between Madrid and Catalan nationalists, over the heads of other parties and forcing through policy in opposition to most voters, was to be repeated in the 2005-6 negotiations for Catalonia's new Statute of Self-Government.

Despite the Pujol governments' strong support for construction (with the accompanying ecological deterioration), private education and private healthcare, all divisive policies consonant with its support for big business, it did achieve considerable consensus in its linguistic programme. At the end of the dictatorship the Catalan language was in a bad way: for forty years no-one had studied it in school. Thus, though it was widely spoken, Catalans were not accustomed to reading or writing in their own language. Added to this was the impact of about two million Castilian-speaking immigrants during the Franco years, few of whom spoke Catalan. This meant that of the six million people in Catalonia in 1980 fifty per cent did not speak Catalan and eighty or ninety per cent did not read or write in it. Pujol's governments set about rectifying this situation. They devoted time and money to "linguistic normalization" campaigns that enjoyed widespread support. Language was the main identifying element in Catalan nationalism, a language spoken since the tenth century, spread to Valencia and the Balearics in medieval conquests and with a rich medieval and modern literature. The fact that national identity was not defined racially or genetically meant that anyone could become Catalan. They merely had to learn Llull's and Verdaguer's language.

This brief account of Catalonia's modernization, in which Tarradellas and Pujol neutralized the left that had led the anti-Franco resistance, should not lead readers to think that Catalan nationalism is only about big business. As this book has shown in several contexts, it is a powerful, historical current with deep roots in Catalan culture and life. It is no accident that today Esquerra Republicana, the more radical of the parliamentary Catalan nationalist parties, governs many of the small country towns of Catalonia.

The political frustration felt by Catalan nationalists has been expressed through a strong movement in recent years for Catalan sports teams. If Wales, Scotland, Northern Ireland and England can all have international teams recognized within the United Kingdom, why cannot Catalonia and the Basque Country have the same within the Spanish state? This demand has been vigorously rejected by all international sporting bodies under strong pressure from Spanish governments. The national question is much more sensitive in Spain than in the UK. Spain has not defeated and integrated its national minorities, despite 500 years of violent effort since Queen Isabel first started undermining Catalan power in the 1490s. The story of Reus' canal money (see p.92) helps explain why.

As second best, for a number of years at Christmas, when there is a break in the Spanish league programme, Catalonia has played friendly soccer matches against international teams. Most galling for Spanish centralists is that Brazil, 2002 world champions, was on occasion the opposition. For these matches the Montjuïc stadium, built for the Olympics and where Espanyol normally play to crowds of 20,000, filled with at least 60,000 people waving Catalan flags and asserting Catalonia's nationhood.

The whole of the recent history of Catalonia is dominated by the terrible defeat of 1939—1714, but worse—and the country's remarkable struggle to recover. Within Catalonia the question of national rights is taken for granted as a valid demand: in general, a demand for devolution, not independence. This was shown most clearly in the united struggle of native Catalans and immigrants, who in the last years of the dictatorship created a powerful movement for national and democratic rights.

Outside Catalonia, Spanish politicians, following the cry of Calvo Sotelo in the 1930s "Better a red Spain than a broken Spain", have spread a tale of Catalans as tight-fisted separatists lacking in solidarity. Such a chauvinist myth gained credence from Catalonia having been always the richest area of a poor state. Spain, 200, 100 or 50 years ago, was dirt-poor. Catalonia, with its seafaring and trading history and then its industrial revolution, was richer. Richard Ford, the Tory who paraded his prejudices on Spain in two classic travel books of the 1840s, reflected this centralist view of Catalans in his normal insolent, brook-no-argument manner, referring to "this rich mart of money-making tasteless traders."

Catalans are, of course, not only traders. We have seen that they are conservative business people, religious artists, revolutionary artists, workers, revolutionary anarchists, rich bohemians, impoverished immigrants and filthy-haired soldiers. In short, much like anywhere else, Catalonia is a collection of diverse people. It is also like anywhere else because its history and culture are so specific to its particular geography: in Catalonia's case, as *terra de pas* between great states and as a narrow coastal strip between twisted mountains and the sea. Visitors come for Catalonia's rugged cliffs and pine-lined beaches, jagged mountains, starred chefs, footballers and art—from Romanesque churches through Gaudí and Art Nouveau, to the canvases of Picasso, Miró and Dalí. Catalonia is there today to be enjoyed, but this peaceful yet lively country has a dark, violent history, still nurturing profound resentments and frustrated hopes with (in Montalbán's words) a certain schizophrenia.

This last chapter has looked at how in contemporary times of relative peace sport can be a metaphor for politics, just as in tougher times politics turns into war. As well as Ronaldinho and Rijkaard, Barça has a third black star, Samuel Eto'o from Cameroon. As Africans flee poverty and war for Spain, working in Catalonia mainly on construction sites, in domestic labour or in agriculture and often without legal status, Eto'o enjoys wealth and the acclaim of Catalonia. To his credit, he has faced frontally, with passion and dignity, the widespread racism on Spain's football terraces. The challenge for Catalonia today, with its population risen from six to eight million people in just fifteen years due to foreign immigration, is whether it can offer to its newcomers the democratic rights, welfare and recognition that it, as an oppressed nation, has long demanded for itself.

Further Reading

Agustí, Ignacio, *Mariona Rebull*. Barcelona: Planeta, 2001.

Allison Peers, Edgar, *Catalonia Infelix*. London: Methuen, 1937.

Andrews, Colman, *Catalan Cuisine*. London: Headline, 1989.

Arts Council of Great Britain (ed.), *Homage to Barcelona. The City and its Art 1888-1936*. London: Arts Council, 1986.

Balcells, Albert, *Catalan Nationalism*. London: Macmillan, 1996.

Ballard, J. G., *The Kindness of Women*. London: Harper Collins, 1991.

Bataille, Georges, *Blue of Noon*. London: Penguin, 2001.

Berger, John, *The Success and Failure of Picasso*. London: Penguin, 1965.

Bonner, Anthony (ed.), *Doctor Illuminatus: a Ramon Llull Reader*. Princeton: Princeton University Press, 1994.

Bookchin, Murray, *The Spanish Anarchists*. New York: Harper Colophon, 1978.

Boyd, Alastair, *The Essence of Catalonia*. Barcelona: Muchnik, 1988.

Brecht, Bertolt, *Poems 1913-1956*. London: Methuen, 1976.

Brenan, Gerald, *The Literature of the Spanish People*. London: Peregrine, 1963.

Burckhardt, Jacob, *The Civilisation of the Renaissance in Italy*. London: Folio Society, London 2004.

Burns, Jimmy, *Barça, a People's Passion*. London: Bloomsbury, 2000.

Burton, Richard, *Prague: a Cultural and Literary History*. Oxford: Signal, 2003.

Carr, Raymond, *Modern Spain. 1875-1980*. Oxford: OUP, 1991.

Castellar-Gassol, J., *Barcelona, a History*. Barcelona: Edicions de 1984, 2000.

Cela, Camilo José, *Viaje al Pirineo de Lérida*. Barcelona: Noguer, 1965.

Cirlot, Juan-Eduardo, *Gaudí, an Introduction*. Barcelona: Triangle, 2002.

Cunningham, Valentine (ed.), *The Penguin Book of Spanish Civil War Verse*. London: Penguin, 1980.

Davison, Peter (ed.), *Orwell in Spain*. London: Penguin, 2001.

Ealham, Chris, *Class, Culture and Conflict in Barcelona, 1898-1937*. London: Routledge, 2004.

El País (ed.), *Imatges de Catalunya*. Madrid: El País Aguilar, 1995.

Erben, Walter, *Miró*. Cologne: Taschen, 2003.

Foment de Ciutat Vella, SA (ed.), *Memòria 2001-2002*. Barcelona: Foment, 2003.

Ford, Richard, *Handbook for Spain 1845 Vol. 2*. London: Centaur, 1966.

Fraser, Ronald, *Blood of Spain*. London: Penguin, 1981.

Galeano, Eduardo, *Conversaciones con Raimon*. Barcelona: Gedisa, 1987.

García Márquez, Gabriel, *Tramontana* in *Strange Pilgrims*. London: Penguin, 1994.

Garcia-Soler, Jordi, *Crònica Apassionada de la Nova Cançó*. Barcelona: Flor del Vent, 1996.

Genet, Jean, *The Thief's Journal*. London: Penguin, 1967.

Gibson, Ian, *The Shameful Life of Salvador Dalí*. London: Faber & Faber, 1997.

Goytisolo, Juan, *Forbidden Territory*. London: Verso, 2003.

Graves, Tomás, *Tuning Up at Dawn*. London: Fourth Estate, 2004.

Heeren, Stefanie von, *La Remodelación de Ciutat Vella. Un Análisis Crítico del Modelo Barcelona*. Barcelona: Veïns en defensa de la Barcelona vella, 2002.

Hemingway, Ernest, *Death in the Afternoon*. London: Penguin, 1966.

Hemingway, Ernest, *The First Forty-Nine*. London: Jonathan Cape, 1956.

Hemingway, Ernest, *By-line*. London: Penguin, 1970.

Hughes, Robert, *Barcelona*. London: Harvill, 1992.

Jackson, Angela, *Beyond the Battlefield*. Pontypool: Warren Pell, 2005.

Jacobs, Michael, *Barcelona Blue Guide*. London: A & C Black, 1991.

Langdon-Davies, John, *Gatherings from Catalonia*. London: Cassell, 1953.

Lee, Laurie, *A Moment of War*. London: Penguin, 1992.

Lewis, Norman, *Voices of the Old Sea*. London: Penguin, 1985.

Macaulay, Rose, *Fabled Shore*. London: Hamish Hamilton, 1949.

Mackay, David, *Modern Architecture in Barcelona (1854-1939)*. Sheffield: The Anglo-Catalan Society, 1985.

Mandiargues, André Pieyre de, *Al margen*. Barcelona: Áltera, 1996.

Martorell, Joanot, *Tirant lo Blanc*. Badalona: Sàpiens, 2000.

Menai Williams, Alun, *From the Rhondda to the Ebro*. Pontypool: Warren Pell, 2004.

Mendoza, Cristina, *Ramon Casas, el pintor del modernisme*. Barcelona: MNAC, 2001.

Mendoza, Cristina & Eduardo, *Barcelona modernista*. Barcelona: Planeta, 1989.

Moncada, Jesús, *The Towpath*. London: Harvill, 1994.

Morris, Jan, *Spain*. London: Penguin, 1982.

Nooteboom, Cees, *The Roads to Santiago*. London: Harvill, 1997.

O'Brian, Patrick, *Picasso*. London: Harvill, 1997.

Orwell, George, *Homage to Catalonia* and *Looking Back on the Spanish War*. London: Penguin, 1970.

Orwell, George, *Nineteen Eighty-four*. London: Penguin, 1955.

Payne, John, *Catalonia, Portrait of a Nation*. London: Century, 1991.

Payne, John, *Catalonia: History and Culture*. Nottingham: Five Leaves, 2004.

Permanyer, Lluis, *Miró, la vida d'una passió*. Barcelona: Edicions de 1984, 2003.

Pla, Josep, *Antoni Gaudí*. Barcelona: El Observador, 1991.

Pla, Josep, *El quadern gris*. Badalona: Sàpiens, 2005.

Pla, Josep, *L'Empordà*. Barcelona: El Observador, 1991.

Reverte, Jorge, *La batalla del Ebro*. Madrid: Crítica, 2003.

Reynolds, Jack, *Saltaire*. Bradford: Art Galleries and Museums, 1985.

Riera, Ignasi, *Viatgers de Barcelona*. Madrid: Ollero & Ramos, 2000.

Ruscalleda, Carme, *Un any amb Carme Ruscalleda*. Barcelona: Empúries, 2004.

Sagarra, Josep Maria de, *Vida privada*. Barcelona: Cercle de lectors, 1991.

Sala, Toni, *Rodalies*. Barcelona: Edicions 62, 2004.

Sand, George, *Winter in Majorca*. Mallorca: Valldemosa, 1956.

Serge, Víctor, *Birth of Our Power*. London: Writers and Readers, 1977.

Sitwell, Sacheverell, *Spain*. London: Batsford, 1975.

Sobrequés, Jaume, *FC Barcelona, Cent anys d'història*. Barcelona: edi-Liber, 1998.

Solé Sabaté, Josep M. (ed.), *El Franquisme a Catalunya 1939-1977. I. La dictadura totalitària (1939-1945)*. Edicions 62, 2005.

Spender, Stephen, *World within World*. London: Readers Union, 1953.

Terry, Arthur, *Catalan Literature*. London: Ernest Benn, 1972.

Tóibín, Colm, *Homage to Barcelona*. London: Simon and Schuster, 1994.

Tóibín, Colm, *The South*. London: Picador, 1995.

Tree, Matthew, *CAT*. Barcelona: Columna, 2000.

Vargas, Claudia, *Antoni Gaudí*. Bogotá: Panamericana, 2005.

Vázquez Montalbán, Manuel, *El pianista*. Barcelona: Seix Barral, 1985.

Vázquez Montalbán, Manuel, *Barcelonas*. London: Verso, 1992.

Verdaguer, Jacint, *Canigó*. Badalona: Sàpiens, 2005.

Williams, Raymond, *Orwell*. London: Flamingo, 1984.

Glossary

The following are some of the Catalan words used in the text. Catalan is used throughout in preference to Castilian Spanish, though in some cases where Spanish usage is so common in English (e.g. Ramblas or Ebro), I have used the Spanish.

aiguamolls	wetlands
almogàvers	ferocious mediaeval Catalan warriors
Art Nouveau or *modernisme*	The style of painting, architecture or literature in fashion at the cusp of the nineteenth to twentieth centuries
barretina	Traditional red floppy cap
barri	quarter/neighbourhood
bolets	wild mushrooms
butaner	person delivering butane gas cylinders
caca	shit
caganer	'shitter' (Christmas nativity figure)
call	Jewish quarter
camp nou	New Ground (of FC Barcelona)
can/cal	Like 'chez' in French... at the house of
cantautor	singer/song-writer
carrer	street
cassola	casserole pot/ casserole
crit cantat	sung shout
Desperta ferro!	Wake up iron! (War-cry of the almogàvers)
embotits	cold meats
esponjament	'sponging out' ... creation of small open spaces in densely populated areas
Generalitat	Autonomous Government of Catalonia
modernista	(adjective) in the style of *modernisme*
noi	lad/kid
noucentisme	Style of architecture, painting and literature, classical in tone, in fashion in the early 1900s

nova cançó	new song
Palau	palace/ mansion
plaça	square
rauxa	rage
Renaixença	Renaissance
seny	good sense
senyera	the four-barred flag of Catalonia
terra de pas	thoroughfare
tertúlia	discussion meeting
turó	hill

Index of Literary & Historical Names

Index of Places & Landmarks